BARRIERS AND HAZARDS IN COUNSELING

Dorothy E. Johnson

Purdue University, Calumet Campus

Mary J. Vestermark

Ball State University

HOUGHTON MIFFLIN COMPANY   BOSTON

New York   Atlanta   Geneva, Ill.   Dallas   Palo Alto

ACKNOWLEDGMENTS

We thank the following publishers and copyright holders for permission to quote from their materials in this volume:

Abingdon Press for quotations from Seward Hiltner, *The Counselor in Counseling*, 1952.

Appleton-Century-Crofts, Educational Division, Meredith Corporation for quotations from Leona E. Tyler, *The Work of the Counselor*, Second Edition, 1961, and Third Edition, 1969. Also for quotations from: *Impact and Change: A Study of Counseling Relationships*. By Bill L. Kell and William J. Mueller. Copyright © 1966 by Meredith Corporation. Reprinted by permission of Appleton-Century-Crofts.

Harper & Row, Publishers, for quotations from C. H. Patterson, *Counseling and Psychotherapy*, 1959.

Holt, Rinehart and Winston, Inc., for quotations from B. C. Berenson and R. R. Carkhuff (eds.), *Sources of Gain in Counseling and Psychotherapy*, 1967.

Houghton Mifflin Company for quotations from Alfred Benjamin, *The Helping Interview*, 1969. From Fred McKinney, *Counseling for Personal Adjustment in Schools and Colleges*, 1958. From Bruce Shertzer and Shelley C. Stone, *Fundamentals of Counseling*, 1968.

Prentice-Hall, Inc., for quotations from Lawrence M. Brammer & Everett Shostrom, *Therapeutic Psychology*, Second Edition, Fundamentals of Actualization Counseling and Psychotherapy © by Prentice-Hall, Inc.

Van Nostrand Reinhold Company for quotations from *The Experience of Psychotherapy* by William H. Fitts, Copyright © 1965, by Litton Educational Publishing, Inc., by permission of Van Nostrand Reinhold Company.

EDITOR'S INTRODUCTION

"God give me the courage to change the things that can be changed, the patience to endure the things that can't be changed, and the wisdom to know the difference." This paraphrase of a classic which has been attributed to several famous people, is as applicable to counselors as any bit of folklore that I know. Counselors seem always to be fighting the Unbeatable Foe, righting the Unrightable Wrong, dreaming the Impossible Dream. They may be jousting with windmills or they may be fighting real battles against loneliness, confusion, and ignorance. Whatever the fray, the weapons used are seldom equal to the nonrational and evasive complexity of their client's humanness. Their mission, nevertheless, whether in relating to an individual face-to-face or in a group, is to help the client sort out the unchangeable and learn how to live with it. Beyond this, of course, the counselor works to enable the client to recognize the changeable in himself and "get with it." Perhaps also the counselor's task is to help the client recognize his assets and not be frightened by his liabilities.

Counselors are great idealists: they truly want to change the world or at least to change an individual. They often unwittingly impose their goals upon the client; they often want him to change at their pace rather than his. Counselors need to know *their* needs as well as those of the client, for both must be recognized in the counseling encounter. They also need to know the solid barriers that frustrate their task and to be able to distinguish them from undesirable professional habits or attitudes which can be more easily tackled.

This book is about counseling barriers and hazards, the unchangeable or hard to change and "the pitfalls the alert counselor might readily avoid." It attempts to provide some guidelines for the counselor's development of "the wisdom to know the difference." The barriers and hazards which may be found within the counselor, within the client, and in the interaction process itself comprise the chapters of this book. The distinction between barriers and hazards is maintained throughout. There is never any doubt what the book is about.

As I read the chapters on barriers I developed a strong feeling that *these* are the profound issues for the counselor, the ones of which he is least aware — lack of self-knowledge and a clear self-image, the temptation to acquire a sense of power, the evasion of social realities through self-encapsulation, etc. But then when I read about the hazards — unconscious intellectualization of client needs, becoming a quasi-parent in attitude, imposing one's own values — it became apparent that these also are often buried within the counselor and hidden from his awareness.

I am glad that this book gives primacy to the barriers and hazards *within the counselor*, rather than those within the client or the process. The professional education of a counselor often deals extensively with the nature of the client and the dimensions of the counseling process, but seldom gives attention to the person and individuality of the counselor. Yet who the counselor is as a person becomes the crux of what goes right or wrong in the counseling relationship and outcomes. The counselor is his own most sensitive instrument, his most powerful tool. Someday (it is true in a few institutions even now) the planned professional education of a counselor will deal extensively with the counselor's awareness of himself.

Johnson and Vestermark have made a valuable contribution to the ability of the counselor to see himself in the counseling process. Their insights are equally penetrating when dealing with client and with process, but the counselor needs desperately first to "look at himself" — with open eyes and an understanding heart.

The authors of this book write with deep perception on many psychological topics often given scant or superficial attention. It is sensitive writing, clear writing, sympathetic writing — it is a book that I wish I had written myself!

C. Gilbert Wrenn

PREFACE

The origin of this book can be traced to a rather casual conversation the authors had concerning the detrimental effect of counselor fatigue upon work with clients. (It was a particularly busy time of year.) We soon found ourselves citing other influences — personal and circumstantial — that seemed to inhibit us in counseling. From experience we realized that individuals seeking counseling also grapple with factors which hinder the counseling process.

Several conversations later we decided to put some of our thoughts in order. Early in this organizational period, we recognized that we were dealing with very real, everyday reactions and consequences that jeopardize optimum functioning in counseling and that these aspects of counseling are seldom discussed with counselors-in-training or with working counselors. We decided, furthermore, that there might be some merit in sharing these thoughts. Thus *Barriers and Hazards in Counseling* took shape.

Since counseling is a relationship involving two or more individuals, it is influenced by whatever each may contribute or fail to contribute. Their present feelings, past experiences, values, commitments, apprehensions, expectations, and patterns of behavior all come into play in the interpersonal process. In addition, the effect one has upon the other — the "mix" of counselor and counselee — may inhibit or enhance the process. Blocks and pitfalls exist for both the counselor and the counselee, and their combination in a given situation can jeopardize the interaction. We therefore divided the contents of the book into three parts: The Counselor, The Counselee, and Interaction.

Involving individuals as it does, counseling is so personal a process that one cannot be prescriptive in treating it. All we hope to accomplish with this book is to alert counselors-in-training and working counselors to barriers and hazards sometimes encountered in counseling. An awareness of these inhibiting influences may enable counselors to anticipate and consequently avoid them or minimize their effect. Or early identification of such influences as they impinge upon the process may enable counselors to understand them better and accommodate them more readily in counseling.

Two sections are appended to the text: Appendix A, "Cases for Discussion and Development," was prepared by David Redfering. It presents situations that might provoke discussion or be used as a basis for role playing so as to prepare the student to recognize and deal with barriers and hazards in counseling. Appendix B is a list of films and audio tapes that seem relevant to the content of the book.

We expect this volume to be useful to students gaining experience in the preparatory program and to counselors on the job receiving inservice training. It might supplement the text in theories and techniques courses, in addition to aiding students in the counseling practicum, interns, and working counselors.

Finally, it is impossible to acknowledge properly all those individuals — colleagues, counselees, students, authors — who have touched us along the way and have contributed richly to our thinking and being. Specifically, however, we wish to express our appreciation to Dr. C. Gilbert Wrenn for his encouragement at the beginning of this undertaking and for his suggestions as the work progressed. We wish also to thank David Redfering not only for having prepared the cases in Appendix A, but also for his enthusiastic support of the total task of getting a manuscript together.

Dorothy E. Johnson
Mary J. Vestermark

CONTENTS

BARRIERS AND HAZARDS IN COUNSELING

1

Structuring

When a four-year-old boy in nursery school said, in describing his classmates, "Nancy is the girl who doesn't know how to share," he was referring to the budding interactive process, obviously being fostered by his nursery school teacher. Increasingly, thoughtful people concerned with the education of youth are turning their attention to interactive skills. No longer is it sufficient that schools — at any level — focus upon cognitive competence alone, or even cognitive and affective development. As Bettelheim (1969) points out, children are not unhappy because they do not know the facts of the Napoleonic Wars, but because they cannot effectively relate to the psychological and social environment in which they find themselves. Seemingly, the business of relating in a satisfactory manner to other individuals is a difficult task, especially as people grow and mature and, of necessity, adopt the defenses and subterfuges of the adult world. So that he may be attuned to the process of being and becoming, it is essential that the child be given opportunities early in life — and continuously — to develop the art of relating to others, to equip himself with interpersonal skills.

The word *alienation* is not to be reserved to describe the condition of those in economic poverty or minority groups, or of anyone considered to live outside the mainstream. The word applies even to those who are found at the very wellspring of the mainstream. One need not look far or hard for evidence to support the contention that a feeling of alienation is prevalent in our society. Note the rising divorce rate; study the statistics on suicides; read about the generation gap; count the continually spiraling crime cases; or witness the rush to T-groups, sensitivity training, and drugs.

The point is not to pass judgment on these coping behaviors, but rather to recognize their existence and attempt to interpret their implications. Is it because we have not learned the skill of listening to each other, or indeed even of hearing ourselves, that we feel alienated? Have the schools been remiss? Can skills of interpersonal relations be learned? Some people think so. Rubin and his associates (1969) challenge the schools to provide opportunities for interaction, so that youth may learn to participate effectively in interpersonal relationships. Effective interaction can occur only in process, Rubin observes. It is like learning to play tennis. One cannot become even an adequate tennis player by reading or by being lectured about the game. To achieve skill in the sport, a person must have a racquet and a ball and step onto a court to practice with at least one other person similarly equipped. So it is in acquiring skill in developing effective interpersonal relationships.

An Interpersonal Relationship

It is somewhat difficult to characterize "an interpersonal relationship," since interaction between or among many different types of people in innumerable settings will qualify as interpersonal encounters. A special openness, warmth, acceptance — these qualities must exist regardless of the principals or the place. An interpersonal relationship may exist between parent and child, between husband and wife, between friends, between teacher and student, between colleagues, between supervisor and the supervised, between counselor and counselee, in an educational or in a noneducational setting, in the office of a professional person, in the living room or kitchen of someone's home, in a bar, or at a drugstore counter. The setting is really not important. The encounter is important; and to the principals involved, the quality of the encounter is terribly important.

Seeley (1969, p. 116) sees the interpersonal relationship as existing when two people are *being together*. For him, the "skill of being" is the essential and enabling factor of being together. The "skill of being" encompasses a knowledge of who each individual is and "people knowledge": the "trinity of 'me knowledge,' 'them knowledge,' and 'us knowledge.' " The experience and the rewards of interrelating for Seeley are predicated upon a knowledge of self and of loving and of being free to interact with one another.

Awareness, warmth, acceptance, honesty, genuineness, sincerity, self-knowledge, sensitivity, humaneness — this is the stuff an effective interpersonal relationship is made of. Any number of studies can be cited in support of the association of these qualities with effective relationships. Identification of the qualities is relatively simple. Accommodating them as part of the self is more difficult. Seeley (1969, p. 115) suggests that these qualities, these "skills of being" are "derived from living and relatedness, not skills taught and learned." Opportunities to develop such skills, to acquire such qualities can be provided. The individual must want to embrace them. The question is, "How diligently is the individual prepared to work to make these qualities part of himself?"

The extent to which the public in general is turning to varieties of sensitivity training in a kind of desperate search for what Bettelheim (1969) terms "inner freedom, personal autonomy" suggests a deep and widespread need to escape from alienation by interaction with others. Nor is sensitivity training a panacea; indeed, in the hands of an inept leader, it can be harmful. Qualities facilitating an effective interpersonal relationship must be nurtured by constant attention. Any amount of sensitivity training will avail the individual nothing if he does not remain alert and aware and open outside the sessions. Like the beagle pup who was a "star pupil" in obedience school but would not even respond to her name outside the training sessions, the individual who does not continue to practice "sensitivity" outside the meetings will fail to learn to relate effectively in his daily life.

Counseling Interaction

Perhaps the persons to whom effective interpersonal relationships are most vital are those who have chosen as their life's work an involvement with others in the form of a helping relationship. Counselors, therapists, and teachers may be so classified. Since our focus here is upon counselors and therapists, we now address ourselves to that special and most significant interpersonal encounter, the counseling relationship.

As a consequence of having studied many therapeutic relationships involving individuals with varying kinds of problems and questions, in a variety of settings, Rogers (1962) concluded that it is the quality of the personal encounter, "the attitudinal ingredients" counselors bring to it, that more than anything else determines the effectiveness of the relationship. He sees three conditions as being essential to a successful interpersonal relationship: congruence, empathy, and unconditional positive regard. In other words, the counselor must be himself, be genuine; he must be able to sense the other's "personal meanings as if they were his own"; and he must accept unconditionally the other person as he is, as a person of worth.

Counseling involves not only the counselor but also the counselee. Each brings to the relationship his own uniqueness to make the encounter itself a unique experience. As Wertz (1957) suggests, interaction of two personalities, involving both verbal and nonverbal behavior, is operating in counseling. The structure of each personality will have a marked effect upon the total interaction process. Professional or nonprofessional, counselor or counselee, each individual brings to the counseling relationship the sum total of his experience up to that point in time. And the process is influenced by what each one is, how each perceives himself and views the other, what each one expects of the experience, the skills each has in communicating himself and receiving the other, and more. All these qualities and conditions and competencies and deficiencies may help or hinder or affect not at all the relationship. The challenge for the counselor is to be perceptively aware and maximally understanding of the flow of feelings and thought operating in the counseling relationship. He must strive for a sense of "being with" the counselee as he maintains the equilibrium that derives from knowing himself.

The purpose of this volume is to focus upon the counselor and the counselee in the counseling relationship and to identify some stumbling blocks and pitfalls that tend to render the process less effective that it might otherwise be. Suggestions are offered as to how difficulties might be avoided or surmounted. It is important to note right now, however, that counseling is an extremely personal business, and in the end, counselor and counselee must themselves work through difficulties, employing methods that are suited to the situation and in harmony with their individual styles. In discussing the challenge of the counseling task, especially as it exists in the initial interview, Tyler (1969, p. 63) observes: "Each person constitutes for us a new adventure in understanding. Each is destined to broaden our own lives in directions as yet uncharted."

Barriers and Hazards Defined

In this book, "barriers" are viewed as real obstacles of varying degrees of seriousness, whereas "hazards" are seen as pitfalls the alert counselor might readily avoid. Although this distinction is seen as a real one, inevitably there are areas of overlap. Both barriers and hazards exist for the counselor and for the counselee alike. They are also present in counseling interaction, evolving simply because two or more individuals come together. These blocks to effective functioning may be caused by circumstances beyond the control of either individual, by the sex of the counselor, for example. Or there may be some personal "hang-up" that impairs effectiveness, such as the counselee's anxiety regarding confidentiality, or the counselor's subtly imposing his own values. Or the counseling process itself may be slowed down as a consequence of prior conditioning or dependency developments. No one can anticipate all possible contingencies, and having anticipated some, one counselor cannot tell another precisely how to act and what to say. But he can, hopefully, suggest some general policies for consideration.

Part One
*

The
Counselor

2

Barriers for the Counselor

Certain blocks to effectiveness in the process of counseling flow from the counselor himself. Such blocks or barriers may exist simply because the counselor is who he is, because he finds himself in a given setting, restricted by externals over which he either has little or no control or views himself as having little or no control. The counselor may experience difficulties because of his own temporary needs, affecting his relationship with only specific types of counselees, or only at certain periods; or he may run into blocks because he himself has not completely solved some of his own problems.

This chapter will focus upon some barriers that may be associated principally with the counselor and will render the counseling process less effective than it might otherwise be. Doubtless other barriers might well be identified, but we have chosen to concentrate on five dimensions seen as potential or real blocks in counseling: the image the counselor has of himself and his role; the position in which he finds himself because of his many and diverse commitments; the limitations established by time boundaries; his encapsulation; and the uneasiness that accompanies functioning when a philosophical base is lacking.

Self-Image and "Professional" Role Concept

If one subscribes to the view that the most significant element the counselor brings to the relationship is himself, then the way the counselor sees himself and his role is paramount in this interpersonal process. The image the counselor has of himself and his professional role, together with his actions and reactions, influence the degree to which the counseling relationship is effective, ineffective, or nonexistent.

THE SELF-LIMITING COUNSELOR

For the counselor who sees his responsibilities extending to educational and vocational matters only, there can be no effective personal-social counseling because the counselor removes himself from the possibility of becoming involved with this type of counseling. Indeed, the counselor who cuts off personal matters limits his effectiveness in helping counselees in educational and vocational decision making, the very areas in which he sees his greatest potential for contribution to counselees. Consider an example of how a counselor fails a counselee who comes to him for help in choosing a college. Jim is a junior in high school, seriously thinking about college application:

> *Jim:* Well, you see, my parents met at XYZ College, and they've always had it in mind that I should go there.
>
> *Counselor:* And you are not enthusiastic about XYZ College?
>
> *Jim:* It's not that I don't think it's a good school — I'm sure it is. But it's . . . it's a small college in a small town . . . and I . . . I'd rather go to State University.
>
> *Counselor:* You'd enjoy a larger campus with more activities than XYZ College has?

Jim: Yes, I guess I would, but . . . well, you see, XYZ has chapel every day, and I'm not sure I could buy that. I've tried to talk to Mom and Dad about it, but I don't want to hurt their feelings. And, anyway, I got blasted just last week when I said I didn't want to go to church on Sunday . . . .

Counselor: Oh, I see. Well, . . . it seems to me that you should meet the requirements for State University. Shall we look at your record with State in mind?

Jim: Yeah . . . I guess so . . . .

This counselor was functioning fairly well with Jim. He had established a relationship with Jim that was sufficiently accepting so that, after one attempt to evade the real reason for his rejection of XYZ College, he blurted out his conflict. But the counselor refused to deal with this hot issue and turned to the safety of Jim's scholastic record, leaving the boy to resolve the religious conflict and its numerous implications by himself. The counselor blocked further effectiveness by his inability to respond to Jim's request for help with a personal problem, one that is central to college choice.

Conversely, some counselors view themselves as being highly competent in counseling individuals with primarily personal and emotional problems. They do not think that they are really counseling unless they can uncover a "good problem." Effective counseling may well take place between these counselors and some of their counselees when a real problem does exist. But the danger here, as is all too obvious, is that counselors who consider themselves just a step removed from a psychiatrist may force a counselee to expose himself before he is ready to do so, or to invent a problem simply to satisfy the counselor. (See Chapter 6 for further discussion of this type of counselor functioning.)

Here is an example of how a counselor, eager to display his competence in personal conflict situations, backed Sara, a college freshman, into a corner.

Sara: I really don't know what's wrong with me recently. I can't seem to concentrate on my

> courses or anything . . . and it's getting worse and worse. I'm falling further and further behind and I just can't get caught up. And then I seem to fly off the handle. Why, just last weekend while I was home, my sister and I had a real battle. I don't know what my trouble is. . . .

Counselor: You feel hostile toward your sister.

Sara: No, it's not that . . . oh, it was really a silly fight as I look back on it. I just don't know. . . .

Counselor: It's all right, Sara. You can speak freely with me. In here you can say all those things you couldn't say to just anyone. You're really feeling pretty hostile toward your sister. . . .

Sara: No . . . no . . . not really. At least I don't think so. . . .

Counselor: Actually, there are times when you almost hate your sister.

Sara: Well, . . . I . . . I . . . Well, I guess she does make me mad every now and then.

Counselor: There, now it's in the open . . . and you're feeling better about it.

Sara: (*Silence*)

The counselor ignored completely Sara's frustration over her courses, with its attendant irritation and feeling of hopelessness, and went straight to the relationship with the sister. Fortunately for Sara, she need not return to the counselor, but unfortunately, this encounter could have planted a seed in Sara's mind that might well provide pain for her in the future. This counselor, too, has thrown up a barrier to his effectiveness for Sara and has missed an opportunity to help her.

Counselors in school settings who are constantly finding deep personal-emotional problems in their counselees might well look at themselves and assess their own needs. Are they using counselees to satisfy needs they themselves have? Are they using counselees to enhance the image they have of themselves as counselors? And those counselors whose counselees seem to have only superficial concerns that are always quite efficiently resolved might ask themselves whether they are really hearing their counselees. Or do they turn them off when the going gets rough, as Jim's counselor did to him?

The counselor who really protects himself, though, is the one who completely surrounds himself with "things" so that he has no time for people. Complaining all the while, this counselor assumes more and more busy-work tasks, completely insulating himself from counselees. He would like to counsel but he has no time; and students quickly realize that he has no time. The barrier is firm and impenetrable. Until and unless the counselor revises his view of himself and his role, the barrier will remain intact. More attention will be given to this type of "counselor" later in this chapter.

The overly eager counselor, impressed with himself as someone who knows something other people do not, also limits his potential for effectiveness. This individual feels superior, considers himself the "compleat counselor," sees problems on all sides, and attempts to counsel both students and colleagues inside his office and outside; friends, relatives, everyone is fair game, regardless of the setting. This course can lead only to rejection for the counselor. Ohlsen (1955, p. 290) aptly describes the situation:

> The eager counselor who tries to help everyone may run into another problem with his colleagues. If in and out of school he always attempts to make clinical judgments about what people say and do, he will be rejected by them. He creates problems for himself and his program by attempting to be counselor for everyone who talks with him. His colleagues resent his effort to maneuver every contact into a counseling relationship.

One might add "and students" after "colleagues." It is important to remember that reputations are built outside the office as well as within.

THE QUASI-ADMINISTRATOR

A classic example of the counselor who renders himself ineffective by the way he sees himself and his role is the individual who has chosen counseling as a stepping-stone to administration. He sees himself as getting close to where the action is as he works more intimately with the administration. Assisted often by the principal, the counselor finds his way into his role of quasi-administrator — or Junior God, as Shostrom (1968) might describe him — quite rapidly. Although he may see himself as having had these administrative functions thrust upon him, he would have to admit, if he really knew himself and could really be honest, that he permitted himself to be used in these ways. Actually, he enjoys the status that derives from identification with the administration. It might even be suggested that the counselor is afraid of what Shostrom calls *contact* (1968, p. 33), communication between the "two inner cores of actualizing potentials" of two individuals. Manipulation, on the other hand, is "communication between the two peripheries of outer rings of personalities of two individuals. . . . contact is a form of loving or trusting another person in a relationship of closeness or touching, whereas manipulation is a relationship to distance that represents a withdrawal to less personal intense forms of communication."

Furthermore, being a junior administrator can endanger one's position as counselor in other ways. Not only do teachers associate the counselor with the administration, but, more importantly, students see him this way, too. In their minds, the counselor is in a position of authority and control, and they expect from the counselor the same kinds of reactions they associate with the principal or assistant principal. Viewing the counselor, then, as an individual who controls and manipulates, students tend to be reluctant to involve themselves with him in any but the most superficial ways. And so the counselor is someone the students seek out when schedules are due, to get a program changed, to locate information about post–high school education, to request help in completing an application form, to learn about financial aid, to buy a season ticket to basketball games, and so forth. Rarely, if ever, does this counselor have an opportunity to serve students in that special way for which he has been specifically prepared — as a counselor in a counseling relationship.

If the work of the counselor described in the preceding paragraph sounds familiar, it is because, unhappily, this situation obtains in too many school settings. It is a betrayal of both personal and professional potential. And the condition will be perpetuated as long as individuals see their counseling role in this way. Studies too numerous to mention have demonstrated that the way students, teachers, parents, and administrators view counselors is a reflection of the way counselors view themselves. The image of the counselor originates with the counselor himself and his understanding of his role.

THE COUNSELOR AS FRIEND

The counselor who views himself as the students' friend, and then behaves as if he were, cheats himself of the opportunity for real effectiveness. The counselor who says, verbally or nonverbally, "I am your friend," "I want to be your friend," misinterprets his role and fails to make the distinction between "being a friend" and "being friendly." While the counselor brings warmth and friendliness to the relationship, the offer of friendship may be misunderstood. The counselor who attempts to place himself in the position of "friend" to his counselees is not authentic, and he is likely to confuse counselees, confound colleagues, and alienate administrators.

Further, the counselor-friend places himself in an untenable position in the organizational setting. His colleagues may wonder just what his position is with reference to other staff members. When a counselor stresses his role as the students' "friend," is he suggesting that he is unique in this respect? Cannot teachers and other staff members be students' friends, also? What implications exist here for barriers not only to effectiveness in counseling, but also to a cooperative and friendly relationship between the counselor and his colleagues? To look at the matter from another point of view, what should the counselor-friend do if he comes upon two students scuffling in the hall? (This question is frequently raised by counselor trainees who are uncertain of their role, incidentally.) Does the counselor-friend look the other way? Or does he betray the friendship and suddenly become a member of the school staff? Does he give his colleagues further evidence of his lack of responsibility? Or, more importantly, does he enter into a kind of conspiracy with the students and give the impression that he approves? What support can he expect from his colleagues for the counseling and guidance effort in the school? And what respect from the students?

The easy, open relationship the counselor hopes to foster is likely to become too easy, too confusing to students. A situation reminiscent of the predicament in which some student teachers find themselves may develop. Eager to be liked and accepted by students, student teachers sometimes approach students as friends, as one of them. Suddenly the situation is out of hand and the student teacher cannot really assume the role of teacher; he seems only to be playing at it. He finds that he cannot command the respect and confidence of students and he loses confidence in himself. His footing is unsure and his direction is uncontrolled. The students, in the meantime, are searching, even pushing, for limits.

This is not to say that the counselor should not be friendly, warm, accepting, and open. He must be, if he is to relate effectively to counselees. But let the counselor interact with his counselees as a professional person, as a counselor, not as the "friend" he can never truly be. Let the counselor say, "I want to be your counselor. I want to enter into a relationship with you that will help you to grow and better understand yourself."

SELF-KNOWLEDGE AS THE BASE

The counselor is, first of all, a human being with needs and frailties, competencies and strengths. If he makes a practice of striving constantly for increased self-knowledge, he will understand more clearly who he is and what he can be to others. Teacher, administrative assistant, friend, adviser, confidant, educator, psychologist — what is the "true and proper" role for the counselor?

The task of self-understanding is primary to developing a professional role concept. Other dimensions enter, of course: understanding of principles and objectives of counseling; comprehension of needs to be satisfied, those of counselees as well as one's own; knowledge of theories and techniques; respect for limits, one's own as well as those of others; and so forth. But in the end, the individual counselor must come to know who he is and what his work is to be. And having arrived at some satisfactory conclusions, perhaps some compromise between consensus and individual competence, he must test his effectiveness in the role. If he is successful, he must communicate this role to others — to counselees, parents, teachers, administrators, and the public. The best way to communicate roles is to be seen performing those functions with which one wishes to be associated. It is extremely simple: When people are asked what the counselor's role is, in any setting, they report what they have seen the counselor doing.

Finally, and by way of summary, these questions are posed: What image do you wish to project as a counselor? Will this image most effectively serve the counselee? What barriers to effectiveness do you see for yourself? Can you be authentic in this role? If not, what recourse do you have? If so, how can you most effectively project the image?

Multiplicity of Commitment

A second category of blocks to counseling effectiveness may be subsumed under the general heading "multiplicity of commitment" — commitment to things and to people. Any consideration of the wide variety of responsibilities a counselor has must include recognition of the person as a member of society. Counselors must be seen as husband, father, wife, mother, community workers, in short, as individuals. The counselor must be viewed as someone who, like his counselees, has a life outside the school or agency setting. He needs diversion and relaxation the same as anyone else. And we must recognize his need for time to pursue his own interests, both professional and nonprofessional — time for being a human being.

The scope of this section, however, extends to the counselor only as he functions "on the job." Focus is upon the "multiplicity of professional commitments" as they tend to inhibit or block effectiveness in counseling.

SELF-REPORTS

One way to learn how working counselors spend their time is to ask them. A group of students in an introductory course in counseling and guidance interviewed school counselors to find out how they spend their time and what counselors do.

Those persons selected for interview were counselors in the schools where the interviewers were teachers or administrators, or were simply known either professionally or personally by the interviewers. The interviewees were chosen for no particular reasons. Following are typical responses to the question, "What responsibilities do you have as a school counselor?"

A counselor in a senior high school made these statements:

> Students use the guidance service as a source of information where they ask all the million and one questions they have about college, grades, program changes, job requirements, etc. They also use the guidance center as a testing service where they attempt to find out what the student is best suited for and as a placement center where students, among other things, obtain job and college applications.
>
> In addition, I help students improve study habits; I counsel all failing students and every prospective dropout. I am also involved in teacher consultation and parent conferences. Then, too, I arrange for visits for at least three outside speakers a week to discuss occupations and post–high school education. As a staff member, I must attend all athletic events and dances.

An elementary school counselor reported that she counsels fifty to sixty students a week, in groups and individually. She also was responsible for coordinating the school's testing program and evaluated and interpreted test results.

Another high school counselor reported that she "keeps up the records" for 500 students, including figuring the cumulative index for all seniors. In addition, she coaches the majorettes one period each day.

A "counselor" who worked with boys only, reported that he was assigned two periods a day for teaching, one period for preparation, and two periods for guidance. The "balance" of his time was devoted to being assistant principal. During the two periods set aside for guidance, he was engaged in "scheduling, vocational guidance, working with personal problems of students, working with teachers, and trying to resolve teacher-student conflicts."

Counselors sometimes function also as directors of guidance, as does one who said he spends about two-thirds of his time on clerical tasks. He also maintains permanent record cards; enrolls and withdraws students; handles transcripts for students transferring in and out; administers the testing program and is responsible for interpreting the results to students in grades 7–12; schedules classes for grades 9–12; distributes vocational and educational information to students and teachers; counsels — all phases; coordinates and supervises college nights and career days; is involved in curriculum improvement; signs admission slips each morning; stands noon-hour cafeteria duty; and coordinates all guidance services for the school district.

When Mrs. M, a junior high school counselor, was asked what changes she would recommend that would improve her situation, she responded:

> The major change I would like to make would be to have the entire day for guidance activities. I feel that with my many responsibilities as a counselor, being required to teach three classes a day and supervise student teachers is ridiculous. Many students who would like to talk with me are slighted simply because I do not have enough released time for guidance.

Mrs. M has a clear view of her situation and what is needed to improve it. There is a very good chance that, given the opportunity, Mrs. M might become an effective counselor. The question now becomes, "What steps will Mrs. M take to effect the changes she feels are necessary?"

The counselor described below works in a new, progressive consolidation. She is a counselor in a high school that is proud of its flexible scheduling, team teaching, and independent study program. The interview took place in one of the attractive counseling rooms of a tastefully decorated and well-equipped counseling and guidance suite in a new building. The counselor displayed materials she had prepared for this new school in the new consolidation: a guidebook for students, a handbook for teachers, the teachers' master schedule, and other similar documents. Obviously much time and effort had gone into the materials. They were attractive, comprehensive, well written, and necessary. The conversation turned to the time required for the preparation of such materials — and to the question as to when she found time for counseling students. "Oh," she replied, "I seem to be able to make enough time to see the students who come in to see me. Not many come, so it works out all right. Anyway, I really like doing these things."

And herein lies the key to most dilemmas posed by a multiplicity of commitments. Counselors frequently would rather prepare written materials, or take attendance, or perform a myriad of other functions, than counsel. Counseling is demanding and requires far more skill and risk than does signing admission slips each morning.

THE DILEMMA

Like it or not, everyone is bound by the twenty-four-hour day and limited by his own reservoir of energy. Each individual must set up some priority with reference to where he will place his efforts. A counselor cannot be all things to all people and yet be an effective counselor. He may be an effective guidance worker, or an effective clerk, or an effective sponsor of activities, but is any one of these roles justified for someone employed as a counselor?

The difficulties a person can find himself in when he pushes beyond his limits to fatigue are touched upon in the next chapter. It is recognized that some tasks not accurately classified as counseling and guidance functions sometimes fall to counselors in certain settings. It is often hard to say no to requests to "help out for a little while." But the counselor must protect himself, both professionally and personally. He must refuse to assume certain responsibilities, and he must establish a rank order of importance among the commitments he feels he must in all conscience assume.

Wrenn (1965b, p. 60) suggests criteria counselors might use in determining whether to undertake certain duties:

> Is the nature of the school task to be performed by the counselor likely to support the image of the counselor that both principal and counselor want others to have of him? Or does it distort that image and make it harder for the counselor to be of help to students? These constitute the basis

for decision, not whether the counselor likes the nature of the housekeeping duty. This suggests that the counselor must have a clear idea of the image he wishes to project and that his principal shares this perception.

Here again is the question of counselor image. What image does the counselor wish to project? He may find himself pressed on one side by chores he feels obligated to undertake and on the other by the knowledge that time and energy spent on these tasks are at the expense of the more critical commitment to counseling. Assuredly, it is easier to view the dilemma objectively, to point out these clerical tasks and those administrative duties, and to say: "Eliminate them. They can be done by someone else. They are not the counselor's responsibility." For the working counselor, such distinctions and decisions may not come so easily. For a variety of reasons, the counselor in the situation may experience some real frustrations in eliminating nonprofessional duties and establishing priorities among those responsibilities he has assumed. We end with the question with which we began, and we shall return to it again and again, for it is basic to the entire dilemma: What image does the counselor wish to project? For some it may help to word it this way: What image *should* a counselor project?

Some mention must be made here of the conflicting responsibilities that develop as a consequence of a teaching-counseling assignment. Despite the recommendation of the American School Counselor Association (1964) that counselors be assigned on a full-time basis, many persons are still employed for a split assignment. And, indeed, on the college level, many institutions employ counselors for service part-time in instruction and part-time in counseling centers. Those persons advocating a split assignment in the public schools point to such advantages for the system as: (a) enabling counselors to know the students better through teaching, (b) providing for better rapport with teachers, (c) gaining and maintaining a deeper understanding of classroom problems, and so forth. The argument in favor of assigning college counselors to both instruction and counseling is to provide counselor-educators with a continuing opportunity to maintain and improve their skills in areas which they instruct.

However, regardless of the sincerity of the individual, a dual assignment necessarily results in a fragmentation of commitment. Frustrations stemming from the split assignment are reflected in the response of counselors to suggestions for improving the counseling service. A majority of those counselors who are part-time instructor and part-time counselor see the necessity for a full-time assignment in counseling or instruction for total commitment and involvement. Feelings of guilt, annoyance, frustration, and fatigue dog the counselor-teacher. And the result is frequently a depressed effectiveness in either or both areas.

SPECIALIST-GENERALIST CONTROVERSY

The controversy relating to the counselor as a specialist or the counselor as a generalist has continued through several years. Should the school counselor spend all or most of his time in counseling? Or should the school counselor be involved in guidance activities as well as in counseling? Support can be found for both points of view. Those who support the specialist concept do so because like Dugan (1963), they see a need for individuals with advanced-level training to provide really effective counseling. Counselors are needed who can give priority to counseling. Dugan points out that counseling in the 1960s was of "minimal effectiveness, partly as a result of the encroachment of many needed but time-consuming general guidance duties." The exclusive service of counseling will be reserved, as Dugan views the future, for the counseling specialist. The many other functions counselors frequently perform — " . . . orientation, group guidance, registration, class scheduling, course changes, cumulative record development, testing and other appraisal, special class placement, scholarship and college application information, parent conferences, and other administrative duties . . ." — would be performed by guidance workers (Dugan, 1963, p. 98). Dugan sees two types of counselors serving in the schools: guidance workers, with preparation similar to that which many working counselors now have; and counseling specialists, persons with two years of advanced or graduate study. As the situation exists in American public schools today, it would appear that Dugan's prediction for the 1970s will be realized only partially. A more realistic expectation might be for more highly trained individuals who will indeed spend most of their time counseling students and working with parents, teachers, and other school and community personnel. But the guidance workers described by Dugan may have only the amount of preparation of counselors now serving in schools. A new group of subprofessionals or support personnel is entering the educational scene. These persons, possibly similar in training to teacher aides, may perform the guidance functions that currently consume so much counselor time.

Tyler (1969, p. 242) projects an almost utopian social environment in which little corrective or remedial effort will be needed, and where anxiety will be restricted or controlled:

> To the extent that counseling is aimed at improving the psychological welfare of unhappy, maladjusted, and handicapped members of society, it may gradually "wither away."

But the "world of the day after tomorrow," as Tyler sees it, will be very populous and very complex, and a major challenge will be that of human beings interacting well with each other:

> . . . it is to be expected that considerable care and attention will need to be devoted to making combinations of individuals work. One role that can be projected for the counselor, then, is that of a *consultant on human relations* (Tyler, 1969, pp. 242–243).

THE COUNSELOR'S PRESENT PROBLEM

For the present, however, the counselor must face the immediate challenge and make a decision about where his commitments lie. Time is running out. He must establish priorities among his tasks, and he must disentangle himself from nonproductive, interfering duties, those that serve as barriers to effective counseling. He must decide just where he will place his time and energy. And, having made that decision, he must ask himself whether he is projecting himself as a counselor, or simply as a guidance worker, teacher, or junior administrator. Does he, as did the lady described earlier, really like writing handbook materials or scheduling or testing to the extent that he is willing to spend most of his time on these activities? If so, perhaps a more descriptive word than "counselor" needs to be found to indicate his function.

Shertzer and Stone (1963, p. 689) have stated the situation well:

> . . . if one hires an individual to do one thing, loads him down with a second and a third and a fourth set of tasks, he is unable to perform his *presumed* original assignment very competently.

The fundamental issue is why the counselor permits this sequence of events to occur. An even more disturbing thought of concern to counselors is in a subtle and shrewd way they avoid facing perhaps the issue of a real test of their skills and services by tacit acceptance of inappropriate assignment or passive tolerance of such assignments.

There are, on the other hand, some counselors who truly wish to divest themselves of duties they do not consider theirs as counselor. And there are some ways to approach the problem:

1. Keep a daily log of activities, weekly or monthly, and summarize the time spent in each activity: consulting with parents, consulting with teachers, keeping student records up-to-date, counseling students, teaching group guidance class, signing admission slips, filing information materials, ordering information materials, working on schedules, conferring with administrators, administering and/or scoring tests, etc. Some of these activities can be combined, for example, clerical, consultation, etc., and percentages worked out. The first step is to have some evidence as to just how time is spent. A series of weekly or monthly reports will begin to show a pattern and serve as a basis for requesting a change of procedure. But be certain to have on hand a recommendation for the new procedure. Reliable office clerks have been used most effectively for signing admission slips or keeping student records up-to-date, for example. And Office Practice students can take over the chore of ordering and filing information materials. Test-scoring services admittedly do a better, more accurate job of scoring standardized tests than do counselors or teachers — and are really less expensive.

2. Keep careful records during the year and make an annual report, using these records, of time spent on various duties, gains from crucial functions (such as counseling), projected gains if certain procedures are changed, improvements or progress over the last year, recommendations (carefully documented) for the next year.

3. Choose one or two appropriate counselor functions and concentrate on improving the service. Make students, teachers, other school personnel, parents, and the community aware that the counselor is functioning this way. Be certain to give teachers feedback when a student they have referred is seen, for example. (This can easily be done without betraying confidences.) Enhance the image of the counselor functioning as a counselor.

    Involve teachers by sharing information related to their subject area or appropriate for their grade level. Ask them to send materials they receive your way. Plan some really good and needed case conferences and follow through on them. Project a strong counselor image.

4. Channel some relevant, well-written articles concerning the field to your supervisor or principal. Underline the important points, if necessary, to save him reading time. Also send along articles pertaining to his field (if it is different from yours) to demonstrate an interest in what he does, too.

5. Try to carry on a little research. Collect some information that you get routinely but that simply needs ordering and packaging for presentation. It is best if it relates to students and serves a real need.

6. If there are no job descriptions for the various positions in the school, find another disgruntled specialist (it should be easy) and discuss the matter, casually at first. Perhaps by the end of the year a full-blown document of philosophy, objectives, job descriptions, and short- and long-range plans may have emerged. Or perhaps the project will be on the agenda for next year.

These are only a few suggestions. A dissatisfied working counselor with some motivation and concentration could doubtlessly add to the list many more suggestions. If the reader detects manipulation in these suggestions, he is correct. Desperate conditions call for desperate measures.

Time and Physical Setting

While the environment in which a counselor works may not be directly related to the person of the counselor himself, as are self-image and multiplicity of commitment, time and setting do influence the counseling climate. Time and setting, therefore, are dimensions of the counseling relationship and perforce are potential barriers to counseling, if they are such that they interfere with the process.

TIME

Earlier in this chapter, "time" was presented as a barrier to counseling simply because "time for counseling" did not exist. The counselor permitted himself to become too heavily involved in other activities and consequently had no time left for counseling. In this section the focus is upon time that does exist and yet is a barrier because of the way it is used — or misused.

For some reason that is not readily apparent, one hour seems to be considered the optimum time for counseling. At least it is accepted as an appropriate period of time by college counselors, community counselors, and therapists generally. And although the counselors and therapists usually schedule their time in hour blocks, interviews may occasionally run long or short, depending upon the needs of the counselee and what happens during the session. If a counselee comes to a scheduled hour's interview and reports that he has made that decision toward which he has been working, any dialogue that extends beyond a half-hour may be not only nonproductive but even anticlimactic and irritating.

On the other hand, imagine that toward the latter part of her third counseling session, a college sophomore finally is able to express the feelings that she has been repressing and at the end of the hour, she is in tears. A sensitive counselor can hardly say, "Well, time is up for today," and usher her out through a reception room of students awaiting their appointments.

Consider now the school counselor whose typical counseling interview is scheduled for twenty minutes. How much counseling can take place in this period of time? It cannot be denied that occasionally the twenty minutes can be extremely effective, but more often than not the time factor determines that the interaction will be kept on a superficial level. The school counselor is constantly aware of the hot breath of time, since no doubt another interview has been scheduled for the next twenty minutes. If he does not get this counselee out of his office on time, the bell will ring before the next interview can be completed, and the student will have to go on to class. School counselors are continuously vying with time, and the subtle and insidious effect of the time element takes its toll in counseling.

The counselor caught in the time bind can, of course, work out another appointment for the same or the next day with the counselee and hope to recapture some of the dynamics of the present interview. Or, if it seems necessary to stay with the counselee, he can ignore the clock and the bell. The counselor can ignore the passing of time, but sometimes the counselee cannot, so conditioned is he by the bell system in the school. Perhaps some counselors are fortunate enough to arrange to have no bells ring in the counseling suite.

Another aspect of time as a barrier has to do with the discouragement of long-term counseling in school settings. Aware of his responsibility to many students, the school or college counselor may try to hasten progress in the interest of time, at the expense of effectiveness.

Consider the counselor caught between the time barrier and Jack's plight. Jack is a seventh-semester senior, an able student, who has been considering pre-med. It is the fall of the year and the counselor is checking with members of the senior class to determine how he can best help each one.

Counselor: Well, Jack, the last time we talked about your plans after graduation you mentioned pre-med. Still thinking about this?

Jack: I know . . . I was pretty excited about being a doctor . . . but you know that Bill . . . you remember Bill. He's a sophomore at the University this year, and just last spring he decided to switch to pre-med. Dad said that one doctor in the family is enough, so I've been thinking about other things.

Counselor: Uh, huh . . . and are you coming up with some ideas?

Jack: I guess so. You know that math and science are my best subjects — and I really enjoy them . . . so I'm thinking about engineering.

The counselor in this case was not imperceptive. He wanted to help Jack explore his feelings; he sensed that Jack was disappointed about pre-med. How does Jack feel about his brother? And his father? More importantly, how does Jack feel about himself and his current choice? But there is no time now for these questions. The counselor will make a note in his files: "Check back soon with Jack regarding his choice of pre-engineering." But there is little likelihood that the counselor will have time to get back to it, and the time is ripe now, but the next client is probably already in the reception room. If he begins to run late at this time of day, he will never be able to meet all his scheduled appointments. Thus time aborted counseling. Perhaps this counselor's solution is simply to review his scheduling procedure and to leave some time open in the day, so that he can answer the need for counseling as it comes.

Other examples of how time aborts counseling can be taken from the whole category of cases in which counseling must break off automatically at the end of the academic year. Like learning, decisions and concerns do not simply stop in June and resume in September. For such matters there is no summer vacation. It would be convenient if problems and decisions could be contained within the nine-and-one-half-month school year. But growth and development and the need for decision making and problem solving are not necessarily in rhythm with the opening and closing of school. The case of Judy will illustrate the loss of ground suffered by a child during the summer when most of the significant supportive individuals and activities are withdrawn.

Judy, a seventh grader, had come to the attention of the school counselor because she seemed unable to make friends. She wanted very much — too much — to be accepted by her peers, but she simply turned them off. The counselor saw Judy on an individual basis several times and together they identified some of Judy's needs and how she was attempting to satisfy them. They examined how she behaved with her peers and the way they responded to her, and why. Soon she was ready — and eager — to join a group of students who met once a week where, among other things, concern was with getting along with other people.

In addition, Judy joined the school chorus in time to get ready for the spring music festival. Judy's teachers assisted by providing opportunities in the classroom for Judy to achieve and get recognition. She was beginning to feel "involved," that she had a role to play. When school closed in June, all counseling ceased, both individual and group, and all contact with the school staff was removed, as was the opportunity to be with her peers in the chorus.

When school reopened in the fall, Judy had regressed in her ability to relate with people. Though Judy was not in the extreme situation she was the previous spring, she had lost a good part of the gain she had made.

The block to student progress — or in some cases, loss — deriving from summer vacations provides a real barrier for continuous improvement. Not only do present procedures result in a loss of personal gain for individual students but they also result in a loss of time and effort for counselors, and for that matter, for the entire school staff. Consequently, many school corporations have extended counselors' contracts beyond those for teachers, and some are considering employing counselors on an eleven-month basis so that they can work with students through the summer months.

PHYSICAL SETTING

In the American School Counselor Association's promulgation (ASCA, 1964) concerning the counselor's role and working conditions, the following statement is made:

... he should have physical facilities appropriate to his work. This would include a private office which offers visual as well as auditory privacy, and provides a relaxed, comfortable atmosphere in which he may communicate with pupils and others in confidence and without interruption.

We recognize that much counseling takes place in less than adequate surroundings, that in many schools, colleges, and agencies, the requirements drawn up by ASCA for counseling facilities are not met. We recognize, too, that some of the counseling that occurs in a "substandard" physical setting is effective. And we subscribe to the argument that it is the quality of the interaction and not the environment that determines the value of counseling outcomes. Effective counseling, like effective teaching, can be accomplished in an old, outdated physical plant, in a small room or a large one, in a renovated classroom or a loft. But it must be noted that the potential for quality interaction is enhanced when the surroundings are pleasant — not extravagant or lavish — just as the potential for quality teaching is enhanced — not guaranteed — by a modern building with up-to-date instructional equipment and materials. Nevertheless, lack of privacy and frequent interruptions represent real barriers to the development of a close counseling relationship.

That an interpersonal relationship of a fairly high level can be achieved under less than ideal circumstances is attested to by the cases presented by Sachs (1966) who brought together and analyzed examples of diagnostic, teaching, and therapeutic interviews. Sachs, a skilled counselor, interviewed students in whatever space was available, from a small conference room to a study hall large enough to accommodate one hundred students. But even Sachs experienced difficulties. In an interview with a male student, for example, in less than "optimum conditions," the relationship deteriorated as a consequence of three interruptions. Finally, when a third person slipped into the room and "unobtrusively" seated himself in the corner, the counselee virtually removed himself from the relationship, responding chiefly with single words or short phrases: "I guess so," "Yeah," "Sure," "No," etc. Sachs himself was forced to observe, ". . . thus the interview never reached as high a peak as it had reached before this interruption" (Sachs, 1966, p. 53).

It is clear that a certain basic level of adequacy with respect to the physical setting is essential. Privacy and freedom from interruption are requisites for satisfactory interaction. A physical setting that is semi-private, with halfway partitions separating counseling stations, does not provide adequate privacy. Aside from the question counselees might have — expressed or not expressed — regarding whether or not they can be heard by people in the next counseling station, there is another factor that deserves mention. Conversations, telephones, intercoms, sweeping, and all manner of movement can be heard from one station to the next. Not only is privacy lacking, but these external noises serve as distractions and interruptions.

Imagine, for example, a rather immature and shy young man, a college freshman, who finally manages to present himself to the Counseling Center as a desperate last resort. Communal living is new to Bob and he is having problems adjusting to it. He has never dated much and is not dating now; he envies the way some of the guys in the residence hall make conversation easily, seem to be developing friendships and generally are having a good time and making it academically, too. He has had some secret questions about his "manhood," and he thinks more than ever that somehow he's different. Bob's frustrations are affecting his grades; he can't concentrate. He is desperate, and so he presents himself for counseling on the pretext that he is worried about his grades and his study habits.

Imagine, too, that Bob's counselor is perceptive and accepting, and that Bob soon feels safe enough to express his real concerns. A few cubicles away two or three of the counselor's colleagues are chatting during a coffee break. As Bob is groping to reveal some of his inner feelings, the sound of laughter comes from the nearby cubicle. He laughs nervously and then shrugs his shoulders and says: "Well, you know how it is." The moment has passed and it can never be recaptured quite that way again. The interaction returns to a superficial level.

The telephone, the intercom, someone opening the door to see if the counselor is *really* busy are other kinds of interruptions that can seriously damage the counseling climate — or turn off a counselee altogether. Take the following exchange, for example, between Marge, a high school sophomore, and a counselor:

Marge: Well, these dreams, nightmares, like . . . they keep happening . . . I can't explain it. . . .

Counselor: And it's really scary?

Marge: Yes, and sometimes I'm almost afraid to go to bed. I keep imagining I hear noises and stuff. My dad travels some and Mom lets me sleep in her room when he's gone. But now she says I'm being silly and . . .
(*The phone rings*)

Counselor: (*Picks up the phone and identifies self. After a brief pause*) Well, I'm busy now. Can you call back later? . . . OK, thanks. (*Replaces the receiver in the cradle. Turns to counselee*) Your Mom is losing patience.

Marge: That's right. She says I have to sleep in my own room . . . if only I'd just stop dreaming and hearing sounds . . . I didn't used to be like this . . .

Counselor: How long have you been feeling like this?

Marge: Oh, I dunno . . . I guess . . . well, I guess ever since my grandmother . . .
(*The phone rings*)

Counselor: Oh, excuse me, again. (*Picks up phone, the same as before*) Well, I can't right now. Perhaps this afternoon. (*Checking calendar*) How about 2:30? Yes, I'll have it ready by then. (*Turns to Marge*)

Marge: Well, you're pretty busy. My grandmother died about a month ago, and I guess, . . . I guess it's been happening since then. Well . . . I dunno . . . well, you're busy, and I've taken up a lot of your time already. . . .

To function with any degree of adequacy, a counselor must be protected from interruptions. If he cannot get a secretary of his own, perhaps he can arrange for student clerks to take calls while he is counseling. Or perhaps he can arrange for an attachment on his phone to transmit his calls to an office secretary or clerk when he is with counselees.

Sometimes counselors complain that both students and staff members ignore a closed door and pop in. Again, in the absence of a secretary or student staff to head off this type of interruption, the counselor must devise some method of protecting himself and his counselees, even if it means hanging out a "Do not disturb" sign. In preference to this, however, a counselor can adopt an open-door policy and let it be known that the only time the door is closed is when he is in conference or is not in the office, at which time the door should be locked. He must not depart from this procedure. He must not close the door to get caught up on paperwork or reading. Often counselors who complain of being interrupted in conference are those who close the door frequently, hoping they will be left alone to catch up on their chores. Then when someone knocks on the door or opens it and says, "Are you busy?" the counselor almost has to say, "Oh no. Come on in." The closed door may or may not signal a conference.

One more aspect of physical setting that serves as a barrier and bears brief mention relates to the location of the counseling and guidance suite. If counselors and the administrator in charge of school discipline share a reception room, students may be reluctant to refer themselves for counseling and risk being mistaken as someone who has "been sent to the office." Similarly, students may feel self-conscious about sitting in a reception room in the "fairway" of the main stream of traffic. On the other hand, if the counseling and guidance suite is difficult to reach or is too far removed from the main stream of traffic, students may not readily find their way to counselors. Students may feel that they do not have time right now to make the trip clear to the other part of the building. Or they do not think of calling on counselors for assistance because on their daily route they are never near the counseling suite.

On one college campus, students offered as one reason for being reluctant to use the services of the counseling center the fact that it was located on the third floor of a walk-up building. Already apprehensive and anxious students had to climb the stairs to the third floor, anxiety mounting as they climbed. Some changed their minds in the process and, halfway up, turned around and walked down. Those who did mount to the third floor were then asked to sit in a waiting room just inside an open door, quite obvious not only to all who entered the center but to everyone and anyone who had business on that floor. The establishment of satellite centers, located for example in residence halls makes counseling more accessible to students. Often students who would not otherwise present themselves for counseling will take advantage of the opportunity for counseling if it is made more accessible. In any case, residence hall centers provided a solution for the situation mentioned above.

To the planners or the architects drawing up blueprints for a total school or college complex, the location of the counseling suite, the mechanics or procedures employed in receiving students for counseling, and the flow of students in and out of the area may seem relatively unimportant. But experienced counselors know otherwise, and it is hoped that experienced administrators will give counselors a voice in planning the physical setting, including design of counseling stations, ordering equipment, plan for routine procedures related to counseling, the flow of traffic, and so forth. In some cases, experienced counselors may have to shout a bit to be heard, and it is their responsibility to do so if necessary.

Encapsulation

In this section, we shall look at counselor encapsulation as a barrier to counseling. Encapsulation as viewed here involves surrounding oneself with a protective cover. Like a capsule, from which the concept of encapsulation derives, an encapsulated counselor is one who has encased himself in a cover that is hard to break. In an expression that captures the resulting feeling of warmth and security, Wrenn (1965a) describes encapsulation as surrounding oneself "with *a cocoon of pretended reality*."

The encapsulated counselor covers himself over with beliefs, values, attitudes, concepts that keep intact his security, that protect him from the necessity to change, that cause him to be rigid, and that interfere with his perception of people and things as they really are. Encapsulation is thus a barrier to counseling. To value only that which is valued by the middle class in today's society, for example, is encapsulation. To long for "the good old days" is encapsulation. To live by "old saws" — adults know better because they are older — is encapsulation. To associate oneself always with the "pretty side of town" because anything else is uncomfortable — this is encapsulation.

NATURE OF ENCAPSULATION

Encapsulation comes in many shapes and varieties. It may be subtle or it may be blatant; it may be consciously nurtured as one reaches for certain security, or it may exist because of ignorance or lack of awareness. It may be expressed emotionally or intellectually, verbally or nonverbally. Tunnel vision, ivory-towerism, dogmatism, egocentrism, and prejudice all involve encapsulation. Indeed, a closed system of any kind manifests itself in encapsulation.

Wrenn (1965a, p. 219) describes encapsulation this way:

> . . . we protect ourselves from the disturbing reality of change by surrounding ourselves with *a cocoon of pretended reality* — a reality which is based on the past and the known, upon seeing that which is as though it would always be. This is "cultural encapsulation," an encapsulation within our world, within our culture and subculture, within a pretense that the present is enduring.

Cloak (1969), an anthropologist, views the rapidity with which changes are occurring. He not only stresses the urgent need to accept present realities but also strongly argues for replacing outdated and maladaptive behaviors with more appropriate ones: ". . . we must change our repertories all the faster, to adapt to this ever more changing environment." In the extreme condition, Cloak (1969, p. 665) posits a devastating prospect if we do not meet the challenge of this rapidly changing environment:

> . . . if the alternative is to allow our behavioral repertories to fall farther and farther behind adaptive reality, then western civilization, and perhaps the entire species *Homo sapiens*, will follow the dodo and the dinosaur into oblivion.

If counselors are to help others develop "adaptive behavioral repertories" to meet "present realities" and continue to develop appropriate behaviors, they must themselves be capable of doing so. And the key is awareness of change. While it is recognized that change is risky and threatening, it is in its own way dangerous to surround oneself, in the name of security, with outmoded values, beliefs, and methods. And it is especially dangerous for a counselor to do so, for it renders him ineffectual.

Wrenn (1965a, pp. 220–222) enumerates some examples of cultural encapsulation:

1. The tendency of counselors and others to be reluctant to admit the possibility of changes in what they considered to be "enduring truths." New knowledge, recent discoveries, changed points of view are often difficult to accept, especially if one has lived half a lifetime "knowing" something quite different.

2. Clinging to certain beliefs (resting in "academic cocoons"), validated by tradition, though they have little relevance for the total present culture. Examples are the belief in the essentially cognitive and traditional curriculums for all students, learning takes place primarily in school, rewarding students who "fit in" and do not create waves, anyone can "succeed" — all he needs is the will.

3. Reliance by the counselor upon his own educational and vocational experience for a frame of reference in counseling students. A counselor who assumes that what was good for me will be good for my counselees is indeed "out of it." The counselor is obviously ignoring not only the changes that have occurred within the past 10 or 20 years, but is assuming that conditions will remain static for the next 5 or 6. He has, so to speak, lost touch with the "real" world, to say nothing of having neglected the essential individuality of the counselee.

Kagan (1964) points out three factors that "perpetuate the cultural encapsulation of counselors." The first factor he refers to as the "wholesale translocation of sociological concepts." Translocation involves stereotyping people. It is the application of a concept to whole groups falling within a given classification. A person guilty of stereotyping misunderstands statistical studies and "typical" descriptions. To find an "average," the statistician borrows from both ends of the continuum. And it can be a serious error to assume that because a given individual comes from a poverty-stricken home, he does not bathe regularly or his parents are anti-school. Kagan's comment that educators in general tend to "advocate programs based on modality" is uncomfortably true.

Kagan's second dimension is an indictment of some counselor education programs but has application also for working counselors, as well as for educators in general. It is the "assumption that cognitive experiences are likely to alter deep-rooted attitudes and beliefs in students of counseling." As Kagan points out, counseling is an "affect-oriented" process and, as research suggests, didactic courses, purely cognitive experiences are not eminently successful in changing long and deeply held attitudes.

Finally, Kagan presents the "error" of defining the counselor's role "in terms of techniques, methods, and theories rather than in terms of the desired outcomes of their attitudes." He would rather have counselors consider what is possible for counselees to gain from counseling and the "areas of potential to be enhanced" than to focus upon such matters as privacy, full-time assignment, and confidentiality.

Encapsulation, then, has many faces. It is rigidity; it is the easy dismissal of potentially uncomfortable situations: "Why should he complain? He never had it so good." It is underlying indifference to others while we mouth the proper pronouncements; it is knowing there is only one right way; it is never questioning a thought or action because "we've always done it that way"; it is always being bustlingly busy — an excellent way of keeping away from people and uncomfortable thoughts.

THE ENCAPSULATED COUNSELOR

Because encapsulation may well be subtle and the counselor sincere, the existence of encapsulation is sometimes difficult to detect. The condition derives, as has been mentioned previously, from a lack of awareness or an unwillingness to be aware. Perhaps it might be revealing to look at several illustrations depicting the encapsulated counselor at work.

A conference between a counselor and a teacher concerning a third-grade girl from an impoverished home leads them to the conclusion that if any significant improvement in the child's feeling about herself is to be realized, the school needs the parents' cooperation. "But," says the counselor, "I don't suppose we can expect any help from them!"

This statement exemplifies stereotyping, a dimension of encapsulation described by Kagan (1964). The counselor assumed — and how many educators do! — that because the child is a product of poverty, the parents are not interested or willing to cooperate. On the other hand, a reverse kind of stereotyping is to assume that all parents who are themselves college graduates and financially comfortable (not affluent) are helping their children develop positive attitudes toward school. But in what direction are a child's values headed when her college-bred parents refer to her kindergarten experience as "kindergarbage?"

Examples of Kagan's "wholesale translocation of sociological concepts" are multitudinous. How many can you recall from your experience?

Lack of perception and encapsulation on the part of the counselor can cut off even a relationship that has been relatively good in the past. Consider, for example, Don, a high school junior, and his "encapsulated" counselor. Don is an academically above-average student who plans to attend college when he graduates. His family will help him financially, but Don has been working ever since he was old enough to do so — carrying papers, mowing lawns, etc. — to save money for school and to be able to have those "extras" that most adolescent boys need. The counselor has called Don in because his grades slipped last marking period. In talking it over with Don, the counselor learns that Don, who is now packing bags at the supermarket, has been working as many hours as he can and is having trouble keeping up with school work.

Counselor: Money troubles, Don?

Don: In a way, yeah. I'm trying to save money for college, of course, and then, too, it takes money to run a car. . . .

Counselor:	A car? You have a car, now?
Don:	Uh . . . yeah . . . uh . . . I finally saved enough money to buy this car . . . well, Dad helped me some, but I have to keep up the payments and keep it in good shape.
Counselor:	Well, of course, it's up to you. From what you say I guess a car is pretty important to you — but grades can be important, too. When I was your age and saving money for school, I didn't have a car — I walked.

Here the counselor exposes his lack of perception, of understanding of the meaning a car has for Don. He has failed, too, to recognize that the mode of living for young people has changed since he was a boy. In "his day," high school students typically walked or rode bicycles to school.

Sachs (1966, p. 15) speaks to the same type of encapsulation when he says

> . . . when a student expresses this feeling of loneliness overtly, a reprimand is often directed at him. The adult will point out that youngsters today can drive cars earlier, can get more education, and have television. . . . It is as though the adult refuses to recall his own feelings of alienation, his own worries about where his future would lie, and how he might establish his niche in the world.

The adult "has it made." (Or has he?) In any case, he has engulfed himself in a comfortable "cocoon" that efficiently blocks out his capacity to understand how it is with youngsters today. He has permitted himself to be encapsulated in his adulthood, a point to which we shall return in a later chapter.

Yet another — and very frequently noted — instance of counselor encapsulation is reflected in persuasive efforts of counselors to direct the majority of students toward four-year colleges. Some counselors assume that because *they* value a college education that it is good for all individuals.

COMBATTING ENCAPSULATION

The counselor who would keep pace must, first of all, cultivate openness and awareness and reject rigidity of thought and action. Cloak (1969, p. 665) comments on the need to eliminate inappropriate dicta, those whose "sole function is to produce conformity and continuity in behavior." He says:

> We must cultivate not only freedom to choose from the past, but also diversity in the present. Each student must be positively encouraged to do his own thing, and defended against pressure to conform from teachers, schoolmates, and parents. This is not for his good, and certainly not for his enjoyment (many will find it most painful), but for the survival of our society.

Wrenn (1965a, pp. 222–223) offers some measures that may suggest to the counselor ways in which he may avoid encapsulation:

1. He should persist in a regimen of "unlearning" something each day.
2. He should accept as an obligation the encouragement of students whose thinking is different from his own.
3. He must batter down any tendency to be self-righteous.

Finally, Sachs (1966, p. 284) has a very simple and wise suggestion for counselors who would escape encapsulation: "It becomes important . . . not to perceive empathy as identification with a culture, nor with an event or series of events, but rather with man." Counselors who can do this, who can develop and maintain empathy with man, can hardly fall victims to the encapsulation barrier.

Indeterminate Philosophical Base

"No field of endeavor which touches human lives can afford to leave its philosophical presuppositions unexamined." With this statement, Beck (1963, p. 1) introduced his survey of the literature involving philosophical aspects of guidance. He found "only forty philosophical articles" in the "literature of guidance or in that of closely related fields" (Beck, 1963, p. 30) during the years 1952 to 1957. The decade of the 1960s, however, witnessed a movement toward professionalization of counseling and guidance, which was accompanied by increased attention to philosophical and theoretical bases for the field, especially for counseling.

THE TASK OF PHILOSOPHY

Whether we recognize it or not, all facets of our behavior, the way we treat other people, our choices and decisions, our reactions, our values, our responsibleness or lack of it, are embedded in a philosophical base. Whether or not we are philosophically aware, we function one way or another depending upon what we believe. Our philosophical beliefs are more often than not only vaguely sensed, more shadow than substance. Asked to delineate our philosophical tenets, most of us would deny ever having considered the subject. And yet our philosophical beliefs determine our response to our environment, and to the individuals who people it.

Consider, for example, how one would react if he believed on the one hand that man is essentially good, or on the other, that man is essentially evil; if he were an idealist or a pragmatist; if he believed man to be a rational being or a nonrational being; if he believed in free will and freedom of choice or if he believed in determinism and predestination; if he operated from a scientific base or from a religious one.

Man is essentially good.	Trust in man, individually and collectively.
Man is essentially evil.	Distrust.
Idealist	Search for the absolute, the perfect in terms of goodness, truth, etc.
Pragmatist	Concentration on the present; "what works is good, useful."
Man is a Rational Being.	If man has the facts, he will solve his problems and work through to a logical conclusion.
Man is a Nonrational Being.	Emotions play a major role in man's decisions; information alone won't guarantee a solution and an end to problems.
Free Will	Man has freedom to make choices, and can be the major architect of his future.
Determinism	Man is a victim of his environment, has no choices, and is the victim rather than the master of fate.

Scientific Orientation	Concern with objectivity, logic, and empiricism.
Religious Orientation	Concern with subjectivity, faith, and inspiration.

The counselor, as one working in a field that, to understate the situation, "touches human lives" must decide where he stands with regard to fundamental philosophical beliefs. Patterson (1966, pp. 20–21) poses five basic philosophical questions which, he suggests, counselors undertake to answer:

1. What is the nature of human nature, the nature of man?
2. What is the nature of human development?
3. What is the nature of the "good life" and "the good?"
4. What is the nature of the determination of the "good life" and who determines what is "good?"
5. What is the nature of the universe and what is man's relationship to that universe?

The task of philosophy, then, is to provide counselors (or anyone) with a base for a working theory or set of principles from which to operate. Theories, as Stefflre (1965) points out, are like road maps; they let us know where we are and where we are going. He reminds us also that:

. . . theories do not appear at random. If we are to understand why certain theories are constructed and accepted, we need to know something about the philosophical assumptions that the theory builders and the theory holders operated from (Stefflre, 1965, pp. 7–8).

Barclay (1968, p. 10) places philosophical concepts within the context of counseling in the following terms:

Certainly the study of the philosophical meaning of counseling should contribute to the formulation of a consistent set of beliefs to give direction to his counseling. As a man thinks, so should he act. If there is a wide discrepancy between patterns of thinking and acting, one would hope, especially in the case of the counselor engaged in practice, that this conflict could be resolved either by beginning to think more in accordance with his acts or vice versa. Indeed, in view of the personal nature of the counseling relationship and the commitment to a process of growth and development in the lives of others, a failure to examine our own beliefs and understandings is a tacit acknowledgment of hypocrisy.

Developing a theory of counseling demands the discipline of self-inquiry and starts with an understanding of the major philosophical systems.[1] Counselors need a working theory of counseling. As Stefflre (1965, p. 3) points out, the question is not "whether we shall operate from a theory since we have no choice in this matter, but rather what theories shall we use and how shall we use theories."

THE USES OF A THEORY OF COUNSELING

A theory of counseling provides the counselor with "a way of organizing relevant, available knowledge about human nature in a way that enables the user to be useful to other people within the framework of a counseling relationship" (Blocher, 1966, p. 25). It provides, too, a means by which the counselor can organize, conceptualize, and accommodate the many pieces of information he learns about his counselees (Tyler, 1969).

Theory gives direction to the work of the counselor, and it permits him to hypothesize regarding behavior. It provides a vehicle by which his beliefs and values can be translated into a working system. It offers a means of making consistent what one believes and the way one behaves in the counseling interview. A counselor's interaction with his counselees is more likely to be seen as genuine if the counselor is functioning in a way that is consistent with his philosophical commitments than when he is not. And a counselee is likely to place more confidence in a counselor when he senses that he is "going somewhere" than when he feels the counseling sessions produce just aimless conversations. As Stefflre (1965, p. 263) notes, " . . . the counselor's notion of what he *should do* . . . is a value related to his total theoretical position on counseling."

Even the topics stressed during counseling may be dictated

[1] An examination of philosophical systems is beyond the scope of this book. The major philosophies on which counseling theory may be grounded are well covered in books such as James R. Barclay, *Counseling and Philosophy: A Theoretical Exposition*; Carlton E. Beck, *Philosophical Foundations of Guidance*; and Donald H. Blocher, *Developmental Counseling*. See also C. Gilbert Wrenn, "Philosophical and Psychological Bases of Personnel Services in Education," in *Fifty-Eighth Yearbook of the NSSE*, 1959, Pt. II, pp. 41–81.

by the model the counselor embraces. Schofield (1967, p. 141) suggests that topics "may well differ systematically":

> In accordance with one theory, the therapist may empha-
> size certain topics for exploration (and explanation) to the
> exclusion of others, and in a variety of ways restrict the
> therapeutic conversation to these topics. Another school will
> emphasize that the topics for discussion should be arrived at
> spontaneously and determined primarily by the patient. One
> theory may emphasize the self-concept as the topic of thera-
> peutic conversation while another may focus on specific
> symptomatology.

Finally, a counselor needs some type of theoretical con-
ceptualization to translate his philosophy into a working relationship, to guide him as he attempts to help others. It need
not be "precise, elegant, or absolute," but as Tyler (1969, p.
21) points out " . . . an organized set of concepts about life
and human nature greatly facilitates his work." Operating
from an indeterminate philosophical base without a model to
serve as a "direction finder," he has no way of knowing why
he was effective — or why he was not. He cannot know why
one day the counseling seemed to move, and another day it
bogged down. Though he may experience "success" with
a given counselee, he will not know why, or what he did (or
did not do) that caused a favorable response or outcome. He
has no basis for hypotheses; his approach is hit-or-miss. Because he has no model to test, he has no yardstick by which
to measure his effectiveness. The signs along the way somehow escape him, because he has no map to tell him what to
look for. Most serious, however, is that he has no safeguards
against stagnation, no way to know that he is changing, no
vehicle for growth and development as a counselor. He is
likely to be perpetually the "erratically eclectic" beginner
described by Stefflre (1965, p. 240):

> The beginner in the field of secondary school counseling
> either tends to become erratically eclectic, piecing together
> remnants of theory, or he allies himself with a particular
> theory and clings to it, whether suited to himself and pupil
> needs or not.

THE "FULLY FUNCTIONING" COUNSELOR

We know that there is no individual who might truly be termed a "fully functioning counselor," just as there is no "fully functioning" individual. Perhaps a modifier should be inserted to make this section read "The More Fully Functioning Counselor," since a difference in functioning is a relative matter. In any case, the purpose here is to describe how counselors who are aware function. Or, in other words, what is adequate functioning? What alternative does the "erratically eclectic" counselor have? Some examples of how theoretical postulates guide the counselor's behavior are given below.

The first example comes from an article (Bates and Johnson, 1969, pp. 247–248) in which the authors' purpose is to distinguish between the way nondirective and existentialist counselors respond to counselees, each from his own theoretical frame of reference. To this and to the example that follows will be added a response representative of that which might be offered by a "nontheory" counselor.

Concept: Man defines himself only through his actions. Good intentions are irrelevant. Man can define himself only through what he does, not what he says he is going to do, or what he intended to do.

Client: I'm not sure what I want to be. Sometimes I think nursing, then again no. I think I would like to be a secretary. I'm just not sure at all.

Nondirective: The whole picture of choosing a job seems pretty dim to you right now.

Existentialist: Right now you seem to have at least two choices in mind. Could we think out loud what's in each job for you?

Nontheorist: What courses are you taking right now?

Both the nondirective and the existentialist counselors have considered vocational development theory and accept vocational decision making as a task that involves the whole person and especially the way the individual views himself. They are moving in the direction of helping the student explore possibilities in terms of herself. The "nontheory" counselor merely brushes the surface and sees occupational choice as involving educational requirements, omitting the most significant dimension in decision making — the way the counselee feels.

The following dialogue represents a contrast between responses of the behaviorally oriented counselor and the nontheory counselor.

Counselee: Well, I finally got myself to the Science Club meeting on Tuesday.

Behaviorist: Good. Now that you've done it once, it will be easier to go next time and the next and the next.

Nontheorist: You did?

Although this example is somewhat oversimplified, it does point up the difference between the counselor who has some direction and the one who is stabbing in the dark. The behaviorist here reinforces the counselee's action with verbal approval and moves along to the counselee's reaction to the experience. The nontheorist simply lets the counselee hang in midair. What private reaction can we imagine the counselee might have to the counselor's response, and what verbal response can he possibly make in return? And where does the interview go from here? Kemp (1967, p. xi) has noted that "the degree to which counseling succeeds is finally dependent upon the response of the counselee."

The counselor is urged to develop a working theory of counseling that will enable him to be most broadly and deeply himself and that will at the same time be flexible enough to meet the needs of the greatest number of his counselees. It is important that counselors know why they respond as they do, why they behave as they do in the counseling relationship. Stefflre (1965) reminds us that a skillful counselor works out a theory of his own, starting by identifying with some orientation with which he feels comfortable, and modifying as experiences dictate. The counselor must recognize that he will change, that theories change, that they are based on present knowledge and present needs and present conditions. All of these may change with time and experience, rendering the presently held theory obsolete.

Blocher (1966, pp. 40–41) offers criteria in the form of questions a counselor might put to himself in building or evaluating his personal theory of counseling:

General Criteria

1. How does the theory deal with the process of human development?

2. How does the theory explain the nature of human learning?

3. How does the theory deal with individual differences?

4. Does the theory offer some central set of constructs or principles for organizing and explaining behavior?

5. How does the theory provide a rationale for counselor behavior?

6. How well does the theory offer possibilities for empirical testing and modification?

Personal Criteria

1. Is the counseling role implied by this theory one that I can assume?

2. Are the techniques and understandings required by this approach ones that I can master?

3. Are the goals recommended by this theory ones with which I can comfortably identify?

In delineating sources of gain in psychotherapy, Hobbs (1967) includes the opportunity afforded the client to develop a "personal cosmology" that is appropriate for him. Hobbs' concept with regard to the personal cosmology has relevance also to the counselor in search of personal theory of counseling. The personal theory of counseling, like the personal cosmology, must be convincing to the counselor; it should be perceived by the individual as being reasonably consistent, but it should contain "some dissonances," either external or internal, to keep the individual sufficiently challenged "to work to strengthen his major propositions about himself and his world." Hobbs' closing note is of major significance: "Finally, it should have built-in requirements for revision, for to live is to change, and to remain static is to die" (1967, p. 124).

3

Hazards for the Counselor

In the counseling relationship, the counselor can easily slip into various nonproductive ways of functioning. The continued negative responses of the counselee may cause him to realize that all is not well. Or he may sense that nothing at all appears to be happening. But it is still difficult for him to know why. It occurs to him that he has been or is functioning in a way that hinders, but he cannot identify the particular behavioral pitfalls to which he has succumbed.

If counselors are aware, in advance, of some of the hazards which can so readily ensnare them, hopefully they will be in a stronger position to combat or avert them. On this premise, this chapter discusses five common detrimental patterns: intellectualizing, or focusing upon externals; inadvertently functioning in a parental role in lieu of that of counselor; counseling when fatigued; becoming enmeshed in emotional and social entanglements; and falling into the trap of subtly imposing the counselor's own values upon the counselee.

Intellectualization

In response to what the counselee is attempting to express, the counselor may "externalize" the situation. Instead of furthering the emergence of the actual problem, he volubly addresses himself to the more obvious surface content of what is being said and talks *around* and *about* it to the counselee. When he does this he is "intellectualizing."

There are a number of reasons why intellectualizing is likely to happen. Seldom if ever does the counselor deliberately or consciously intend to be evasive. When he does fall into this particular hazard, it is because it is for him a very natural and comfortable way of responding. It is natural, because the counselor, by virtue of his educational training and aptitudes, is typically quite verbally adept. Understanding concepts and explaining or dealing with them is not likely to be difficult for him. He feels "at home" in doing so, and so does it readily.

Thus intellectualizing on the part of the counselor is a particularly subtle hazard. Basically, as has been implied above, it is an avoidance technique. By selecting certain "safe" aspects of what the counselee is saying, albeit unintentionally, the counselor actually is attempting to be in control of the interview. It is an attempt to hold the situation within respectable or manageable boundaries, to guard against emotionally disturbing trends which might otherwise erupt.

An illustration may help. Jim is an intelligent young man who has almost completed his junior year at the university. When he comes to the counselor, he is tense and troubled:

> *Jim:* I think I'm going to have to drop out of school. I can't go on any more. It's been bad since my mother died last spring. There's just no need to continue having to put out the money any more.

> *Counselor:* If money is a problem for you now, Jim, I'm sure the situation can be worked out. There are a number of student loans available, and part-time employment opportunities too, if you are interested in working.

Jim: It really isn't the money. It's just that . . . well, ever since mother died, nothing is the same. Probably no one can really understand . . . (*silence*) My grades sure have gone down, too.

Counselor: It's understandable that it would be harder to study and to concentrate. But making the effort can help you, Jim. You don't have too much longer before your degree, you know.

Jim: Yes, I know. But I just can't do it now. Her death changed things too much.

All of the emotional content and the real concerns that Jim was trying to express about what his mother's death meant to him were sealed off. They were skirted and detoured, as the counselor picked up only some of the more obvious and external facts. Maybe finances and the values of study were not consciously set up as shields against the counselor's possible anxiety and disinclination to discuss death, but that is exactly what they were. The counselor has intellectualized.

Let's look at another example. When Ruth comes to the counseling session, she is struggling hard, and not very successfully, to keep from crying. The counselor attempts to help her to relax and to establish rapport; he does this, however, by completely disregarding her emotionalized state:

Counselor: Sit down, Ruth. I'm glad you wanted to come in today.

Ruth: Yes . . . I . . . well, I guess I *need* to be here. I don't know who else I could talk to about this. I feel awful and I don't care if I die. My parents *can't* know, and I hope I never see Jack again — ever.

Counselor: Is Jack your boy friend?

Ruth: Yes . . . well, he *was*. And now I just hate him. He got me into this nightmare mess. I thought he loved me, but now he hasn't called me for three whole weeks. And I don't know what to do.

Counselor: You realize this is near the end of the quarter and final exams start in two days. Maybe he has had a lot to do lately.

Ruth is trying to tell the counselor that she is pregnant and that she is desperate and alone. But again, avoiding the real messages, the intellectualizing counselor selectively tunes in on the cognitive level only. Ruth feels even more alone and upset. But the counselor's needs have been met.

Preconceptions of what the counselee is like may also initiate the hazard of counselor intellectualization. It is as if the counselor has, in Gestalt psychological terms, prematurely completed a configuration. He jumps to hasty "closures" and conclusions. It may be, for example, that something the counselee says reminds him of a similar interview (there are no "similar" interviews!) with another counselee. Or he links it up with some of the data he recalls having read from this counselee's record, so he feels he can fully interpret the whole problem. But by not allowing the counselee the freedom and time to explore his own experience, the counselor is revealing that it is probably also difficult for him as a person to continue with anxieties of uncertainty. Intellectualizing — in this case, presenting a completed configuration — serves as a refuge:

Counselee: I've cut so many times in that class . . . I just felt I couldn't face it in there any more. I feel . . .

Counselor: This is somewhat of a pattern for you, isn't it, Jim? Cutting classes, I mean.

Counselee: Not really . . . I mean, I don't really want to do it, ever. But in *this* class now, it really bothers me . . .

Counselor: Well, I guess you do know what the consequences will be, though, if you keep on missing class.

The counselee is stranded, left alone to struggle with the disturbing feelings he has about why he is so upset about this class. No real communication has occurred.

Similarly, an intellectualized picture may be presented the

counselee because the counselor's personal prejudices have been touched upon. His bias may have been activated from the counselee's remarks:

> *Jane:* (*a white student*) I really like this guy an awful lot and I've dated him five times. But . . . well, the trouble is, he's a Negro. If my parents ever found out, it'd be like a bomb explosion. They'd pull me immediately out of school too, I guess.

> *Counselor:* What caused you to first start dating this boy?

> *Jane:* It was on a double date with my roommate. Her date wasn't colored, but he was a friend of Ron's, and he respects him. Ron is nice looking, and his skin really isn't too dark. I wanted to see what he'd be like.

> *Counselor:* You didn't think then that doing this could cause serious problems? It would seem you would have had many reservations. Your parents undoubtedly have real reasons for their strong objections.

> *Jane:* Well, *they're* prejudiced — I'm not. Ron is such a wonderful person. I think I like him better than anyone I've ever met. But still, I'm not sure what to do. . . .

The counselor has tightened up; feeling that he has the whole picture very clearly in mind, he has intellectualized in terms of his own prejudice. Jane is not helped to clarify her mixed feelings; she may now only feel a mounting defiance and resistance toward the counselor. Certainly she will not disclose many more real feelings.

Intellectualizing can be used to "save face," if and when the counselor feels temporarily inadequate or embarrassed as he listens to the counselee. He feels at a loss as to how to respond, yet feels called upon to demonstrate his competence. He may ask questions, but the questions probably are again directed to the peripheral and factual externals and serve as intellectualized devices to bypass the immediate unpleasantness.

     Bob: After I had the accident and got these scars on my face and all, I guess she just couldn't take it. Last Friday night she gave me my ring back — just like that. Wham! So I don't think anyone can ever care about me again. I don't care what happens to me any more. . . .

Counselor: But you do know that your family cares? And that the accident could have been so much worse? You still have so much to be thankful for.

Bob's miserable feelings have been totally ignored. The counselor shied away, lest the situation become even more painful. He poses questions, safe factual questions, to bring the situation around to more comfortable ground.

Still another form of intellectualization when the counselor feels ill at ease and unsure as to how to respond may be an overly brusque, quick reassurance to the counselee. For example, Karen, highly nervous, is talking to the counselor:

    Karen: So I did finally go to the doctor. And he said yes, I do have to have an operation. A major one, and right away. But I just *can't!* Since Jim and I are both in school now, there just isn't any money. And the baby is just 5½ months. I'm awfully afraid, too. . . .

Counselor: Most people are a little scared when they think about having an operation. But probably everything will work out just fine. Even the bills. And of course you will be completely unconscious from the anesthetic when you have the surgery — you won't feel a thing.

It is as if the counselor, in swiftly intellectualizing the whole matter, is saying, "I'm not worried one bit. Why should you be, after all?" A somewhat similar instance, and one particularly hazardous for the inexperienced counselor, arises when the temptation exists to be overly supportive to the counselee. On an intellectualized level, the counselor might "take up" the problem himself and talk to the counselee about what might neatly "solve" his dilemma. It is true that the counselee may have asked for such answers. But it is interesting to note that frequently such requests are asked in consequence of a *prior* intellectualizing by the counselor. When feelings are detoured, the counselee may feel he should respond within the intellectualized structure. Thus, if the interchange between counselor and counselee has evolved to a very factual or cognitive level, the counselee may attempt to use the counselor on this basis.

> The intellectual process is easy, but it is superficial and oversimplifying. It does not engage the whole person with all his relationships, or stand by him in the ongoing search for his unique destiny among his fellows. . . . The problem goes far beyond 'information please,' because it is in reality an ongoing quest for new life in which to outgrow the old life (Johnson, 1967, pp. 178, 182).

Intellectualization in counseling is like a sand trap in golf: all forward movement becomes bogged down during the time that this hazard engulfs the play. In the interview, the counselee is hindered and stopped, blocked in what he really needs to tell the counselor in seeking release from his tensions. The counselee is not freed whenever the counselor focuses on externals, interposes his own high-sounding knowledges, or intellectualizes with prematurely phrased interpretations. As Jourard (1968, p. 42) sees it:

> Every time a therapist meets his patient in the privacy of the consulting room, a secret society has just sprung into being. The purpose for which the society came into being is freedom. . . . If the therapist is an unwitting agent of the status quo, he may well hinder his patient's struggle.

Intellectualizing is a hazard most likely to happen to the counselor who is insecure and unsure of himself. It should be recognized that considerable moral courage is needed in real counseling. If the counselor is not to be the "unwitting agent of the status quo," he must somehow develop the inner strength not to avoid, but to face and deal with the counselee's emotional problems, painful as they are. He also has to become willing to set aside his own defenses in the relationship. For if evasiveness and detouring by way of intellectualizations are not stopped, counseling will be.

Intellectualization blunts sensitivity for future counseling. It becomes easier to tune out the real messages and feelings which counselees are struggling to express. The counselor grows more immune to them, less of a perceptive listener. Surely the counselor does not *want* this to happen, but it does. Then, as he senses lack of counselee growth and response, his own doubts about himself as a counselor and helping person increase.

Thus the hazard of intellectualization is both a potent and a pernicious one. However, counselors, and not just counselees, can gain in self-insight and come to modify their behaviors, even though it is not easy to do so. Hiltner (1952, p. 82), speaking in this regard of himself as counselor, says:

> If I develop an almost overpowering impulse to stop listening to a teen-ager talk about which college he is going to apply for, and give him the real dope, and I catch myself in the act, I may now be strong enough to be able to admit to myself that showing what I know, even just to myself, is something on which I rely for propping up self-esteem. Not a very pleasant insight. But if it is true, and if I avoid it, the tendency will pop out in repeated temptations to inject my knowledge where it has no relevance. *If I take the pain of the insight, I become in some measure free from a compulsion.* [Italics ours]

Assumption of Parental Roles

There are all kinds of parents and parent-child relationships. There are authoritarian parents, parents who are overly protective and possessive, indulgent parents who attempt to give their sons and daughters everything possible which they themselves might not have had. Then there are the very permissive parents, the *laissez-faire* ones who adopt this policy either because they no longer feel adequate to cope with problems or because of cumulative indifference which actually reveals their feelings of rejection. But of course there is also that very large group who do respect the emerging personalities of their children and earnestly try to help and to understand their unique growth patterns.

In common with this latter group, counselors experience feelings of genuine and intelligent concern and caring. However, in any parent-child relationship, in one form or another, there are some inevitable emotional factors and involvements. These represent the hazards. For the counselor must function as counselor, not as a parent or as a parental representative. The *in loco parentis* concept may have been examined academically and legally, but insufficient attention has been given to it therapeutically.

Whether or not the counselor actually is a parent, such parental behaviors as overprotectiveness, authoritarian or judgmental roles, manipulation, or punitive response patterns can be real pitfalls. It could be helpful, therefore, to consider how and when these are likely to occur in counseling.

Functionally, the boundary between empathy and sympathy is thin. It is not hard for the unwary counselor to abandon the more objective aspect of empathy and to sympathize. And sympathizing, he may identify with the counselee's problem to the extent that he feels a strong desire to help the counselee avert certain consequences. So he steps in to help in some direct way, to "fix things," much as a protective parent would do. When Marie, a high school student on the verge of despair, tells the counselor that if she does not have an acceptable theme ready for her sixth-period class she will not only fail in English but will be ridiculed before the class, and that she just can't "take it" any more, the counselor may offer then and there to help her write it. Or when Paul, a junior high school boy, tells of a very upsetting personal misunderstanding which occurred yesterday between him and some of his friends who ride the school bus, the counselor offers to give him a ride home or to loan him the money for a taxi. But, as Tyler (1961, p. 226) points out, these actions do not help the counselee "work through" his problems to the end that he is enabled to cope on his own behalf.

> It is usually inadvisable for a counselor to lend a client money although he may have a strong impulse to dispose of some of the client's problems in this simple way. Ordinarily

he should not take action on the client's behalf — clear up a misunderstanding with an instructor, petition for an exception to academic regulations, or get him a job. . . . Such acts shape the counseling relationship for an overdependent client into the familiar pattern in which he manages to get along, though not very successfully, by inducing people to take care of him. It is precisely that pattern which the counselor is attempting to enable him to break away from.

Monitoring the counselee's behavior, responding in terms of the counselor's own "shoulds" or "should nots" or in terms of how he, the counselor, regards the sanctions of societal norms is another form of "parent trap." The counselor moralizes. Resenting being preached at, as he no doubt frequently has been on many past occasions by his parents, the counselee instantly is put on the defensive. He becomes either sullen or silent. Let's look at Don's situation:

> Don: (*a high school senior*) It was about 3:30 in the morning when I took her home. Sure was hard to take her to the door, when I saw the lights were on, and knew her folks were probably up and waiting. But I do care a lot about Sue and I want to see her again.

> Counselor: Well, as you know, that just is far too late an hour to take a nice girl back home. If you did feel you wanted to see her again I'm surprised you didn't see that she was home much earlier than that.

> Don: (*Silence*)

It might be argued here that some moralizing on occasion is not only justified but necessary. But as Benjamin (1969, p. 141) observes, it is wise to consider if doing so ever really helps the counselee:

Moralizing can be overwhelming. At best, it helps the interviewee see how society judges him, how others look upon his behavior. At worst, it blocks examination of self and self-motivated actions and stifles further expression of feelings and attitudes. It can result in insightless submission or stubborn defiance.

Closely allied with moralizing is the hazardous tendency to chide or berate the counselee, even though this response may be disguised. The counselor, acting in the role of parental substitute, feels called upon to express strong personal disapprovals and criticisms. He may be more likely to respond in this manner when the counselee is referred because of some specific offense or deviant behavior pattern. In the following example, Ann, a junior high school student, has been asked by her home room teacher to see the counselor:

Counselor: Come in, Ann. Miss Ames tells me that it could help you if we talked together.

     Ann: Uh-huh.

Counselor: Can you tell me what the trouble is?

     Ann: Wh — Well, I didn't come to school yesterday. And I didn't have an excuse from my mother.

Counselor: Ann, you know this is against the rules, don't you?

The counselee is very accustomed to this parental type of chastisement. He or she also is familiar with such responses as marked facial expressions of disapproval or an ignoring of much of what he may be trying to say. Similarly, he shrinks inside himself, again, if he hears a counselor say to him something like, "You probably realize this did disappoint your father very much" or "Your mother probably does have a basis for trusting you less." What happens here is that rather than being enabled to talk and to gain insights and release from his present feelings of guilt, the counselee feels that now he must push these feelings down even more. Shame often is used by parents, intentionally or unintentionally, as a motivational device to get their children to repudiate undesirable or obnoxious behaviors. But seldom, if ever, do parents realize the hidden psychological damages that can occur from repeatedly adding to guilts and very rarely do they see the hoped-for results from regular practice of this motivational route. However, it may be understood that a parent does this because he does not realize the harm he may be causing and because he does not know what else to do; his outraged expressions may be simple and direct. The counselor, on the other hand, should understand the perniciousness of cumulative guilt; the hazard is that despite this knowledge, he frequently may fail to act accordingly.

A counselee may go to a counselor because of his unresolved and snarled relationships. Mixed up, he has the need to open up his conflicts. He may have ambivalent feelings toward a friend, toward the person he has dated or wants to date, or about the particular social group he would like to join. Now he wants to be freed and to get "in the clear" on his own. Perhaps he has already tried to broach some of this with his parents, but it did not work. They may have been concerned, but anxious. Possibly they did not approve of this or that attachment, and firmly said so. In all likelihood, they did give him considerable direct advice. It well could be that now they are a part of his present relationship problems!

If the counselor becomes motivated to do in part the same type of thing, the counseling will be pretty sterile for our counselee. Why would the counselor be likely to feel on occasion that he should assume a supervisory role? Or why would he consider it necessary to impose strong views about the counselee's interpersonal relationships and to be very free with advice? These are questions it would be well for him to ask himself. In addition, he needs to analyze thoughtfully the probable effects of such responses upon the counselee. Benjamin (1969, p. 132) provides some perceptive observations:

> It is essential that the interviewer ask himself whether he has a need to give advice, in specific instances or generally. Such a need may interfere with the interviewee's struggle to decide what is best for him. The interviewer's need to advise may prematurely cut off the joint examination of the matter under discussion. If the interviewer can become aware of this need, he may think twice before giving advice and ask himself whether it has been solicited and whether it is, in fact, required.

All of this is not to say that there are not times when open-ended suggestions or interpretations may not be offered to the counselee. The hazard is one of encroachment. If he is to grow, the counselee should retain the freedom to consider, "filter," and accept or reject all such proposals.

Overly protective behavior can be manifested in many forms. Parents often feel that they cannot allow or trust their sons and daughters, even in later adolescence, to be autonomous in making decisions. It is difficult for them to transfer freedom rights and keep abreast with the advancing maturity of their "children"; they feel their "voice of experience" still needs to be heard.

The counselor may sometimes feel very much the same. If he is honest, he may admit that he cannot bring himself to fully trust the counselee; the counselee *could* do that which he *should not*. "I must come in at this point," the counselor reasons to himself, "or a very unwise choice might be made." But as Shostrom (1968, p. 65) observes:

> His active demanding and "shoulding" are . . . forms of omnipotence that deeply distrust the potential for independent action on the part of the other person.

The counselee has the need to explore and sort out his own feelings before making a decision. If the counselor pushes him, hands out a packaged solution, reinforces strongly some possible actions over others, or probes with questions indicative of doubt and distrust, the counselee cannot open up his own situation to himself. He also, in some measure, will forfeit the experience of taking consequences, for the counselor in reality will have assumed them. Growth is blocked, in that he feels less self-reliant and that probably his own judgment in new and untried situations should not be risked.

Sue:	I think I'd really like to join the sorority. But Tom doesn't like the idea and my parents think it might cost too much. But I still think I'd like to do it.
Counselor:	Do your parents also feel that it might lower your grade-point average? Would you have less time for your studies, if you did?
Sue:	Maybe . . . but I don't think so. I think I'd enjoy being with those girls, and living in the house . . .
Counselor:	But there are probably many things, too, that may not be positive about it, don't you think?

The counselor seems to be pushing for Sue to make a negative decision here. And certainly Sue cannot be oblivious to the parent-like overtones in the counselor's responses. She probably feels now that somehow she does not want to discuss the situation any more — she will just keep things to herself.

It is a grave hazard indeed for the counselor to become excessively involved in the decision-making process. Paul Johnson (1967, p. 99) understands this when he comments:

> The [true] counselor sustains the person in his search for identity from which he can see more clearly who he is, and come to basic decisions in his situation.

Parents are prone to feel that because they are parents, respect should naturally be their due from their sons and daughters, irrespective of whether such respect has been deserved and earned. For some counselors, although they may be unaware of it, a like feeling may be present. They really feel that their title and role *per se* qualify them to receive only expressions of liking and respect. In common with many parents, they find it extremely difficult, for any reason, ever to serve as a "target" for counselee hostility. This would shake them and strike a real blow to their self-concepts. Their own feelings of security would be in jeopardy. There is a real hazard to the counseling process here. If the hazard is to be avoided, somehow the counselor must acquire the strength and security to be able to receive *all* counselee feelings, to encourage and promote full catharsis. When counselees grope and try to accept and understand their troubled feelings, some emotional entanglements may temporarily be displaced to the person of the counselor, as Freud well knew. If the counselor is unable to absorb them, he will, in the words of Paul Johnson (1967, p. 162) tend to act as do many parents — "label children as bad when they act out their feelings."

A deep reason why many parents find it difficult to accept failures of their children is that they feel this reflects on their own egos, reputations, and self-esteem. They feel that they too have failed. But of course, in the growing process, not only do children and adolescents inevitably fail on many occasions and in many ways, but they actually need to know *how* to fail and what these failures can teach them. These valuable learning experiences can be shunted and blocked by both parents and counselors. For many counselors react here as do parents; counselee failures may be interjected into their own feelings and needs for adequacy. The counselee's self-concept needs could then receive diluted attention. But just at these times of defeat and failure, the self-regard of the counselee will certainly have dropped to a very low point. Despair may be close. Now he has an especial need for the "unconditional positive regard" of the counselor to be continued and unchanged. But if his retrogression personally disappoints the counselor, what then? The counselor might feel that as he and the counselee had been exploring in this particular area for some time, such present failure reflects upon his own competence and helping abilities as a counselor. "My" counselee has failed. But how unlike the parent who also finds it difficult to assimilate failures would this response actually be?

Because counseling is an interaction, further hazards arise in response to parent-like behaviors. Maneuvering and manipulative devices are likely to be employed by the counselee as a form of response generalization. When the counselor behaves in certain parental ways, he provides a stimulus situation similar to that of the counselee-parent relationship. As part of the counselee's problems may have been grounded in just this context, he may have been attempting to cope with his conflicts at home by means of various devious maneuvers. In consequence, the counselor who has assumed the parental role could find himself vulnerable to these same manipulative techniques. To the counselee, he may appear as someone to be used, outwitted, or cleverly resisted. In reality, the counselee has an especial need to be freed from this form of behavior. As Fitts (1965, p. 30) says, it is as if he were saying to the counselor, "Are you strong enough *not* to be what I [apparently] want you to be, even if I use all of my tricks on you?"

As we look in review at some of these hazards for the counselor of assuming various parental roles, it would appear that such behaviors contribute to a blocking of counselee catharsis and growth. The counseling situation is not too different from the home situation, and the counselee still feels either somewhat protected, censored, judged, or partially rejected. He therefore cannot change.

It may well be that the counselor who falls too easily into an adoption of these responses is himself responding too readily to past conditionings. He tends to respond as *his* parents responded to him. As McKinney (1958, pp. 232–233) says:

> There is perforce a wide gap between the understanding of an accepting attitude and the practice of it. In a counseling session, we may tend, particularly under pressure and emotion to fall back on previously established reactions. More often than not, these will consist of passing judgment, scapegoating, taking an authoritative role, condemning behavior that is unconventional — in short, continuing the role of teacher or parent.

Fatigue and Insensitivity

If clients are to be really helped to improve because of the counseling experience, according to Carkhuff and Berenson (1967), there are certain identifiable "core factors" that must be manifested by the counselor. These primary factors or conditions are similar to Rogers' congruence, empathy, and unconditional positive regard and are "facilitative." Carkhuff and Berenson list the core factors as empathic understanding, positive regard or respect, genuineness, and concreteness. Obviously these qualities are not operative to any noticeable degree in weary, dispirited counselors. This is to say that even those counselors who usually do express such personal attributes cannot do so well when they are fatigued and spent.

Counseling is work, and the psychological demands made upon the counselor are very real. In the counseling interview, the counselor has the professional obligation to the particular counselee then with him. Each client presents himself because his needs and problems require help beyond his own efforts. He hopes, sometimes desperately, that maybe here with the counselor, a person prepared to understand inner personal problems, he can work through all of his dilemmas. Of course the counselor wants this, too. But what if, at the start of the interview, the counselor finds himself dulled, tired, and consequently incapable of responding fully?

This is a recurrent hazard which many counselors do not wholly recognize; or if they do, it may be one they are reluctant to admit or tend to ignore. Fatigue has a way of being subtly cumulative. Because he is very aware that many counselees are waiting to be interviewed, and that there are numerous other urgent allied responsibilities to be discharged, the counselor may simply press on day after day, even when really fatigued. He postpones or omits entirely some of the recreational activities he used to enjoy and too frequently may curtail needed hours for rest and sleep. Thus it can easily happen that these negative functional patterns become established ones.

Wrenn clearly perceives the hazards involved here and understands as well the generative sources of such fatigue. He speaks of the development in the counselor, as in other personnel workers, of a "kind of nervous fatigue, unlike that experienced in most other fields." The counselor's task involves daily unique human contacts, in which there exists the "necessity for attempting to see beneath the surface and to infer attitudes and conflicts from exterior behavior and verbalization." Wrenn (1962b, p. 564) further observes that a highly significant danger lies in what can then happen to the tired counselor in the counseling process, inasmuch as the fatigue "mask" can be expressed

> . . . in inattention or insensitivity which is revealed by a wandering of the counselor's gaze, or the wandering of his mind, or in preoccupation with superficialities because he is too tired or too lazy to deal with the fundamental human dynamics involved.

When the counselor thus does not concentrate and center upon the needs and problems of the counselee, the counseling process truly is "thinned." The counselee feels the full impact of these counselor responses to him which have become mechanical, superficial, or slightly irrelevant. He feels the counselor is not too concerned, not "with" him, and does not understand what troubles him. In other words, the counselor is not *empathizing* with him any more.

EMPATHIC UNDERSTANDING

We have noted Carkhuff and Berenson's citing of empathic understanding on the part of the counselor as one of the "core facilitative dimensions" in the relationship, if the counselee is to be helped. What exactly is meant by the term *empathy*? Hiltner (1952, p. 163) attempts to define it functionally, as well as to underscore its significance for the counselor:

> To put it positively and unsystematically, the counselor needs . . . the ability to convince his client that he is genuinely interested in him and to have this true in fact, the capacity to lay aside temporarily his own problems and concentrate understandingly on the person and problems of the client and the ability to retain his sensitivity to the nuances of communication.

To illustrate what might occur in the counseling process when empathic understanding is present and when it is not, let us look at two examples. In the first instance, the counselor obviously has *not* "retained his sensitivity to the nuances of communication":

> *Ruth:* It bothers me a lot. I don't think John really loves me. I just don't think I'm *important* to him. He never tries to really understand how I feel about anything.
>
> *Counselor:* But you are engaged to him now?
>
> *Ruth:* Yes. But I wonder if we should be. We've been engaged since last summer when my parents announced it.
>
> *Counselor:* Your parents do approve of him, then?
>
> *Ruth:* Uh-huh. (*Silence*)

At this point, when counseling seems to have halted on a chilly plateau, Ruth may feel that John and the counselor have some things in common. Neither of them do tune in to what she is trying to tell them.

Let's look at what might have occurred had the counselor been receiving and responding on Ruth's wave-length. We will start with Ruth's same initial expression:

> *Ruth:* It bothers me a lot. I don't think John really loves me. I just don't think I'm *important* to him. He never tries to understand how I really feel about anything.
>
> *Counselor:* You feel that if you really mattered to John, he would try to understand you more as a person.
>
> *Ruth:* Yes! That's just it. But he doesn't listen to me. He doesn't even know what I'm really like.
>
> *Counselor:* If he would just really hear what you try to tell him, he could come to understand you as you are.
>
> *Ruth:* And if he cared, he would do this, wouldn't he? I guess this is just what worries me so much about us. . . .

Counseling continues; the counselor understands. Ruth is enabled to unburden herself, to express more and more of the conflicting feelings she has been experiencing.

In empathic understanding, the essential component is perceptual sensitivity. It is the type of sensitivity called into play when the counselor actually hears and understands what the counselee is saying. The hazard, of course, is that the counselor may not be sufficiently alert to respond in this manner.

To gain a further understanding of fatigue, temporary or chronic, as it can affect the counselor in counseling, let us briefly focus on the other three core dimensions in turn.

GENUINE RESPECT

Respect for the counselee, communicated by the counselor so that the counselee really experiences it, is the second essential dimension. The counseling relationship is a pseudo one without this basic factor. Every individual has the deep intrinsic need to feel important as a unique person. He needs to be accepted just as he is, to know that he matters and has worth. How multiple, complex, and distorted are the relationship problems which develop because this crying need has been denied or blocked! It is not surprising, therefore, that when a counselee, who in all likelihood has in some form been experiencing hurts in this area, feels that he *is* receiving true respect, he gains a sense of nourishment and release.

The counselor does know these psychological realities. But, fundamentally, if he is actually to respect each counselee just as he is, receive and interact with him in an honest endeavor to understand him as he has developed up to the present time, the counselor has to function from the firm basis of his own self-respect. Many subtle implications are involved here, but we are especially concerned with the effects of fatigue. If the counselor has become chronically fatigued, he undoubtedly feels less competent in counseling; he has been the recipient of various negative feedback clues. These feelings can generate doubts about future adequacy. Thus, anxieties and self-distrust can undercut the counselor's self-regard and respect; at this point, he may even feel he needs to be a counselee! He certainly needs renewal and recharging if he is to be able to extend, in all sincerity, the essence of genuine respect to counselees. Also involved in respect is the willingness to trust the counselee. This of course varies in degree, according to the philosophy held by the counselor. But to the extent that the counselor conveys his belief that the counselee is able to grapple with and work through his own problems, the counselee experiences self-respect. However, even those counselors who do feel this way toward their counselees are less likely to convey this communication when fatigue is present. Any counselor whose sensibilities are temporarily dulled is far less likely to encourage real counselee involvement and problem exploration; he, the counselor, is more tuned in to the time boundaries of the interview, as well as to his own present needs and concerns.

GENUINENESS

The third dimension of *genuineness* on the part of the counselor closely approximates what Rogers means when he speaks of "congruence." There must be psychological integration within the counselor. While how he actually feels about the counselee usually may not or should not be fully or overtly expressed in deference to counselee benefit, all such feelings must nevertheless be recognized and accepted. It is necessary that the counselor be aware of any of his own negative emotions or intruding needs, and that he accept rather than resist them if he is to be authentic in the relationship. But the fatigued counselor may find this vigilance very difficult; either achieving or retrieving genuineness or congruence may temporarily be impossible for him. However, it should be said here that while fatigue can indeed be a hazard with respect to genuineness, the counselor who recognizes he is depleted and can admit this fact to the counselee, has not forfeited authenticity. Thus, with some improvisations upon an example cited by Benjamin (1969, p. 31), the counselor might respond in this manner:

Counselor: You know, Helen, I'm very glad we had this talk today. We'll have to stop now, though. Frankly, I realize I'm fatigued and can be of less help to you.

Helen: I still haven't told you what Dad said when he came to see me last week. I didn't know he was coming, and I was in the middle of . . .

Counselor: I'm glad you want to talk about that, but if you continue now, as I say, I realize I won't be listening very well. So why don't we meet on Thursday at the same time and discuss this the way we both want to.

CONCRETENESS

The final primary core dimension which Carkhuff and Berenson cite is that of *concreteness*. Counselor expressions need to be directed specifically to that which is relevant to the counselee; the focus must be kept on that which is of real concern to him. It does not help when the counselor generalizes, "objectivizes," or reverts to analogous experiences of his own or of other counselees. These comparisons may not be at all pertinent to the counselee. Instead, the counselor needs to concentrate on the unique, below-the-surface emotional content of what this particular counselee is communicating. It may be that the counselee hesitantly, or casually, makes certain subtle but significant allusions. Or he may consistently avoid or omit discussing certain aspects of his problem. It is the counselor's task *not* to circumvent these areas, nor dismiss them lightly. The counselee's real needs can be right there. Counselor responses, then, must continue to be truly relevant and meaningful to the counselee; they must "concretely" speak to him in his present situation. The counselee must be helped to uncover and discuss personally meaningful contents. Obviously, fatigue can gravely handicap the counselor here. He may fail in his effort to concentrate on the deeper aspects of what the counselee is saying; instead, he may respond very broadly or superficially. Carkhuff and Berenson (1967, p. 35) provide an example:

Client: Oh . . . I get so mad at my supervisor — every time I come up with a creative idea, he cuts me to ribbons. He's just a bunch of old sour grapes!

Therapist: I guess you get angry at a lot of people.

Client: Well — no, not really — just at irrational authority.

Therapist: But, don't you find irrational authority everywhere?

Client: No . . . no, I don't think so. I came in here angry, and I think I had a right to be angry . . . But you — you don't seem to understand it.

Therapist: Well, that's all I'm trying to do . . . simply trying to understand you here. Lots of people define "angry" differently . . . how do you define it?

We conclude then that fatigue is indeed a potent hazard for the counselor. If the counseling process is not to deteriorate, the counselor must keep himself receptive and alert; it is necessary for him to be continually aware of his periods of depletion, and not to engage in counseling at such times. To avoid chronic fatigue, he must somehow discover and implement those ways and means which for him will provide renewal. For, as Wrenn (1962b, p. 564) notes,

To allow ourselves to be licked by the human fatigue factor, to become insensitive to the nuances of human behavior, is to lose our distinctiveness as specialists in human behavior and human need.

Emotional and Social Entanglements

Despite his training and the fact that he hopefully is a relatively secure, "well adjusted" human being, the counselor possesses no insured immunity from his own recurrent intrapsychic or emotional and interpersonal problems. In fact, some of the very qualities enabling him to counsel, such as being sensitive and perceptive, may cause him to be more vulnerable to various pitfalls and entanglements. Some of these hazards arise either directly or indirectly from the counseling process itself.

HOSTILITY

Hostility is such a hazard. On occasion, the counselor may see a counselee who arouses these feelings inside himself. He may realize that he feels very negative or experiences an active dislike toward this counselee and what he is saying. Very aware of such reactions, he may simply try to accept them. However, if he feels he is having little success in doing so, what should he do? How can he continue with counseling?

At such times, the pitfalls are to be found in what he should *not* do. As he is feeling strongly, yet probably trying to mask how he feels, these hazards are at once more subtle and more likely to occur. For example, in the well-known defense mechanism of reaction-formation, a response is made in terms of the opposite, positive feelings. Such a response attempts to camouflage the unacceptable and dangerous reaction, and to lessen the anxiety. But it is a sham response. If the counselor even mildly employs this technique, unintentionally, the chances are very good indeed that the counselee will pick up and feel the real counselor reaction. Certainly the counseling is not furthered. A second pitfall might be for the counselor to attempt to manipulate the trend of the counselee's remarks. As much of what the counselee expresses seems to strike wrong chords within the counselor, he attempts to harmonize the theme. He tries subtly to maneuver and adjust and correct the content; his overly directive efforts, however, are really an attempt to be of help to himself and not to the counselee. The detriments here to counseling are too obvious to require any comment. Still a third pitfall could occur if the counselor should enter too actively into the situation and overtalk the counselee. He could do this, defensively, as a needed catharsis for his own feelings. He feels the need to "cover up" but yet to express himself.

The question remains: how are these and other like hazards to be avoided when the counselor does feel hostile?

Tyler (1969, pp. 58–59) suggests that time can help. If the counselor, in spite of his present feelings, can yet manage to retain an open-minded focus upon the counselee, his antipathies may recede. From this effort to understand more about why this counselee appears and acts as he does, this may happen:

> In cases where one starts out with negative attitudes it is well to allow oneself a little time before deciding that one really dislikes the client. There is a curious perceptual shift that sometimes takes place during an interview with an individual who initially makes an unfavorable impression. . . . All we can be sure of is that we are most likely to achieve the experience if we concentrate all our efforts on trying to see the client's life from his own viewpoint.

Another positive course of action could be to express forthrightly the negative, critical feelings. Although it may seem paradoxical, the counselee may be benefited. Not only is the dimension of "concreteness" increased, but the counselee perceives the authenticity of the counselor's response. For the first time he may acquire a realistic understanding of how he actually "comes across" to another person. An example may illustrate this:

Counselor: It sounds to me as if you are a hypocrite and a phony.

Counselee: I don't know what you mean. . . .

Counselor: Well, aren't you telling him these things which you really don't mean, just to try to get what you want from him?

FAMILIARITY

Sometimes the counselee, possibly to bolster his self-esteem or to feel more comfortable with the counselor, calls the counselor by his first name. It may be that there are other ways in which he attempts to "familiarize" the counseling situation. What hazards, if any, are here for the counselor? We may say that the answer is dependent on the emotional maturity level of the counselor. If the counselor's own emotional needs cause him to be too receptive in this regard, there could be unhealthy developments in the counseling relationship. If the counselor, for example, feels that he always must be warmly liked and accepted and seen as a pal by his counselees, he may be showing some of the same security needs as the counselee. The counselor needs, therefore, to be honestly aware of his own emotional motivations in order to determine whether he can constructively utilize these informalized behaviors of the counselee and can maintain the essential dynamics of the counseling relationship. No harm need occur; rapport and genuineness may even be furthered. Fitts (1965, p. 91) believes it is possible for these positive developments to happen:

> Many therapists will be shocked to discover . . . how often clients call me Bill. They disapprove of this practice as "unprofessional" and say that this is getting too "involved" with the client. My own feeling is that unless I can get truly involved with another person to the extent of being a real person for him, and in this respect laying my own self on the line, then I am short-changing my client.

COUNSELOR INVOLVEMENT

In counseling, the counselor obviously should subjugate his own concerns in order to give his full attention to the counselee. It is the counselee's situation and the problems he faces with which the counselor must be empathically engaged. Yet, because the counselor himself has experienced crises and emotional conflicts in the past and may be struggling right now with some personal problem, he may discover that he easily interjects himself into what the counselee is saying. This hazard of "counselor involvement" is very real and can happen so "naturally." Maybe the counselee's father was recently killed in a car accident, and the counselee is struggling with his feelings and with all the present adjustments in the home. This touches off the remembrance in the counselor when some years ago his father died suddenly. So he really reacts again to and from his own experience. Or maybe a counselee confides to the counselor that she is now in love with a boy of a different religious faith. She worries about whether things can work out for them if they marry, and also how her family will accept the situation. The counselor feels he has some knowledge here. Possibly this had been a problem for him or for a member of his family; it is easy for him to respond now with some of his views and solutions. He need not always have special associations, however; counselor involvement can happen because of special curiosities, too. Patterson (1959, p. 50) points out several of the hazards:

> On the one hand, the counselor may be preoccupied with his problems, and may be seeking a solution to them. As a result, he may be sensitized to certain problem areas, or may even project his own problems into the client. This may also reflect itself in an overwhelming curiosity about certain areas of his clients' lives, the sexual, for example, so that he tends to probe into these areas and uncover all the details. On the other hand, his own conflicts may blind him to certain problems, so that he avoids them or is unable to understand what the client is saying. It also sometimes happens that a counselor who has found, or feels he has found, a solution to his own problems, attempts to impose his solution upon his clients.

Other problems can arise from the counselor's involvements and relationships with colleagues. Or there may be special problems if and when he counsels the parents of a counselee. Counseling is not always a situation in which but one counselee is seen at a time, and there are other categories of persons who, when counseled together, pose difficulties for the counselor.

PARTNERS AS COUNSELEES

Thus, if both parties to a relationship come to the counselor together, the complexity of the counseling task is greatly increased. It may be, for example, that the father of a troubled junior high school boy comes with his son, or that two college girls who are roommates and are having compatibility problems want to discuss their situation with the counselor. People in many other possible relationships might seek counseling together.

In double counseling, the counselor is involved in emotional crosscurrents, as it were. When the partners to the relationship have their differences, each one is motivated to tell the counselor how *he* feels. Yet, these expressions to the counselor are likely to be somewhat restrained, for each of the persons realizes he is speaking in the presence of the one with whom he is emotionally involved. The counselor needs to realize this fact, and also needs to assess as sensitively as he can other dynamics of their relationship. His full concentration too is required throughout the interview if he is to grasp the actual and deeper meanings of what is communicated, meanings which may only be implied. The counselor has no simple nor easy task as he attempts to relate and empathically understand from their respective frames of reference!

A further hazard is that the counselor may "take sides." This could happen quite readily if he is not on guard, for he well may have his own biases, views, or possible preconceptions about one of the persons. The counselor needs to catch himself if he finds that he is listening and giving more time and attention to one person than the other, for in this case neither of the counselees is helped. Because the counselor himself serves as a potent reinforcing influence, the less "received" party of the duo now may feel only added resentments or anxieties. Obviously such feelings hardly improve the subsequent relationship.

Let us look at Kay and Bob's situation: Kay is a high school senior who has been seeing the counselor for some time. She has been having special problems in her relationship with Bob, the boy with whom she has been going steady for the past year and a half. He is very jealous of her, she reports, objecting if she so much as looks at another boy. She can't even think of what he would do if she accepted a date with anyone else. She doesn't really think she wants to, but what really bothers her is that the situation is so unfair. Her friends keep telling her how Bob is not going steady with her, and about the different dates that he has. Even though she feels she can't trust him, she doesn't want to break up with him. She tried that once, but it "tore her to pieces." She asked the counselor if she and Bob could come in together, if Bob would do it. He finally agreed to come, and now here they are. How open and receptive can the counselor be? Has he formed his ideas in advance about Bob, shaped from Kay's resentments and anxieties? Can he actually be free from expressing subtle approval or disapproval of either Kay or Bob? In other words, can he function as counselor to each and to both of them?

PARENT COUNSELING

In order to build a relationship with parents, the counselor needs a considerable amount of tact and patience, combined with a sincere effort to understand their point of view. As parents are intensely emotionally involved with the problems of their son or daughter, they may not be very open or receptive to counseling or even to the counselor. This is not at all to imply that these are the attitudes of all parents; without doubt a large number of parents come to the school counselor sincerely seeking help. But, on the other hand, there are parents who do come with developed feelings of resistance, defense, hostility, prejudice, or stubbornness.

Hazards for the counselor surely are plentiful. In all probability, the counselor has been counseling the son or daughter for some time; he is aware of many emotional needs and concerns. Now he may find that as he attempts to relate with the parents, his own defenses may be very much activated if they express these negative and resistant attitudes. Rapport is difficult. He may want to tell them what to do or what not to do; he may feel he just would like to "let them have it." But, as it is with other counseling, giving advice, lecturing, telling, judging — none of these are effective to any degree. As McKinney (1958, p. 503) succinctly observes, "Rare, too, is the case where improvement in the student's adjustment is achieved by reprimanding the parent."

McKinney points to a further hazard for the counselor in counseling parents. The counselor needs to be aware of the parent who could be working out his or her own problems through the child. Here the counselor must be sensitive to the parent's unique emotional needs and recognize his or her inability at the present time to be realistic about the child's conflicts and concerns. Sensitivity, empathy, and realistic fairness on the part of the counselor are especially needed. In general, McKinney (1958, p. 496) suggests it is wise for the counselor to

> . . . anticipate what kind of relationship he can expect with the parent. . . . He should . . . accept any relationship that exists and then work toward a more positive one.

PROBLEMS WITH COLLEAGUES

Frequently, colleagues or school administrators misunderstand what the counselor is trying to do. Some teachers may even resent the counselor, feeling he or she has an interfering or separatist role in relation to classroom instruction. Or they look to the counselor to handle disciplinary cases. Also, when a teacher refers a student to the counselor for any reason, a full feedback report from the counselor may be expected. Teachers, and administrators too, often do not really respect the students' rights and needs for full privacy in the counseling interview. The counselor may find it very difficult to reconcile all such colleague expectations with his counseling. In trying to satisfy colleagues, the hazards of compromising counseling standards are very real ones.

Outside of the school environment, social entanglements with colleagues and friends can easily cause problems. Over the bridge table, for example, a colleague of the counselor may observe that she really must talk to the counselor about her mother-in-law. ("She's driving me crazy!") Or, on another occasion, a friend of long standing may ask the counselor to "please talk to my Betty. I'll have her come in and see you next week. Fred and I are really worried. She has been going with this boy who has low moral standards. We need your help in straightening her out!"

The counselor would do well to recognize the hazards involved in counseling friends, colleagues, or children of friends or colleagues. Another counselor, free of the emotional and social entanglements, could in all probability serve much better. Some hazards have very red lights indeed.

Subtle Value Impositions

Inevitably, and essentially, values are an integral part of counseling itself. They are a part of the process, and they surely are reflected in the goals. When we speak of the counselor showing respect for the counselee, or of the necessity for the counselor to be genuine in the interview, we are talking about values. Similarly when we hope for a self-actualized growth for the counselee, we are again dealing with values.

Nor is it possible, or desirable, for the counselor to park outside the door all of his own developed values, when he comes to meet the counselee. The philosophy the counselor holds, the way he has come to view the meaning of life and of persons, what to him is important and vital and has worth — all of these are a part of him. Of course all of these also influence his behavior and how he interacts with others, including his counselees. They have influenced him in becoming a counselor in the first place. We might say that probably the greatest hazard for the counselee might be to work with a counselor who was so neutral, so colorless that he had developed *no* meaningful values for himself!

It is very likely that the counselee can perceive the counselor's value orientations. There is no harm in this, *per se*. But the counselee must be left free to decide and choose his own values, which hold meaning for *him*. He needs very much to feel that the counselor sincerely accepts and respects him right now, just as he is. Then, even though he may request or welcome some explicit understanding of the counselor's values, the experience for him might yet be positive. It could prove very helpful to hear and understand the counselor's values, so long as the counselee feels free to evaluate them for himself.

The hazard lies in an imposition of values by the counselor. The danger is great because the counselor may not consciously intend for this to happen. But when it does happen, the counselee feels somewhat pushed down as a person. An implied denial of the worth of his own views and experiences is given to him, and he senses the disapproval and rejection of himself as he is at the moment.

We have mentioned that this hazard can be a subtle one for the counselor, and this is very true. It also is true that it is difficult and sometimes painful for the counselor to realize what he may be doing. One counselor reports how he came to gain self-insights the hard way. It was his first experience in counseling a boy who was a homosexual. The counselee was becoming increasingly exasperated:

"No, that's not what I was talking about! You're the one that keeps bringing *that* up all the time!"

This sharp counselee response brought him up short and made him really look at what was happening. All of the understanding, of course, did not come to him at once. But he slowly began to see things about himself, and about counseling in this whole area of counselor-counselee values that he had not realized before:

> I was obsessed. . . . All I could think of was *of course* he wants to repudiate this kind of life. . . . But I was tuned in improperly. Instead of really listening to him, I heard him only through my own sense of how he *ought* to feel and what he *ought* to want. This could only come through to him as my rejection of him. He could only feel that I had judged him and had no interest in the problem as he saw it. *I did not meet him with sympathetic concern at the point where he was.* In spite of myself, I had a fundamental disrespect for his person (Granberg, 1967, p. 892).

The subtleties of self-pride, in reality the hazards of Phariseeism, comprise the hazards for the counselor here. "I am thankful I am not as this man, with his shoddy, distorted values." Small wonder that realistic insights into such self-motivating behaviors are very painfully won. For many counselors, inner judgmental attitudes toward counselees are persistent hazards.

COUNSELEE LEARNING

Essentially, the experience of counseling is a learning process for the counselee. He must have the latitude and opportunity to be an active participant — exploring, discovering, choosing, and deciding. If the counselee is to grow, if behavioral changes are to result, the counselor can in no way hinder him from doing these things. The reasons for the counselee being here in the interview at all may be because of confusions due to his own value conflicts. He may feel he has no purpose or goal, life seems meaningless, or he is mixed up about how he feels toward "significant others" in his life and about how they regard him. Now he needs the objectivity and the opportunity to "sort out" these values of the counselor, to review and evaluate them. He needs the counselor to be *with* him, but not to overshadow him; he needs not to be told, or to be exhorted, but to be helped to experience his own fresh perspectives. As Arbuckle (1961, p. 231) says:

> . . . if real self learning is to occur, the client, as the learner, will not see the counselor . . . as the one from whom pearls are dropped. He will, rather, see him as a warm and humane person who is involved with him in an adventure of self exploration and self discovery.

Both pride and impatience can prevent the counselor from facilitating this type of learning for the counselee. He may interrupt the explorative process, interposing a value judgment, which he feels is so "right." But here is the hazard: the developmental process has then been undercut. It is like pulling open the petals of a rose bud; the bud has to develop itself from within, if it is to be beautiful and alive. So it is with values. They must be accepted, digested, assimilated, and lived by the person himself. Then for him they *are* values.

CUMULATIVE RISKS

When the counselee is attempting to make a decision, this type of counselor intervention is especially likely to happen. If the counselor is to allow the counselee the opportunity to explore and consider, much patience is required. This is especially true when something the counselee says taps a counselor value. Should the counselor at such a time respond with a comment like, "You probably realize that joining up with him would pull you down, don't you?" or "You probably would not be very wise to do that," he would at once arouse the counselee's defenses. The counselee would resist, responding to an implied criticism and judgment of himself and of his ability to decide ethically. Or he might decide differently from the way he might have otherwise.

In the latter instance, there is a special new type of hazard for the counselor. His intervention could boomerang. By entering the situation and influencing or altering what the counselee decides to do, the counselor assumes a share of responsibility for the outcome. This is rather frightening, or it should be. It is the counselee's life; *he* must live it now and later. The subsequent events and relationships which involve him possess many intricacies. The counselor cannot possibly anticipate nor understand all of these; it may turn out to have been very presumptuous to have pronounced an initial value assertion concerning what the counselee should or should not do, when the counselee needs to make an important decision.

Because of an overreadiness to respond in terms of his own value orientations, the counselor's responses may be too *reactive*. They may not be as perceptive as they should be. He could misunderstand and wrongly interpret the counselee's real meanings and feelings. Negative effects are then compounded. Not only has the counselor been judgmental, but what he said may not even have been relevant. For example:

> *Bill:* I didn't know what she'd say, but I asked her. Guess I'm feeling that way about her now. So I wanted her to come home with me. . . .
>
> *Counselor:* If you respect her, that might not have been too wise, do you think?
>
> *Bill:* Now, wait a minute! I mean I wanted her to come home with me next week and meet my folks!

Bill is outraged and feels completely misunderstood. All rapport at this point is blasted.

COUNSELOR SELF-UNDERSTANDING

When the counselor feels it necessary either to approve or disapprove strongly that which he thinks he hears the counselee saying, he reveals the manner in which he regards his own role. He feels that unquestionably, since he knows what is "best" and "right" and "good," the counselee must be told.

The implication is that, with respect to what is ethical, the counselee is a *tabula rasa*, and instruction or exhortation is needed. But if possible, the counselor should acquire enough insight from an honest self-analysis to ask himself if he is functioning as a *counselor*. Is he really wanting the counselee to be helped in such a way so that he, the counselee, can be the architect of his own, more integrated future development? How does behavioral change and a change in value systems ever really occur, anyway? Samler (1962, p. 135) notes, "We know that in their behavior, defenses, and values, human beings change least of all by exhortation."

In all probability, the counselor views himself as a socialized human being and feels that he has obligations and commitments with respect to societal norms. Any realistic influence he has on others, however, counselees very definitely included, will for the most part evolve from his own life functioning, from what he really is and does. In his role as counselor, there are many questions and hazards concerning attempts to impose conformity behavior patterns upon counselees. As Patterson (1962, p. 153) observes further:

> . . . this does not mean that the counselor refuses to discuss ethics, values, or philosophy. It does not mean that he is not concerned about the influence he has on the client in these areas. He recognizes this, and attempts to be a constructive influence. But he does this not by attempting to manipulate the client in the counseling process. He does it by being himself.

To as full an extent as possible, the counselor should be aware of his own biases, attitudes, and prejudices. He needs to understand what prompts his own motivations during the counseling interview. If some of these emotional value orientations were unwittingly to be expressed, the disclosure could present hazards for the counselee, for it is likely he would react in some way. He could be attracted or repelled, feel resentment or resistance or a lowered respect for the counselor. Or some of the counselor's same bias or prejudice could germinate within him. As we have stated earlier, when values in any form are expressed by the counselor, the counselee should be helped to realize that these are expressions of how the counselor feels. And a counselor needs to recognize the hazards of subtle encroachment upon counselees. These hazards can be largely avoided when the counselor does understand his biases and so, in fairness, does not want to inflict them unconsciously upon the counselee.

In summary, Lowe's (1962, p. 127) comment provides perspective.

We suggest that each counselor have an understanding of the values both of himself and others and that his values be known by all who are personally affected by his professional behavior.

Part Two

*

The
Counselee

Part Two

*

The
Counselor

4

Barriers for the Counselee

As has been mentioned earlier, the counseling relationship involves two selves — the self of the counselor and the self of the counselee. (Of course, if group counseling is involved, the selves would be multiplied by the number of persons in the group.) Chapters 2 and 3 focused upon barriers and hazards associated principally with the counselor that might interfere with progress in counseling. This chapter will address itself to the blocks to which the counselee might be heir.

Like the counselor, the counselee brings to counseling all that he is up to the time of encounter: his attitudes and values; his feelings about himself, his family, and his friends; his past successes and failures; his aspirations and his disappointments; his habits and his world view. In addition, he brings his concerns, his fears, his uncertainties, and his expectations of counseling.

The counselee brings to counseling the many qualities, beliefs, and experiences that are himself. It must be remembered, furthermore, that the counselee exists in an environment, one that may be perceived as friendly or hostile. Influences constantly issue from this environment and impinge upon the counselee, external factors over which he may or may not have control. From a large selection, four aspects of counselee condition have been chosen for examination in this chapter. The counselee-associated blocks to effective counseling singled out for discussion are resistance to involvement in counseling, the way the counselee perceives counseling, his feelings of hostility and fear, and his conflict concerning change. Many more barriers might be mentioned, but we have chosen to concentrate on these four dimensions.

Resistance to Involvement in Counseling

In a forthright comment, McKinney (1958, p. 226) said, "Counselors must face frankly the fact that at times they are avoided!" Any counselor who has served in the public schools can recall repeated instances that substantiate this statement. The boy who is referred for "adjustment counseling" after having been readmitted to school following suspension would like to avoid not only the counselor but the entire school experience. And the girl who finds her way to the counselor's office (a referral, of course) because she has body odor or is overweight enters into counseling most reluctantly. Or consider the plight of the college student (and his counselor) who is told by some insensitive individual in authority to report to the counseling center and " . . . get straightened out or I'll have to recommend that you be asked to leave this campus." And then there is the young lady who is planning to do her student teaching next year but who has some difficulties that should be resolved. She agrees that counseling would probably be helpful (she would agree to anything at this point), but if she goes to the counseling center, this will be an open admission of need for help. How would the fact that she needed counseling look to anyone knowing she planned to be a teacher?

These examples are clear cases of resistance that would block effectiveness in counseling, either because the individuals simply refuse to present themselves for counseling or because they are referred by someone in authority. This is not to say that effective counseling can take place only when it involves self-referrals. Certainly successful counseling relationships with positive outcomes can and do develop with counselees who have been referred by others or who have been called in by the counselor. Often a call-in or a teacher referral may be just the nudge a student needs. Moreover, an initially resistant student fortunate enough to find a sensitive and skillful counselor may eventually derive much benefit from counseling.

More interesting, more subtle, and more difficult to deal with, perhaps, are the resistant self-referrals. Whereas resistance in the examples given above was overt, externalized, and readily understood by both counselor and counselee, resistant behavior of the self-referral is different. This type of behavior is more complex, deriving as it does from internalized conflict.

PROCRASTINATION

Once an individual considers counseling as a possible source of assistance, he may enter into a period marked by vacillation, bewilderment, self-disgust, and indecision as he struggles with himself. He becomes irritable in situations that previously he faced calmly. He finds himself arguing with his family, his friends, and his coworkers. He loses his temper easily, regrets it later, and becomes despondent over the incident: "I don't know what's wrong with me." He seems always distracted, always too tired to make the effort to do things he used to enjoy. He feels alienated, unable to really communicate with others. He dislikes himself. He is suffering, but he cannot quite accept the fact that he cannot "handle this myself."

He may find himself in a virtually paralyzing approach-avoidance conflict. He knows where the counselor is and the procedures for making an appointment, and he thinks that perhaps the counselor can help, but he cannot accept the thought that he needs assistance. Or he is afraid that someone might find out. Or he views the counselor as a "head shrinker," as "someone you go to when you are really out of it." And so he delays, unable to arrive at a decision, as the anxiety mounts. Added to the original problem is the somewhat frightening spectre of himself as someone unable to make up his mind. The paralysis of indecision in major matters spreads to indecision in relatively minor matters. Not until he hurts beyond endurance does he act, but here again he is faced with a decision: He can seek counseling or he can quit school, join the army, go on drugs, get married — anything, rational or irrational, to prove to himself that he can make a decision.

If the individual chooses counseling, he comes resentfully, apprehensively, resistively. He brings with him not only his original problem but all those additional barriers that have been developing during the delay period. It is important for the counselor to recognize the counselee's condition and accept the resistance, giving the counselee an opportunity to verbalize his feelings: "It's sometimes hard for people to come to the counseling center." "It makes you almost angry because you haven't been able to settle things by yourself."

Patience and understanding are required by the counselor as he helps the counselee chip away at the blocks he has erected. If the counselor attempts shortcuts, if he moves too quickly, he may lose the counselee, thus eliminating the possibility of giving him any assistance. Progress will be slow, for here is a person who, reluctant to submit to counseling, will guard against exposing himself.

DEFENSIVENESS

Fitts (1965, p. 17) identifies two steps in "getting started." The first step has to do with coming to the decision that an individual wants to do something about his plight, about himself; and the second is deciding to present himself for counseling. Persons experiencing counseling for the first time are likely to be apprehensive and distrustful. Some cloak their true feelings under a brash "okay-here-I-am-now-go-to-work" attitude. Others, fearful and insecure, find they are unable to express themselves. If the counselee has had prior experience in counseling, he may attempt to establish a kind of "knowing" relationship. He says, in effect, "This is not new to me. I know what it's all about. I know what I'm supposed to say, and I know what you're supposed to say." He converses with the counselor, employs the jargon of psychology, and thus attempts to avoid counseling. Another experienced counselee may spend most of the first sessions telling the counselor how much she has benefited by previous therapy, and this is why she returned: "It's going to be so helpful to me." Finally, there is the bright young woman (or man), frequently found in college counseling centers, who is still undecided about risking herself in counseling. She attempts to keep the exchange on an intellectual level, discussing perhaps the efficacy of counseling. (She gives herself away when occasionally the efficacy of counseling "for someone like me" is allowed to seep into the discussion.) Like the person who has not a superstitious bone in his body yet walks *around* the ladder, the counselee is not quite convinced.

Each of these ploys is used to keep the self intact, to protect the self from exposure. It is not enough for the counselee to be present in the counselor's office. He must have reached the point where he is ready to explore his feelings, look at his inner conflicts. The counselor must find some way to work through the defenses (help modify them, not destroy them) to reach the person. It is vital that the counselor recognize the defensive behaviors and their underlying causes, accept such behavior and do whatever he can to establish a climate conducive to counseling. He must communicate by his behavior his positive feelings toward the counselee: "You are important to me. What is troubling you is important to me. This thing can be worked through, and I want to help you work it through."

Fitts (1965, p. 28) comments on the critical nature of those first interviews when the counselor and counselee are dealing with very fragile feelings:

> Naturally some clients have many disappointing, frustrating, and otherwise negative reactions to their early therapy sessions. Some discontinue therapy when this happens, while others stick it out and work these feelings through with the therapist. The first few sessions are extremely crucial for this reason, for in these early meetings the client is testing the therapist in many different ways.

Support, reassurance, and concern for counselee comfort may have to give way to confrontation if after a few sessions there has been no breakthrough. Timing is important, however, as is sensitivity to such matters as where the counselee is, and how psychologically strong he appears to be. The counselor will of course not be unaware of the counselee's feelings, but he may have to take the initiative, break through the resistance and involve the counselee.

To the young man who dared the counselor to counsel, he may say simply: "You're still fighting me. Who do you think is winning?"

To the one who finds expression difficult, he might offer: "You are still finding it hard to talk. Can you tell me what you were thinking as you were sitting out there waiting to see me?"

To the psychology-wise young man, he may respond: "You seem quite knowledgeable. How does all this fit in with you?"

To the woman who is anticipating so much help from counseling, the counselor may have to take this stance: "I don't think you really feel you've been helped in the past. Let's look at how you felt about coming here today."

Finally, to the intellectualizer, he might say: "This isn't what you came here to discuss. What really brought you here?"

The counselor's approach in each instance was a two-pronged thrust: (1) He told each counselee that he or she was hiding behind a smoke screen; and (2) he posed a question that turned inward upon the counselee. Confrontation will elicit the desired results only in the hands of a sensitive, skillful counselor. Its purpose, of course, is to provide the counselee with an opportunity to look openly at what he is doing; and there is at least an equal chance that it may serve as a nudge to involvement in counseling. It is a risk worth taking.

RATIONALIZATION

Another commonly employed type of resistance to counseling is rationalization. For the person who is really apprehensive about counseling — or for that matter about anything — rationalization is an ideal intellectual tool. It is a well-known technique, for we all employ it daily, some self-consciously, others unconsciously.

For example, take the young man, a college senior, who made inquiries concerning counseling for himself and his wife. When it seemed possible that some arrangement could be made for them to be seen, he explained:

> We don't really need counseling. That is, we don't have any problems, but I think it's a good thing for people to be exposed to counseling — so that they can get to know themselves better. My wife used to have some "hang-ups." And I guess we had the usual adjustments, but we have everything all straightened out now (after one year of marriage).

Incidentally, they never followed up the opportunity for counseling.

Some persons highly approve of counseling — for someone else. A case in point is the mother of a child who had been working with an elementary school counselor. It was evident early that the child's problems stemmed from the home and without improvement of the situation at home, there was little hope for much change in the child. The parents were cooperative, the mother conferring with the school counselor and teachers regularly. Finally, the child was referred to the child clinic where it was suggested that the parents become involved in counseling. Mrs. M was indignant:

> Why should we submit ourselves to that sort of thing? I don't feel the need for that. And anyway, I know what he'll tell us. He'll say that we don't really love our little girl. That we give her lots of things, but we don't really love her. That's what he'll say, and he'll be wrong. Of course, we give Chris everything she needs, and more, because we want her to have the best. And it's just not true that we don't love her. Why should I become involved in that kind of thing when I know what he'll say? It would just be a waste of time.

Here is a woman who has no confidence in counseling, or is afraid to expose herself, and is defensive. Instead of acknowledging such feelings, however, she chooses to rationalize her position. Is she satisfied with her rationalization, one wonders? What steps, if any, should the therapist take at this point?

Then there is the young lady who for several years has experienced long periods of depression, verging on despair. During these periods, she loses confidence in herself, questions her worth, finds it difficult to play out the daily routine of living. She realizes that "something is very wrong" and that "I need help with this." And so she presents herself to the community clinic where she has an initial interview, is informed of the procedures, the costs, and so forth. As she thinks it over, it occurs to her that the fees are too high. She cannot afford to undertake such a financial burden at this time, despite the fact that the cost was only slightly more than an evening's modest entertainment, including cocktails, dinner, and a movie, something she did quite regularly. Using the financial lever, she was able to rationalize herself out of involvement in counseling.

What can the counselor do to overcome the barriers of rationalization? Really, there is not much he can do if the individual simply will not appear for counseling. But he can understand the problem, perhaps be alert of its possibility in an initial interview, anticipate, maybe, what the counselee may do and help the person talk about his conflicting feelings.

Resistance manifests itself in many types of behaviors. We have looked only at three general ways in which people resist. The purpose here has been to draw attention to the fact that not everyone views counseling as a good, beneficial, and safe experience. (Counselors tend to have tunnel vision regarding the efficacy of counseling.) A second point of emphasis is that when individuals do come for counseling, agonizing periods of inner conflict may well have preceded their first interview. Even though the counselee is there, face to face, with the counselor, he may not be "ready" for counseling, but must work through the protective layers. This period frequently requires all the skill, sensitivity, and understanding a counselor can muster. The counselee has tentatively reached out a hand, to test the situation with his sensitive fingertips, in much the way a person makes the toe-in-water test. If the temperature is acceptable, the swimmer will slip into the water. And if the climate is comfortable, the counselee will continue.[1]

Preconceptions of Counseling

The counselee's preconceptions about counseling may serve as a barrier to the process. At least they often determine the nature of the first few sessions. How the counselee perceives counseling derives from his own prior experiences, in or out of counseling, and the nature of his concerns — whether he seeks counseling for help with an educational-vocational decision or a highly charged personal matter. Whether negative or positive, feelings are mixed and often difficult to sort out. In any case, feelings are directed toward the counselor, counseling, or inward upon the counselee himself — or all three (Fitts, 1965). The counselee thus may have expectations about what the counselor does, about what he himself should do, and about what the counseling process itself may entail. These expectations may be quite accurate or they may be entirely different from what normally occurs. Even the counselee who says, "I didn't know what to expect" gives us a clue concerning his notions of the process.

Expectations and preconceptions tend to vary depending upon whether or not the counselee has had previous experience in counseling. And, of course, differences exist from individual to individual among the experienced as well as among the uninitiated. Experienced or not, the one certainty is that the counselee brings with him to counseling a variety of feelings. McKinney (1958, p. 241) sums up the matter well:

> The client comes into the counselor's office with varying feelings and attitudes. He wonders what is going to happen, what he is going to find out, how he is going to show up. He is nervous about whether he will have to tell things about himself that he does not want to say.

[1] For an excellent presentation of the difficulties associated with moving into counseling, see William H. Fitts, *The Experience of Psychotherapy* (Princeton, N.J.: D. Van Nostrand, 1965).

THE EXPERIENCED COUNSELEE

The experienced counselee's preconceptions of counseling will, of course, be influenced by prior experience. If the counselee has had poor prior counseling experience, he will come with negative attitudes. He may bring with him such feelings as resentment, hostility, and fear, and he will be extremely cautious and defensive. He appears unwillingly, but he has made the decision to seek a counselor for any one of a number of reasons: he is desperately uncomfortable and he doesn't know what else to do; his wife or his girlfriend or someone else has told him to "go to see a counselor or else . . . " etc.

Attitudes expressed in such comments as the following provide real blocks to counseling and a challenge to the counselor:

Okay, I'll try but it didn't help one bit the last time.

This person is making a token gesture. Counseling has not been helpful in the past, and he has no hope that it will benefit him this time. A reaction such as this may come from a variety of persons and situations. It may be a husband who is being forced into counseling by his wife "to save the marriage" or it may be a high school junior whose mother is suggesting she see the counselor about getting a scholarship to a business school.

Individuals feeling this way will enter counseling expecting nothing, prepared to do nothing. They will simply be there to satisfy someone else. Most likely they will be unresponsive, forcing the counselor to take the initiative and be responsible for any movement in the process.

I wonder what would happen if I just didn't show up. I hate having to go through all that again. And he'll just sit and look at me and say, "Hmmm" while I pour out my soul. I just hate it, but what can I do? It's no use, I know I'll go. Why did this have to happen to me?

A young woman may be having these thoughts. She resents being in the position of having to seek help again, for she remembers her last experience with shame. She will try this time, though, to keep better control over herself. She does not want to pour out her soul; it is humiliating to her to have to expose herself this way. Perhaps the feeling of humiliation the last time was so pervasive as to prevent effectiveness. The counselor this time will have to grapple with this counselee's resolve not to expose herself and her need to look at her feelings. The counselor's task will be to help the counselee perceive the setting as open and free, nonjudgmental and nonthreatening. And before the counselee can be helped, she must perceive the counselor as accepting and supportive and yet giving her the responsibility for her own destiny, so that she can feel a greater sense of strength and worth.

I don't trust anyone. I don't want anyone poking and probing around, trying to psych me out. And yet if I don't talk to someone, I think I'll explode!

This person enters counseling "up tight" and plans to remain closely held as long as possible, resisting any attempt by the counselor to get to know her, in contradiction to what she is crying out for. The counselee is desperate, even irrational in her feelings about counseling — wanting someone to help — and fearing that someone will get to know her. Slow movement, letting the counselee establish the pace and direction, is important here. A period of testing can be expected, and it will occupy the first few sessions. Probably the counselee will continue to test every so often for a long time.

Individuals who have had good experience in counseling view the process positively. It is likely that they will think of counseling when they face inordinate personal difficulties or, in the school or college settings, when they need help in thinking through a problem or arriving at some decision:

I guess I'll check this out with Mr. Rollins. He sure helped me get straightened out the last time.

Perhaps I quit too soon. But I thought I had it made. If I can just get a little booster, things will work out — I'll call the counseling center.

I have really missed counseling. I should have been going all along but I never got around to contacting anyone in this city. I'd better get started again before things get any worse.

These people have positive feelings toward counseling and are ready, indeed eager, for additional counseling. A person whose prior experience has left him with positive feelings anticipates that counseling will be beneficial the next time. It would thus seem reasonable to expect that a relationship will easily be established and effective counseling readily realized. Unfortunately, cases do not always unfold so happily. Other interventions and expectations may block the way.

The individual may, for example, have difficulty getting an appointment within what he considers a reasonable period of time. He is ready now — and anxiety is building. The waiting period may witness frustration or produce deterioration sufficient to make counseling extremely difficult when the times does come. One woman expressed herself this way:

> The program here is "Something else." Ass that I am, I thought I could waltz right in and the crying towel would be waiting. Ha! As it stands now I'm to see the social worker in two weeks. I might add this is only the beginning; they play bean bag with you until they decide you're worth it, I guess. By the time they get ready to listen to my tale of woe, I won't be able to utter a word, or won't want to (Fitts, 1965, p. 25).

Expectations relate not only to the process itself but also to the counselor. Fully anticipating that counseling will be exactly as it was last time, the counselee is thrown off stride if this time it is somewhat different. Disappointment and bewilderment — and uncertainty as to what to do — may follow. It may even cause him to quit.

Since counselees who have had positive counseling experiences tend to have a warm feeling toward their counselors, they tend also to project his image to all counselors. This type of projection prepares the way for disappointment, for counselor number two can never be counselor number one. Consequently, the counselee may have a negative reaction to the counselor, not for what he is but simply because he is not someone else. It is difficult sometimes for counselors to accept the fact that they are not "measuring up," but it is essential that they understand and accept the situation as it is.

This unexpected reversal, this sad trick of time and process and person may produce totally unpredicted reactions. Counselees who anticipate an easy relationship and quick relief because their prior experience had been beneficial, may find themselves facing difficulty in counseling, simply because they were so sure they knew what to expect. On the other hand, many who approach counseling with a negative or indifferent attitude may be shaken loose by the fact that it is not as they had anticipated. Thus, they are surprised to find that they can establish a close relationship and that counseling is beneficial. In either case, the skillful counselor perceives the counselee's predicament and provides an opportunity for him to talk about it.

THE UNINITIATED COUNSELEE

For the person who has not had counseling experience, preconceptions develop from a combination of things: what he has read; what his friends have told him; what he has seen on TV; what the social expectation is in his circle; and, if the setting is a school, what other staff members think counseling is.

When a high school student walks into the counselor's office and says, "I need your advice," his words are a clue to his expectations. And if the counselor does not tell the student what to do, what then will be his perception of counseling? Or if a junior high school student comes to the counselor's office upon having been called in and asks, "What did I do?" we can assume that his view of counseling is associated with the activity that takes place in the principal's office.

There are some persons, we suspect, who expect to find a couch in the counselor's office, à la psychoanalytic cartoon in popular magazines. Others — not only counselees, but teachers as well — become discouraged if after one or two sessions the problems do not disappear, as if by magic. To these individuals, counseling is some mysterious rite that is supposed to bring about instantaneous change, effect an immediate solution, like instant coffee or instant hemlock, perhaps. How many teachers refer a student for counseling and after the first twenty-minute session expect the student to return to class completely adjusted? And how many individuals have spent an hour with a counselor only to decide not to return?

> It was okay. We had a good talk and all, but I didn't notice anything different. I really don't see why I should go back again.

Sometimes the counselor has to explain what counseling is, what responsibilities are shared by the counselor and the counselee, the limitations of counseling, and what the counselee can reasonably expect. Counseling is, after all, another learning situation, in which the counselee must learn his responsibility. Fitts (1965, p. 30) refers to various counselee reactions as therapy starts and mentions this one as being common:

> . . . the uncertainty and doubt about the therapeutic process or psychotherapy itself. Oftentimes it is difficult for a person to invest so much in something he understands so poorly. And many beginning clients have little real grasp of what psychotherapy really is.

When an individual is uncertain about what is going to occur, or what he is expected to do, he tends to hold himself tightly, and proceeds cautiously. Until he learns the ground rules and has assessed the situation — and the counselor — he is likely to withhold himself. He is not willing to invest much of himself or to expose himself. It is in this context that students appear in the counselor's office to discuss grades or present themselves to the counseling center to request interest inventories. If after assessing the situation and the counselor, the counselee feels safe, he will talk about those concerns that prompted him to come in the first place. Somewhere or somehow he has learned that he could bring problems such as he had to the counselor, but he wanted to find out for himself. The experienced counselor will, like the experienced teacher, meet the counselee (student) where he is and work from there. The experienced counselor knows that a testing period must sometimes precede involvement in counseling. Actually, though, counseling begins during this period of assessment: the relationship is being established, counselor and counselee are getting to know one another, and they are learning what to expect of each other and themselves.

Of the many aspects of counseling that the inexperienced —and sometimes the experienced — counselee does not know, one must be mentioned here: In general, many significant insights come outside counseling. Counseling merely facilitates insight by provoking thought, and understanding breaks through, usually not in the counselor's office, but sometime later as the counselee is riding on the subway or washing his car, or cleaning house. It is this important knowledge that the man who decided prematurely to withdraw from counseling did not acquire. Those unfamiliar with counseling assume that all the "good things" must happen during the counseling session. It just does not work that way, and perhaps this information should be communicated to the counselee.

We have said that counselors may, because of their closeness to it, forget that many persons do not view counseling as particularly helpful. Thus a goodly number of people who approach counseling are unbelieving or indifferent. Also because of our own involvement, we may need to be reminded of the apprehension and naïveté counselees bring with them on their first visit. And because counseling is so commonplace an experience with us, it should be emphasized that the unknown for counselees can be frightening and bewildering. It is important that we stay alert for signs of negative behavior arising from faulty preconceptions that might block counseling, lest we lose the advantage anticipation can provide.

Hostility and Fear

The feelings of hostility and fear a counselee experiences may manifest themselves in various types of resisting or defensive behaviors, such as those mentioned earlier in this section or those that will be taken up in terms of manipulative strategies.

Inevitably there will be overlapping in any discussion touching upon counselee behavior that creates barriers in counseling, since much of it is negative and defensive. In this section, however, we shall restrict the treatment insofar as possible to a consideration of counselee hostility and fear as blocks to counseling, emphasizing the inner feelings rather than outer manifestations.

SUPERFICIAL HOSTILITY

As has been mentioned, a counselee may become hostile toward a counselor simply because he is not exactly like the first counselor. The counselee has been disappointed and thrown off stride; consequently, he becomes hostile and a barrier is inevitably erected. Similarly, a counselee may become hostile because he cannot manipulate a counselor. He simply cannot get the counselor to do as he wishes, and thus frustrated, the counselee may become outwardly hostile. In another instance, a counselee may feel that he is superior to the counselor; he loses respect for him and becomes openly hostile. This again may possibly be a manifestation of frustration and disappointment. The counselee may have placed much hope in being helped by the counseling experience, only to find, once again, that another counselor "let him down."

These feelings of hostility cannot be minimized; they do represent barriers or hazards for counseling that must be met. We have described this type of hostility as superficial, however, and have done so only to distinguish it from a different kind of hostility. For present purposes, "superficial hostility" is viewed as relating to a feeling that tends to be comparatively easily identified, and, more importantly, develops in response to a particular set of circumstances and is likely to be temporary.

AGGRESSIVENESS

To distinguish basic from superficial hostility, we refer here to the essentially hostile individual. This may be the child who finds his way to the counselor's office because he bullies other children or because he always seems to be getting into scraps with his classmates, the aggressive child. "I don't know what to do with Billy. He disrupts the entire class."

In middle school, the aggressive child may find his way to

the counselor's office via referral by the principal: "I'd like you to talk with Jimmy Peters. This is the third time this month he's been sent to my office from the playground because of shoving and fighting with the other boys." Or perhaps Linda, a high school sophomore, is referred by a teacher: "I just don't know how to get to Linda. She shouts out at any time, not caring whether another student or I am talking. And when I try to correct her behavior, she loses her temper, slams her books and her purse around on the desk. I just cannot understand a girl who acts this way."

Or take the case of Jack who had gotten into some skirmishes with the school authorities for carving his initials on desks or writing on the walls in the boys' room. Along with several others, he was picked up by the police for vandalism in a new subdivision. He appears in the counselor's office, referred by his parents and the high school principal: "See if you can find out what's bugging Jack and help him straighten himself out. This time he got off easily, but if he does this sort of thing again, they'll really crack down on him."

Then there are Mr. and Mrs. F who present themselves for counseling. A quiet and insidious erosion of their marriage has been taking place over the past six years. In a somewhat condescending way, Mr. F explains he agreed to accompany his wife, although he has no need of his own for counseling. After the first rather unproductive meeting, Mrs. F phones the counselor and pours out her anguished story. Mr. F belittles her, at home and in front of friends; he treats her as if she were incapable of any intelligent thought. She has lost confidence in herself and is desperate.

Here are angry people, Mr. F and the others. Some are fighting for acceptance, not realizing the self-defeating nature of their aggressiveness. They want acceptance and are hurt because they feel they have been rejected, and they want to hurt others in return. The counselor faces this hostility and aggression when these individuals present themselves for counseling. Hostility has become a way of life, and they feel hostile toward the counselor, too. Unless the counselor finds some way of coping with the hostility such counselees bring with them, the chance for effective counseling is blocked.

When people such as those described here find themselves face-to-face with a counselor, they most likely realize that they are unhappy, but they do not know why. Frequently life seems to them just one frustrating obstacle after another. It is not their fault that everyone is against them. Their very inability to grasp the consequences of their own behavior or to realistically survey their situation serve as blocks to counseling. People behave as they do because of the way they view their present circumstances. From previous experience they have learned that people will reject them or, at best, be indifferent. Billy and Jimmy are making a bid for attention. Mr. F needs the security of feeling superior to someone, and his wife becomes the target. The counselor is just one other person who appears — at first, at least — to be superior.

In any case, Billy and Jimmy and Linda and Jack are in the counselor's office because someone sent them there — not because they chose to consult the counselor. Mr. F, on the other hand, is hiding behind his wife's "need." She appears to be unstable; he sees no need for help himself. The underlying insecurity these people sense, and the general suspicion with which they view others provide a real barrier for the counselor. They must necessarily hold themselves tightly, present a "closed system" to the world, lest the delicate balance they have been able to achieve be toppled. Rigid, surrounded by protective devices that keep intact their image of themselves, hostile individuals in a sense draw a circle around themselves to keep others out. Their behavior is reminiscent of the way boys, who are at the moment enemies, may draw a line in the dirt and dare the other to step over that line. These individuals are at odds with the world because they cannot get into the world. "They don't like me and so I don't like them." The counselor is another one of "them," and defenses are high and firm.

The type of aggression referred to here manifests itself in hostile behavior that is self-defeating. Not only does it hurt others, but since it is also socially destructive, it merely compounds the person's difficulties and strengthens the barriers to satisfactory relationships with others. Individuals toward whom the hostility is directed may be surprised or even angered by behavior they think is unwarranted. Indeed, in some cases even the person himself may be shocked by the fierceness of his feelings, sensing that such outbursts may cause him to lose friends or may cost him his job. He, too, may even recognize the fact that his feeling is far stronger than one would expect under the circumstances (McKinney, 1958).

At the root of such aggressiveness is frustration. D'Evelyn (1957, p. 60) writes of hostile behavior in children:

> . . . we are trying to discover what in the life of the child has disturbed his interpersonal relations with others. The youngster who has good feelings about his own worth and acceptance by others does not have to fight people as the aggressive child does. His aggressive behavior means that he feels that people have pushed him aside, have been unfair to him, have not given him the love and understanding that all children need. He is therefore both fearful and angry. He is afraid of not being acceptable and he is angry at being denied this acceptance.

Aggressive, frustrated persons have difficulty forming friendships; they are usually insecure and are masking their low image of themselves with hostile activity. McKinney (1958, p. 206) suggests that "the counselor can piece together the fragments from the interview that relate to early frustration and find the source of these accumulated aggressive tendencies." The counselor must create a climate in which such counselees feel safe and can talk about their insecurities.

Billy, mentioned earlier, also needs an atmosphere in which he feels safe. For a boy such as this, the counselor may use toys in counseling toward which Billy can direct his aggression. Sometimes talking to Billy through a puppet will provide him an outlet for his aggression. Billy also needs to learn limits. He must realize that he cannot hurt others, cannot disrupt his classmates. At the same time he must feel that he is wanted and accepted. Billy needs to learn self-control, and the counselor must work with both the parents and the teacher to provide opportunities for Billy to gain self-control and to feel better about himself, through experiencing personal, nonaggressive success. Using retaliatory and primitive measures tends only to substantiate such a child's feeling of insecurity and rejection. As D'Evelyn (1957, p. 63) points out:

The aggressive child is always afraid down underneath; he fears that he is unworthy, bad, and unacceptable to others.

Parents and teachers must be helped to understand the causes of frustration and hostility and must be helped to find ways of dealing with aggressive youth, other than using solely primitive measures. A hostile counselee presents a challenge to the counselor, even in some instances a barrier that cannot be pierced. Sometimes, however, a really empathic counselor can reach such counselees.

FEARFULNESS

Separation of hostility and fear is arbitrary at best. As D'Evelyn suggested, the aggressive child is a fearful child. The two feelings are certainly closely related. A separation has been made here, however, to provide a chance to look at certain aspects of fearfulness that offer barriers in counseling. Fear of counseling, fear of self, and fear of change may serve as ways of examining some types of fearfulness the counselee brings to counseling.

FEAR OF SELF

That which is unknown is a possible source of fear. An unidentified noise strikes fear into individuals; an upcoming experience cloaked in the unknown causes apprehension. When the noise is identified, however, recurrent sounds are taken in stride, and when some familiar association is made with the new experience, apprehension is allayed. So it is when focus is turned inward. Indeed, many persons are reluctant to "turn inward" because they are afraid of what they will find. And so fear of self becomes a barrier to counseling. It is this very fear that causes individuals to delay going to a counselor or having decided to consult a counselor, fear of self may result in resistance to involvement in counseling, a matter discussed earlier in this chapter.

Not only does fear of self — fear of exposing oneself, as well as fear of looking at oneself — result in evasive tactics on the part of the counselee, it may also be the reason the counselee makes an effort to remain on a superficial or intellectual level in counseling. Here is safe ground; here the counselee is in charge. He does not trust his feelings, or rather, he does not trust his "feeling self." Or perhaps he has not had much experience with his "feeling self" as it manifests itself in counseling, and he is therefore reluctant to function on a feeling level. This resistance constitutes a block to effective counseling, for it prevents the counselee from functioning on anything but a superficial level. Traditionally, for example, boys and men have been expected to deny their "feeling selves" because to expose feelings has been considered to be a betrayal of their masculinity and a sign of "weakness."

One other aspect of fear of self bears brief mention. Fear of what he will say, or fear that he has exposed himself too much or too fast will cause a counselee to pull back, the way a turtle takes to the protective covering of his shell when he senses danger. A case in point is Rita who, quite outspoken in her feelings about a teacher, remembered suddenly that the counselor and the teacher were friends. Fearful that she might offend the counselor, Rita was determined not to risk additional "slips." Rita pulled over herself a protective covering which the counselor was not able to penetrate during the remainder of that session.

FEAR OF OTHERS

Fear of others refers here to fear of what others — family, peers, society in general — may think of a person who consults a counselor. The fear may derive from some basic attitudes the counselee himself has learned from the significant people in his environment. "Stand on your own two feet." "All counselors are head shrinkers." "You should be able to handle your own problems." The counselee is frightened, uncomfortable, even ambivalent about having referred himself to a counselor. The discomfort, fear, and ambivalence serve only to inhibit the counselee, to cause him to be more uncomfortable because he does not feel free to talk with the counselor. He cannot reap the benefits of an effective counseling relationship because the way is blocked by the counselee's inhibitions. The counselee begins to wonder whether counseling is an answer and he becomes increasingly ambivalent and inhibited. The circle is complete, and the counselor is on the outside.

FEAR OF COUNSELING

If counseling is an unknown, the counselee will approach counseling apprehensively. He may even be afraid of what will happen to him as a consequence of the experience. In a sense, he is ambivalent about counseling — he thinks it may help, but, on the other hand, he is afraid that it might change him — and that thought is frightening. Under such circumstances, counseling moves slowly, if at all. Sometimes the counselor can provide reassurance, but often the counselee is reluctant to respond to such reassurance, so fearful is he. Very often, a counselee who experiences this feeling will decide early that the counselor cannot help and will simply drop out of counseling. Often a counselor needs to explain counseling to people, reviewing the basic premises, mentioning the responsibility of both the counselor and counselee in a counseling session, and touching upon some of the benefits that may be derived from an effective counseling relationship.

Fearful, hostile individuals, because of their fundamental insecurities, create blocks to effective counseling, even as they search — knowingly or unknowingly — for relief from their condition. They continue on their self-destructive course, hemmed in by the very feelings that led them to that course originally. Unless the counselor can break into that cycle, such counselees will not be helped and will be frustrated by another futile attempt at reaching out, without really being able to reach out far enough to make it matter.

Ambivalence Toward Change

"I would be different if I knew how." "I would change if I could." How many times these words are spoken! Apparently the speaker is saying he wants to change, and all too often it is assumed that all that is needed is someone to help him find the way.

But change, even when one thinks he wants it, causes anxiety. On the one hand, the person is dissatisfied with himself and wants to be different. At least, he wants *something* to be different. Sometimes change, any change, appears to be the only alternative to an intolerable situation. Yet there is fear and anxiety. The counselee views being different as a panacea, but often even after he has presented himself for counseling, he encounters an impasse. Unable to continue, the counselee becomes discouraged and falls back. Much like an approach-avoidance conflict, the ambivalence surrounding counselee change may create powerful barriers for counseling.

Typically, the counselor is viewed as a facilitator of growth and change. When an individual goes for counseling, it usually is because he senses that somehow all is not well. Or when a teacher or parent or friend refers another individual for counseling, it is because the referring person senses that all is not well. Although neither the principals involved nor the person making the referral knows what is to occur, each one (except, perhaps, a reluctant referral) hopes that somewhere, somehow, counseling will make a difference. Some change is expected — in thinking, in outlook, in understanding, in behavior.

It should be noted that change, as it is considered in this section, is not concerned with reorganizing or restructuring of the personality — that is the province of psychotherapy. We are addressing ourselves, rather, to ambivalence centering around change in attitudes or insights or understanding or the kind of change sought by individuals who exhibit what Tyler (1969, p. 177) describes as "disadvantageous behavior." Disadvantageous behavior causes the counselee frustration, as in the case of a wife's unfounded jealousy. Or it inhibits development in a desired direction, as in the case of the young man who aspires to a certain position in his company but sees himself as inordinately shy. Or disadvantageous behavior may be found in the capable high school senior whose excessive aggressiveness costs him the support of his peers in his bids for positions of leadership. Each person aspires to become a "different me"; at least, each one wishes part of him were different.

If one subscribes to the concept that each individual strives to enhance and maintain the self, then we can readily accept the notion that change can be very difficult, especially change involving such intimate matters as the image one projects, one's basic beliefs about oneself and others, one's immediate environment, and values. Complex and painful, sometimes, change involves accommodation of new notions about the self, the familiar, the comfortable (though disquieting) reality one has known. The barriers to facilitation of growth and change may be associated with three "stages." The obstacles that must be met in counseling for change are identified here as (a) recognizing and accepting the need to change, (b) making the decision to change, and (c) taking action leading to change.

RECOGNIZING AND ACCEPTING THE NEED FOR CHANGE

Whether the individual presents himself for counseling or is referred by someone else, he may not actually be aware of the need for some type of behavior or attitude modification. He may only vaguely sense his dissatisfaction or wish things were different. The task of helping the counselee understand his plight and reach the point of accepting the need for change may test the counselor's patience and skill as well as the counselee's frustration tolerance. Once the counselee recognizes and accepts the need to change, moreover, the approach toward modification has only just begun.

A young woman, Mrs. L, wife and mother of three children, reported her experience.

When my youngest child entered the first grade, I returned to teaching. Before I returned to work, my husband and children and I discussed the difference it would make in our household and, really, things were working out quite well. The children seemed to be adjusting. My husband was accepting and cooperative. I kept foremost in my thinking that my first obligation was to my husband and my children. Within a few months, however, I found myself increasingly irritable, dissatisfied with myself and my entire situation. I loved my husband and my children and they were responding well. Somehow I felt the growing conflict must be my fault. It was at this time that I decided to consult a counselor.

I spent about six months in counseling. At first it seemed to help, and I guess it was the thing that got me through that first year. But after a time the sessions seemed to be unproductive and I stopped going.

To remain in teaching, it was necessary for me to take graduate work, and so during the second year, I began taking courses for my master's degree. I found myself stimulated by the experience of being back at the University. But that old nagging dissatisfaction and irritability returned also. And once more I began counseling.

For several months after each session I vowed I would not return, for the effort appeared to be totally unproductive — and yet I was afraid to cast myself adrift. Suddenly, one afternoon, there was a breakthrough. During a most productive session, I realized my problem. My guilt about being a "working mother" became clear. The fact was that I enjoyed teaching and taking courses at the University. The conflict between how I had been taught to think a wife and mother should behave and the role in which I currently cast myself was obvious. For years, long before I was married even, I thought of myself in the traditional wife-mother pattern. And now I had stepped out of character, so to speak.

Without being aware of what was happening, my pattern of living and behaving had changed, but I had not yet accepted myself in my new role. I realized, finally, that I would have to accommodate my "different" self into my concept of myself. I think now I am ready to change the way I see myself — as a career woman and as a wife and mother — and I'll have to be able to accept this change in me despite the way my parents feel about it.

The internal dynamics here are, of course, far more complex than this brief report reveals. The point is that it took this young woman almost three years — in and out of counseling — to recognize the problem. Finally Mrs. L accepted the need to change her way of viewing herself. She thinks she's ready, despite pressures of her family and many in her social group. She has taken the first step only.

Mrs. L's experience illustrates Fitts' (1965, p. 17) comment: "It is not unusual for a client to become involved in some kind of regular relationship with a therapist without ever having decided *that he really wants to change himself."* In Mrs. L's case, the barrier was so great that she simply withdrew from counseling once and was close to giving up a second time when the "breakthrough" came.

MAKING THE DECISION TO CHANGE

Once the need is recognized and accepted, the decision to change may be immediately forthcoming. The task then is to "put some teeth" into the decision and take some action. Sometimes, inexperienced counselors, eager for closure, assume that the counselee, having made the decision, will carry out a program of change. At this point, these counselors may prematurely bring the case to a conclusion. But often the decision has not *really* been made.

Anyone who has had experience with children knows only too well how easy it is for them to say, "Oh, yes, I want to do better. I want to change." But the difficult road to change still lies ahead. And having vowed sincerely, promised earnestly, they continue to behave as they did in the past.

Nor is ambivalence toward change limited only to children. Change is threatening, anxiety-producing; even making the decision to change may create fear and doubt. The verbal commitment given today may be rejected at next week's session. Uncomfortable as the present situation may be, anticipation of a foray into the unfamiliar and unknown may be even more uncomfortable. It is often difficult to know whether or not a counselee has *really* made the decision to change. Even the counselee himself may not be aware that he is fighting the decision. And the resolve to change must be firm before the counselee can take that first step. Sometimes counselees consider courses of action, chiefly to please the counselor or some other individual, suspecting all the while that nothing will come of any of it. In such cases both counselee and counselor are playing games, though the counselor may not be aware of it, at least at first.

If and when the counselor realizes that the counselee has really not reached a decision about change, that the conflict still exists, several avenues are open to him: He may continue "playing along" with the counselee, so as not to upset him, hoping that support and understanding will help the counselee *really* make the decision and choose a course of action. Or the counselor may confront the counselee with his present type of behavior as he sees it, hoping to serve as a catalyst to activate the counselee. Or he may suggest that the counselee might work more effectively with someone else.

Indecision may elicit another type of blocking behavior on the part of the counselee. Because he is ambivalent about changing, the counselee embarks upon a program to manipulate the counselor, employing a kind of defensive or delaying action to protect himself because he cannot — or until he can — reach the decision to change. (A more extensive treatment of counselee uses of manipulation appears in Chapter 5.)

Individuals exhibiting various types of disadvantageous or defensive behavior frequently find themselves in a situation where the need is great to make some modification of their behavior, to replace defeating behavior with "more desirable kinds of activity" (Tyler, 1969, p. 177). The ten-year-old girl, who has not yet learned alternatives to temper tantrums when she is frustrated, is unhappy because she has no friends. The college junior, who is on drugs and says she wants to quit, seeks help because she cannot seem to make it without help. And a classic example is the young homosexual who thinks he may want to change.

Let us assume that three such individuals find themselves in the counselor's office saying, "I want to be different from the way I am." The ten-year-old has used this behavior for a number of years, obviously because it has worked. Some alternatives might not be nearly so immediately effective. How important is having friends as compared with this "successful" behavioral device? What role can the adults in her life play in helping her change? How firm is the coed's resolve to stop using drugs when she is alone and scared or despondent? When the counselor is not present to support her and the going gets rough? And young homosexuals have been known to use counseling as a way of determining just whether or not they do indeed wish to change their behavior. For some, even, it is an exciting game; the time for decision is still in the future.

Unless the decision to change has been made and accommodated into the counselee's thinking, real commitment to change is impossible and further development in this area is blocked.

COMMITMENT TO ACTION FOR CHANGE

Often a counselee will see and accept the need for change, will feel that he is ready to change, will commit himself to a plan of action, but will find the conflict too great and the effort too demanding. In this stage, too, when action is needed to carry out a program of behavior or attitude modification, the counselee may bog down and/or give up entirely. The first two stages may be comparatively easy to negotiate, but the final test comes here. It is when the counselee must take action leading to change that any ambivalence he may be feeling provides the most formidable barrier. And it is at this point, too, that counselors may mistakenly judge that the task has been accomplished when the counselee announces his plan of action. Actually, the counselor's support is needed now as never before, to help the counselee take the jolting and sometimes painful steps to reach his desired goal.

It is comparatively easy to talk about needing to change and grow and develop. It is even easy to commit one's self to growth and change — as compared with taking action. Now is the time when the counselor must work with the counselee, helping him say, in effect: "This is what I think I can do." "This is what I need to do." "This is what I'll do." And then help him do it. One danger, of course, is that first attempts may not meet with success. If first attempts at carrying out a plan of action or trying an alternative method of behaving are successful, then the probability for following through is high. If success is not achieved at the outset, the counselee may give up entirely. Unwilling or unable to make the effort, the counselee accepts defeat and simply views the experience as a substantiation of his ineffectiveness.

Both counselor and counselee must find out just how committed to growth and change a counselee is. The process of change is hard; anxiety runs high; old ways are familiar and comfortable. But the test must be made. Tyler (1960) suggests an approach she calls "minimum-change therapy," in which the counselor helps the counselee find an "unblocked path" along which he can move. For Tyler it involves a "change of *direction*." Perhaps if the first attempts can be made in ways that differ from but can be associated with that which is known to the counselee, those first attempts may have a better chance to succeed.

The counselor may also encourage and support any meaningful attempt the counselee may make toward growth and change, to give him courage to move further. A counselor may simply reinforce positive efforts at change, no matter how small they may be, thus providing the counselee with a feeling of achievement. Throughout, however, the counselor must maintain a warm and empathic relationship with the counselee.

The potential barriers to counseling that lie in the counselee's ambivalence toward change are great. The potential for helping the counselee deal with his life in more effective and satisfying ways is there, too. And this is the challenge, of course. But the potential for harm exists, too. Kell and Mueller (1966, p. 20) sum it up well:

> The potency of a relationship resides in the commitment and effective involvement of the client and his counselor; but a commitment to change implies vulnerability. The power of a relationship necessary to effect change can also make failure to change an equally significant event and have a lasting influence upon both participants. For the client, failure may mean confirmation of previous ineffective interpersonal relationships; for the counselor, it may mean that his next counseling relationship labors under residual burden of proof.

5

Hazards
for the
Counselee

Many of the hazards present in counseling involve and affect primarily the counselee. As the vulnerable and "incongruent" person in the relationship, some of the possible dangers may stem from the counselee himself; others are likely to be more indirect. But, in either case, the counselor's responsibility is indicated. As the "more knowing" partner, he has the need to understand as clearly and realistically as possible the nature of some of these concerns.

In this chapter, we direct attention to four such hazards. From the standpoint of the counselee, what are the risks and anxieties concerning confidentiality? When defenses are progressively laid aside, what are the dangers of the counselee becoming more unstable? As he makes his decisions, what are the hazards? And finally, what are for him the subtle dangers associated with manipulative strategies?

Anxieties Concerning Confidentiality

If I did tell you what has really been bothering me so much
. . . well, I guess that if anyone ever found out, I just
couldn't stand it.

How do I know I can trust you about all I might say?

My parents simply can't know this about me. . . .

Expressions like these from counselees reveal their acute
anxieties concerning privacy. For the counselee who has
personal problems, there is little doubt that it has required
considerable courage to come to the counselor at all. The
anxieties motivating him have probably reached such a high
level that he feels unable to try any longer to cope with them
on his own. But he is scared to talk about them too. At least
as he is now, they are his own inside problems; if he un-
covers them, then others might know too. What can he do?
Can he risk opening himself up to a counselor? But, if he
doesn't, his problems might get worse. . . .

These are the ambivalences the counselor must truly understand. The counselee brings not just his problems and
anxieties, but an anxiety *about* his anxieties. He seeks release
but fears the process; he wants the counselor to know and
to understand, and yet he feels it isn't safe to let *anyone*
know.

In varying degrees, an anxiety concerning confidentiality is
probably present in all counselees who come for personal
counseling. The hazard for the counselor is that he may minimize these fears, or even ignore or overlook them entirely.
He may fail to realize how pervasive and deep-seated these
feelings concerning possible exposure can be and that reassurance and trust must be experienced by the counselee throughout all of counseling, if he is to feel secure. Many counselors
regard a simple structuring at the outset of counseling to be
sufficient. The counselee is told that he can feel safe, say
anything that he wants to, and that all will be well. What he
says will not be repeated. But, as in one of the counselee
expressions cited above, how can he *know* that he can trust
to this extent?

COUNSELOR REPUTATION

Intellectually, the counselor realizes the significance and necessity for privileged communication to be a reality. He is professionally concerned that there be an established and recognized legal basis for counselors to have this right. He subscribes to the fact that counselees have to have it. But could it also be that in his own day-to-day functioning as he interacts with his own friends and colleagues that he sometimes is rather careless? When, for example, on a coffee break in the faculty lounge with several colleagues, a certain type of problem situation is mentioned, does he say, "I had a situation just like that recently"? While just meaning to be conversing in a general way, he could easily relate more than he intended to do. Unwittingly, personal identities can be revealed in this way.

It is from such "small" slips that confidentiality is eroded. The word gets around. Students come to know if they can really trust a certain counselor or not; the counselor's reputation, good or otherwise, envelops him and conditions counseling relationships with present and future counselees. Maybe if the counselor fully realized how extremely important confidentiality actually is to each and every counselee, if he empathized with counselee anxieties he would be more scrupulously on guard. The counselee can know that what he says in counseling is strictly respected when he finds evidence that the counselor *does* in fact what he *says* he will do. It is up to the counselor to reconcile and establish the integrity between the two; his reputation will then take care of itself. We are saying that the counselor should realistically be aware that there is a very close relationship between counselee anxieties concerning confidentiality and the reputation he earns for himself as a person to be or not to be completely trusted.

It is far better not to give a blanket promise of confidentiality to the counselee if the counselor himself feels that for some reason, depending on the nature of what the counselee tells him, there might be the need to communicate to others. Nor should the counselor ever be intentionally vague or evasive concerning the matter and leave counselee anxieties dangling and unresolved. If confidentiality is going to require some conditional boundaries the counselee should know these facts in advance. Benjamin (1969, p. 59) points this out:

> . . . we should not promise confidentiality if we are not certain that we can provide it. The question, "If I tell you what happened, do you promise not to tell my teacher?" should not be answered positively unless the interviewer intends to keep the promise. It need not be answered positively, however, for I, the interviewer, may not be prepared to promise something about which I know nothing. I can reply: . . . 'I can't promise without knowing, but I do promise that if you tell me about it, I won't do anything without first letting you know what it is and discussing it with you.'

ANXIETIES ABOUT RECORDS

High school and college students are certainly well aware of the significance of personal records and reports kept by the school. In the past, in various ways, they have realized the effects of communications coming from them. They understand too about permanent or cumulative record folders, that here in addition to grades, test scores and basic background statistics, personal comments and other like entries are frequently included. So now, when a student comes in for counseling, it is hardly surprising that he feels an anxiety as to whether his visits to the counselor will "go down" on this permanent record. Maybe even what happens in counseling will be recorded? And maybe these records can be seen by other teachers or administrators or future employers? Or (and this might worry him the most), maybe now his parents will learn this new information about him?

Some counselees ask the counselor directly about this matter; others may just hope this will not be the case and not express it. But the student counselee who comes for personal reasons undoubtedly has a number of his anxieties centered here. He worries about what might be recorded and known about his coming. A hazard is, does the counselor realize how he feels about this? The counselor could greatly strengthen rapport if he speaks strictly to lessen these fears. He can assure the counselee that no counseling information whatsoever need go into his permanent record.

These anxieties may again be increased, however, if the

counselee observes that the counselor is taking notes. Many counselors do not do this during the interview for just this reason. Other hazards are involved when the counselor takes notes, as Benjamin (1969, p. 58) understands and warns:

> Don't be secretive about the taking of notes lest this arouse the anxiety or curiosity of the interviewee. Finally, when taking notes in the presence of the interviewee, don't write things you are not prepared to have him see.

In any event, the counselee should be assured that all such notes about the interview are reserved for the counselor's use only, and others will not have access to them. Similarly, if the interview is to be taped, the counselee should understand that this will be done *only* if he consents. The counselee also needs to know that the purpose of taping the interview is simply for study and for a better understanding of later interviews. He is also helped by understanding that the tape will be played back only for the counselor, and possibly too for the counselee himself, if this would appear helpful to do. Finally, it cannot be overstressed that all of these assurances given the counselee must be stringently kept.

PERCEPTIONS OF PEER ISOLATION

In all likelihood, relationships for the student who comes in for personal counseling are already strained or difficult. It may be that he feels excluded, when he would very much like to be included by his peers in various social activities. Or maybe he feels that some of his friends, or one special friend, misunderstands the way he really is. Many of his present tensions and anxieties could easily involve problems such as these.

Anxious and troubled, as he now is, he certainly does not want to do anything that might further weaken any present relationships. "What would so-and-so think if she (or he) knew I felt I needed counseling? That would be bad enough, but then if she wanted to know why, or what it was about — that'd be awful. It would probably fix things up for sure!"

As he imagines future worsened social situations, of course his anxieties about presenting himself for counseling greatly increase. He keeps thinking that if some of his friends who particularly matter to him should find out, they will think less of him than they do now. They might be embarrassed to be seen with him because he "has problems and needs help." He does want help and has come to realize he needs it. But he certainly doesn't want his friends to know and to think of him this way!

Maybe the counselor can perceive, empathically, some of these anxieties and the reasons for them; the hazard is that he could to some degree discount and belittle their meaning and importance. It may be helpful to consider two examples: Helen, a senior in high school, has come to the counselor for the first time:

> *Helen:* I don't know why, but I just feel like crying all the time, anymore. So I thought I'd really better talk to you. But no one can know I'm here . . . they won't, will they? I mean . . .
>
> *Counselor:* You felt you needed to come here, but it would embarrass and upset you if your friends learned of it and thought you needed this help?
>
> Helen: (*starting to cry*) Yes. Oh, yes. It sure would.

There is a good chance that this counselor really does understand the reasons for Helen's anxieties about her friends. But let's look at how another less understanding counselor might have responded:

> *Helen:* I don't know why, but I just feel like crying all the time, anymore. So I thought I'd really better talk to you. But no one can know I'm here . . . they won't, will they? I mean . . .
>
> *Counselor:* There is no need for you to feel ashamed of coming in here today. This is the right place to come when you feel depressed or upset.
>
> *Helen:* I know. But . . . I mean, I just don't want any of the kids to know. They'd think I'm funny or something. . . .
>
> *Counselor:* Probably they wouldn't see it that way at all.

ANXIETIES ABOUT PARENTS

❧ In our foregoing discussion we have referred several times to the high level of anxieties which counselees feel if they think that any part of what they say during counseling may be directly or indirectly relayed to their parents. Why should this be such a predominant concern? Why should anxieties about confidentiality here seem to be so crucially central and important?

The present relationship between the counselee and one or both of the parents may have deteriorated, even seemingly to a point where no viable current relationship exists. Or the relationship may apparently be quite positive and strong. In either case, complex and potent emotional factors operate. Hostile and rejective attitudes toward parents can hold especial psychological significance. All child-parent relationships have deep roots; accordingly, they can either be potentially explosive or integrative. But they are never really meaningless or neutral.

We will limit our consideration here to students or other counselees of high school age or beyond, as these individuals have become relatively autonomous in their behavior. (Confidentiality problems become more complicated when counseling children and seldom can privacy here be absolute. One or both parents is usually of necessity brought into the counseling process in some responsible way, or to some extent.)

An important reason why Rogers introduced and emphasized his concept of "*un*conditional positive regard" in counseling as being as therapeutically central and essential as he feels it is, is that a young person may never have known this type of acceptance of himself before. There may always have been strings attached to approval. If he did that which his parents wanted him to do, if he was "good," all was well; all that was necessary was that he not deviate too much from the norm or blueprint which they set up for him. Rogers explains that it is exactly this type of "conditional" regard that accounts for the child's pushing down the "unacceptable" parts of himself to meet the expectations of others. As a person, he was never allowed to be known; what he naturally felt he wanted to explore or understand so often had to be fitted and tailored into an approved mold. Therapy, Rogers feels, should in essence reverse the process. When the individual experiences a sincere *un*conditional regard for himself, the heretofore submerged "unacceptable" parts of himself can come up again. He then has a new opportunity to be literally re-created and reintegrated without fear.

This explanation may have real relevance here, as we consider the genesis of anxieties concerning parents. In the counseling situation, the counselee with pressured emotional conflicts, seeking release, is motivated to get them up and out. But, and in his mind it may be a big "but," he strongly feels the learned threat of what his parents would do or say if they really ever knew this part of himself. Disapproval, rejection, estrangement — these may appear to be the possible costs, if disclosure is risked. No wonder his anxieties concerning whether he can trust the counselor not to tell his parents are running high!

It is not essential that there be a "generation gap." The generalization that this invariably exists is unfair and inaccurate; certainly it is not a new concept. However, the expression, and what it involves, has come into current parlance and preeminence because there so often *is* a considerable divergence in understanding between parents and their young people. In today's fast moving societal context, the communication distance may in many instances be sharply marked. There may be deadlocks in understanding each other. Adolescents and young adults are action-oriented; they are struggling to achieve an identity and to be heard and understood; and they are not to be placated or satisfied either with second-hand experience or authoritarian dicta. There is nothing new about these insurgent behavior patterns of young people, but in times of rapid social, political, and ethical changes and the transition in racial attitudes which we are currently experiencing, they find a dominant and turbulent expression. Many parents may overreact and retreat into negatively judgmental positions. If and when this is the case, it also has relevance here. Student counselees feel that if their parents were made aware or heard how they feel and what they do, the barriers to communication and mutual understanding would only be increased. So again, the anxieties they feel about confidentiality in regard to their parents can be readily understood.

ANXIETIES ABOUT REPRISALS

Counselee anxieties concerning confidentiality may stem from still another source. He may fear that if he tells the counselor some of the things about which he is worried, feels guilty, or is in conflict, the counselor may feel it necessary to report them to those persons in relevant positions of authority. He may feel anxious, in other words, concerning past actions or situations involving himself or others. He feels that if these were known, some form of disciplinary action might result. So he is anxious and ambivalent about revealing them. What should he do now?

What hazards in turn are present here for the counselor? *Can* the counselor, especially in the school context, honor fully the confidentiality of all such "confessions"?

While assuredly there are hazards involved, they are considerably lessened when the counselor has clearly thought through in advance the stand that he will take. *For the counselee has the need and the right to understand his position.* Basically, the counselor must be realistically and sensitively aware of the extent to which he is prepared and able to receive all that is told him in confidence. In addition he needs to know, and come to terms with, how far he feels he can and will retain all confidences with respect to the institutional setting in which he works. Finally, he must implement with courage and consistency what he believes and what he has communicated to the counselee.

Courage is needed by the counselor, for there may be many who do not feel as he does about counselee confidentiality in the area of "misdemeanors." And counselors, of course, themselves differ in their philosophies here. It may be helpful to cite some opinions. McKinney (1958, p. 237) writes:

> There are many on the school roster who can administer discipline; there are very few who can provide the wise acceptance of a troubled individual which will cause him to understand himself and deal with his errors and shortcomings. . . .

The counseling office should be a sanctuary. It is one of the rare places where an individual can come to grips with his own derelictions and use his errors to strengthen his choices in the future.

In Patterson's view (1959, p. 46),

> . . . the counselor should not divulge the details of his knowledge of the client, except with the express permission of the client. People concerned with the client may have some rights to learn about the client. These rights do not include the right to share confidential information. The counselor must decide what he can tell the individual concerned, whether parent, guardian, teacher, or probation officer.

Tyler (1961, p. 98) cites other reasons for her strong personal position against this type of counselor reporting:

> The risk that the counseling service could come to be regarded as an espionage agency is one which is too great to be taken, as it would rule out effective work from that time on. There are other channels through which knowledge of bad conditions can reach the authorities, and it is better that these channels be used. The counselee himself may decide to report the facts to the responsible officials. Another reason for the counselor to take no action himself is his realization that he is always working in the realm of attitudes and beliefs, not facts.

GENERAL PERSPECTIVES FOR THE COUNSELOR

The counselor needs to appreciate realistically and be responsive to the many anxieties counselees have with respect to confidentiality. A few of the many hazards in this area are: (1) the counselor may fail to realize the depth and importance of these anxieties as counselees view them; (2) he may carelessly let some confidences slip out to colleagues and others; (3) he may fail to define clearly his stand, both to himself and to counselees, when it might be controversial. As a professional person, it is essential that he implement his responsibilities to counselees concerning confidentiality with a consistent integrity.

Heightened Instability

When a counselee presents himself for counseling for the first time, either because of being referred or because he comes on his own, in all probability he has many self-doubts and anxieties. Even if he comes for counsel concerning educational or vocational matters, this is likely to be true to some extent. However, it is especially true when he needs assistance because of real personal problems and conflicts; he then, as Rogers puts it, is in a state of "incongruence." Disturbing inner states such as feeling tense or at "odds with himself," doubts of his adequacy to cope any longer with the situations facing him — these are the confusions which have motivated him to come to the counselor. We are concerned here with the counselee who is seeking help with his personal problems.

THE GOALS OF COUNSELING

Probably it could be said that, in one way or another, counselors see themselves as facilitative agents of behavioral change. They differ markedly as to how they view the causes of basic problematic conflicts in counselees requiring change, and they undoubtedly differ even more conspicuously in their beliefs as to how and to what extent they should participate in the changing process.

Because of their differing philosophical positions, therapists also differ as to the definition and type of change which they feel is indicated. Some focus their efforts to provide assistance in modifying external behavior patterns; others seek to aid the counselee in making his own deeper inner and motivational changes. The writers subscribe to the latter view concerning behavioral change. We see counseling as a partnership process in which the counselee is progressively enabled to help himself in his own growth through achieving new realistic insights and understandings. These are understandings meaningful to him because they are in terms of his own experiences and values and are not imposed upon him. Because of the conditions provided during the counseling process, the counselee is allowed to explore and reintegrate his feelings. All of this, however, is much easier to define than to implement. Many hazards are present. Johnson (1967, p. 178) writes:

> There must be uncovering for the person to know himself more deeply; yet it must not be a violent unmasking or clever exposure of his secret, but rather a steady and patient searching faithfully together. There will be ambiguities, vague fears, false expectations, and uncertainties about what to do or how to go forward together.

EGO DEFENSES AROUSED

The "self-concept" of the counselee is his own preconceived image of himself. It is the mental picture which has evolved and been shaped from all of the composite, developmental "feedbacks" which he has assimilated. Criticisms, "labelings," failures, as well as the commendations and successes he has experienced, have all contributed to the way he has come to think of himself. Now, despite the inner conflicts and tensions with which he has been struggling and which have motivated him to see the counselor, he is still trying to keep this subjective view of himself as intact as he can.

No doubt many of the problematic situations with which he has been unsuccessfully attempting to cope have worn down his feelings of adequacy. And under such circumstances it is difficult for him to maintain very much self-regard and self-esteem; the picture he has held of himself is endangered. He feels too that his own image is projected and that others think less of him as well. So when he comes for personal counseling, it is hardly surprising that he probably feels embarrassed and anxious. Fitts (1965, p. 26) quotes the actual comments of a client who later wrote of her reactions during early therapy:

> The first few visits I felt uneasy, tearful, embarrassed, ashamed, guilty and depressed and constantly reminded myself: "Surely I could have done better than this; why did this have to happen to me? What does my Doctor think of me? How could *he* know what I'm going through? Why should he care? Why should he spend his time with me? (Someone else maybe, but I should be capable of straightening this out myself!)"

These feelings concerning self are too deeply rooted to be easily altered. They may persist throughout many counseling sessions, because the counselee's self-esteem is in jeopardy. Probably he will be responding with various defense mechanisms, since this is true. Here are some examples:

> I think you think it was my fault that I'm on probation now. But in every class I had last quarter all the cards were stacked against me.

> So I didn't win the election. But I could have, if the guys in the Hall weren't so jealous of me.

> She said she didn't want to room with me next year. That's O.K. with me — who wants to live with her again anyway?

The counselor must listen sensitively and be understanding. Not only must he realize the basis and cause for such defensive reactions but he must guard against the hazards of expressing responses which might increase anxiety levels of the counselee and keep him from feeling he can begin to "open up." Suppose, for example, that to the three counselee expressions cited above, the counselor should respond, respectively, as follows:

> But the responsibility about your courses was up to you.

> There probably were other reasons why you lost out.

> Why do you really think she doesn't care to room with you again?

The counselor has challenged, instead of empathizing. And the counselee, as his defenses have so clearly indicated, is already feeling very insecure. He can hardly be expected to respond to a challenge at this point and expand his feelings! Kell and Mueller (1966, p. 35) realize that these restricted defensive maneuvers on the part of the counselee should be initially expected by the counselor. Another typical and safer defensive pattern is for the counselee to begin by presenting quite a tightly compressed statement of what has been bothering him:

The compacted experiences of the client serve many functions for him. The client has compressed his experiences for good reasons and one of these is that in its present form, the affect, although anxiety provoking, is not as painful as it would be if it were expanded. The anxiety is more dormant and encysted.

Here the hazards are much the same, and so is the task. Again, the counselor must "loosen" the situation with supportive acceptance and empathic understanding. The counselee needs to be able to experience sufficient safety in the counseling relationship so that he can widen and look into the "compacted picture."

OLD ANXIETIES STIRRED

As we have noted, in personal counseling, a most important function of the counselor is to facilitate the "opening up" process for the counselee. For tension release and subsequent behavioral changes to occur, the psychological wrappings and cover-ups of the counselee's old hurts, problems, and conflicts need to be lifted. This, in essence, is counseling. But it can be painful at times for the counselee, and for both counselor and counselee there are a number of hazards. Former humiliations experienced by the counselee can come to life again. He reexperiences the old hurts. Can the counselor genuinely follow with him at such times? To avoid "leaving" him, the counselor first of all must really want to go on accepting him in full and to allow him to proceed through any of his dark alleys that he chooses. The counselor's disinclinations, own needs, or insecurities, if aroused, cannot intrude or circumvent. Nor can he push or prod. Because the counselee may be recalling at least in part some of the experiences which gave rise to his anxieties and conflicts, he may be hesitant in expression or he may lapse into a complete silence, or he may distort or omit some aspects of what he is saying. His heightened instability will be but confirmed, however, if the counselor fails to make it possible for him to continue and to work through these old anxieties. The hazard is indeed a large and central one if the counselor fails to believe that new perspectives and insights with resultant behavioral change can actually occur. As Kell and Mueller (1966, p. 32) write:

> The counselor's task is to help the client to express his problems. In order to provide a situation in which a client can recall and work out conflicted feelings, the counselor must provide the emotional strength and security for the client to do so.

We are not saying here that the counselor should assume the analyst's role. If and when severe and deeply embedded repressions are recognized, the counselor should perceive that referral is probably indicated. Nevertheless, these instances may not occur as frequently as sometimes is supposed. The sensitive and receptive counselor can usually be of much real assistance to counselees who are anxious and upset, by helping them experience safety and understanding in the relationship. McKinney (1958, p. 78) comments:

> In all successful counseling, the client brings up matters he had no intention of discussing. Because he feels safe with the counselor, he dares to uncover repressed material. He unearths some of his ignorance of himself produced by his anxiety. He becomes aware of himself as he was not before. He gains self-understanding and perspective.

PAINFUL REALIZATIONS AND INSIGHTS

Throughout the counseling process, there remains the very real hazard that the counselor could detour or block counselee expressions. When the counselee begins talking about very painful or unpleasant happenings and the associated feelings which deeply disturb him, it may be that the counselor feels vaguely uneasy in letting him go too far. But what could happen then, although of course he does not intend it at all, is that the counselor may add to the tangled causes of the counselee's instability. Kemp (1967, p. 90) recognizes the danger:

> The counselor is unwilling to share in the desperate feeling of the counselee and, perhaps threatened by the force of the counselee's anxiety, may cause more damage than good. When this occurs, the problems underlying the anxiety go unsolved and become buried in a complicated system of repression.

If, on the other hand, the counselor has been able to avoid this serious pitfall and has made it possible for the counselee to continue with his disclosures, the counselee will undoubtedly understand things about himself he had not realized before. Some of these realizations may be painful and very difficult for him to accept. He may hear himself saying things aloud which he had never dared admit before.

> When my Dad took that trip, I guess what I honestly was thinking when I told him goodbye, was I don't care if you never come home again. I don't care if you die. . . . But that's awful!

Insights such as these, although potentially and temporarily alarming to the counselee, are essential in the therapeutic process. The hazard for the counselor is that at no time or for any reason can his regard for the counselee's intrinsic worth as a person be shaken. It must be, and be perceived by the counselee to be, a steady and genuine "unconditional regard." If the counselee can truly feel sustained by the counselor's authentic and continued warm acceptance of him, he can incorporate and utilize the new hard-won perspectives. He can work through all of these frightening realities, and come out on higher ground. Gradually, his instabilities can progress toward an increased stability.

Expedient Decisions

When a counselee comes in for counseling, he may have planned in advance exactly what he will say to the counselor. All he needs is some help, he may say, in deciding what to do about this or that particular course of action. A boy may presumably simply request help with respect to a vocational or educational choice. A girl may say she is considering dropping out of school for a year to work and "get experience," and she needs the counselor's advice about jobs. While some of these requests may be largely just what they purport to be, a large number of them have emotional roots. Very often the question which is posed serves as an entrée and represents a respectable "front." We have noted that it is common for counselees initially to present a "compacted picture." The counselor must be sensitive in perceiving emotional content behind requests for "simple" decisions. It is hazardous to rush.

LOW FRUSTRATION TOLERANCE

The counselee feels "tight." He is urgently looking for relief and release from cumulative inner frustrations which he feels he cannot continue carrying. He may not be, and probably is not, wholly aware of what motivates him. He only knows he wants to *do* something which will dissipate these uncomfortable feelings of anxiety and unrest.

So when he presents himself to the counselor he is very action-oriented. He is ready to get something decided as soon as possible. For example, Jim, a college sophomore, comes to the counselor asking help. He says he would like some information about other schools, as he wants to transfer next semester to a different type of college. "Can you help me decide which one would be best?"

It well may be that behind such a request lie many feelings of conflict. They have been pushed down; it is painful to grapple with them. And so "the grass looks greener" on a different site. The "Jims" are not realizing that their unresolved tensions within themselves would only accompany them and become even more complex and troublesome. They simply feel that they want to escape from present frustrations.

As a result, because of this typically low frustration tolerance of the counselee, grave hazards are present. Both counselee and counselor might be deceived here. For if the counselor looks away from these needs, he reveals that he too has some needs for early closure. He may relate to the counselee too quickly and too nominally, not fully aware that he too would like to minimize the strains of frustration tolerance. Hiltner (1952, pp. 23–24) warns that it is easy to respond to the counselee on this opening action level and that the counselor may be further deceived by believing that the counselee then has genuinely been helped.

> . . . the evil is not necessarily discussing action, if we know we have deserted counseling itself when we do so. It is in resorting to action-discussion as a substitute for clarification; and then, by a superficial evaluation of results, fixing our-

selves in a practice which, whatever its bright immediacies, will do harm to our people and our own counseling in the long run.

VACILLATION

Although the counselee may be action-oriented and would like nothing better than to do something which would improve his situation, yet it is threatening to him to actually come to a decision. So he wavers back and forth. He asks the counselor what to do.

> I'd like your opinion so I can decide about it.
>
> I lie awake at night wondering what to do. But I still can't make up my mind.
>
> I keep thinking what might happen if I decided to do it. But if I don't, I'll just keep on feeling like I do now.

Why this vacillation? It is, of course, to this "why" that counseling must be directed in each case. The counselee's feelings and confused motivations are fairly crying out to be examined. The counselee vacillates between possible alternatives in order to evade the responsibility of consequences, should he actually do this or that. He feels uneasy and insecure.

The temptation for the counselor is to attempt to be overly helpful. He would like to relieve the immediate stress. On the face of things, he may think this or that course of action appears to be the "right" one for the counselee to follow. It is hard to remember constantly that the "face of things" seldom if ever constitutes the counselee's real situation. Also, whether the counselee himself fully realizes it or not, it is he who has both the need and the right to make his own decisions, circuitous and involved though the process may be.

DOGMATISM

If the counselee comes from a family in which he has experienced extremely strict discipline, if his parents and the other significant adults in his life have been authoritarian and rigid, it is highly probable that in approaching the making of decisions he will be quite narrow-minded. He has learned to take refuge in strongly opinionated and emotionally based stands; to listen to any other points of view is threatening to him. So he has tended to decide hastily, largely by rearranging his prejudices.

But it is significant that now he comes for counseling. He probably has been experiencing many disquieting emotional seepages. Although he tries to ignore emotions which arise from conflicting exposures to other views and experiences, it is becoming more and more difficult. His "system" has encountered challenges, and he feels overwhelmed in attempting to cope with the inner stresses. For example, Steve, a college sophomore who has held strong racial antipathies is asking now for the counselor's reinforcement about deciding to quit his fraternity.

> Some of the fellows in there are nuts. Last night they pushed a vote through to pledge a couple of colored guys!! So I'm going to quit that bunch. You sure can understand there's no point staying in there anymore, can't you?

Or it may be that there are disillusionments experienced with former identification figures. Ada is a high school senior.

> Will you help me get some information about taking a business course next year? I used to think I wanted to go to college and be a teacher. But too many of my teachers are just phonies.

With some of their former moorings and emotional anchorages eroded, the counselee may seek hasty compromises. Because it is anxiety that motivates, the decision presented is likely to be very superficial. The counselee who has been dogmatic in his thinking has tended in the past to overgeneralize, and he does so now. These are hazards the counselor must recognize. Patience and perceptive understanding and a continuous acceptance are all necessary to assist the counselee who is torn by frightening doubts and new conflicts.

Threats also arise for the counselee with respect to his peers and their general acceptance of him. This occurs especially for the student in middle adolescence who fervently seeks to be popular and "to belong." He is afraid to see if he really subscribes to the attitudes and prejudices held by his parents and to the premises which have always dominated his own thinking and behavior. He may now find himself experiencing some exclusion and rejection and being "at odds" with the views of many of his peers. He feels confused and upset, even overwhelmed. He doesn't know what to do. He urgently needs the counselor to assist him in making his own sound decisions concerning where he stands.

UNREALISTIC VIEWS OF SELF

Many of the contemplated choices of the counselee are based upon unrealistic perceptions which he has come to hold about himself. There may be large discrepancies between the way in which he persistently continues to see himself and the way in which others more realistically regard him. It is very difficult, psychologically, to assimilate too many negative experiences. If the counselee has sustained numerous defeats and humiliations, he may have rationalized or suppressed them. In effect he denies them, feeling "I am not like that." It is not acceptable to himself to be "like that." So it is understandable that he frequently tends to choose courses of action which will confirm and defend this more idealized self-picture and which also in part will compensate for the emotional jolts he has experienced. The high school student, on the borderline academically, who comes requesting information about medical schools, and the plain-looking, shy little ninth-grader who wants to know what you have to do to get to be an airline stewardess are examples.

The evaluations of "significant others" have a major role in contributing to the counselee's self-picture. For example, unrealistic parental aspirations can foster distortions, for the developing boy or girl is hardly in a position to be neutral. So now it can happen that a counselee comes to the counselor wanting to make a decision whether to align himself with (or rebel against) these particular parental hopes or expectations. When maternal or paternal expectations lack realistic foundations and are projected upon the young person because of the parent's own unmet needs, unsound decisions are highly probable. Consider, for instance, a mother who had cherished

•

hopes to attend a certain exclusive college in the East. Circumstances made it impossible for her to do it, but for years she has been instilling and projecting these desires upon her daughter. But Sue has done poorly as a student throughout her three years in high school, and she has barely attained her present status as a senior. Now she comes to the counselor for help in applying for admission just to this one particular high-ranking college. Or, consider the case of Tom. Tom's father is in an engineering consultant firm and has pressured his son over a period of time to become an engineer like himself. Tom has increasingly rebelled against this prescribed vocational avenue and for the past year has been going with a hippie group of friends. Although he has a very high I.Q. and his teachers say he could and "should" be making all "A's," like Sue he has barely succeeded in becoming a high school senior. Tom has been referred to the counselor, for he thinks what he wants to do is to drop out of school and go to New York for a while. The decisions proposed by both Sue and Tom are predicated upon extremely unrealistic "self-estimates."

Counseling can assist these counselees gradually to understand themselves as they are. But can the counselor perceive and understand their deep needs clearly enough for this insightful process to occur? Can he supply genuine, continued, and unconditional acceptance so that they are enabled progressively to resolve their own inconsistencies and come truly to accept themselves? Realistic decisions cannot be made until then. These are the defined hazards.

EXTERNAL PRESSURES

John is a counselee whose opening remarks to the counselor are that he is here because he has to decide right now (at least before next Monday morning when he has to register) what his college major will be. For another counselee, a job offer has been made and he must accept or reject it immediately. Or maybe it is a problem of personal relationship, and the counselee feels the other partner is pushing for a decision. So the counselee asks for the counselor's advice. Marie is a high school senior, who on her first visit to the counselor presents this latter type of dilemma:

> So now that graduation is in two weeks, Mike says I've got to make up my mind or else we're through. We've been going round and round on this business about his being Catholic and that I'm not. I don't know . . . maybe it doesn't make any difference, and I don't want to lose Mike. But I've got to decide *now*.

There are many other instances in which the counselee, because of pressures from parents or teachers or because of deadlines or other circumstantial pressures, feels that a decision *has* to be made without delay.

The counselee in these instances almost always, to some degree, feels anxious and pushed. He feels the pressures and the urgency. But some of the situations presented do have more flexible time boundaries and latitudes than apparently are present. The counselee needs to know these facts. In the case of Marie, for example, she has enough at stake in the decision to refuse to be stampeded into her final commitment by an ultimatum.

It is true that there are decisions which have to be made at once. When the context calls for this kind of action, it obviously is a hazard to counseling itself. There actually may not be time enough for counselee and the counselor to uncover together the counselee's feelings which may underlie a decision in either direction. But some hazards for the counselee can be skirted if this fact simply is understood. If the counselee is ambivalent, yet can realize he is making a decision under pressure, he may be able to decide the minimum to satisfy the present requirements. He could thus leave the road as open as possible for further exploration and understanding with the counselor. But pressured decisions, like other decisions, should always be fully his own. Tyler (1961, p. 202) comments:

> In such instances it is well to make sure that the difference between an arbitrary decision and a genuine one is clear to the client, so that the way will still be open for him to work toward a genuine one. The client rather than the counselor should make this arbitrary decision.

Some illustrations may be of help here. John may tentatively decide to major in economics and register for courses in the social sciences. But these courses also answer requirements for graduation and could apply just as well at this point to a major in political science or history. John feels that after graduation he may want to teach history, but that he might prefer to go into business. If he goes into business, the economics would be important to him. If a decision must be made about a present job offer, and the counselee has doubts and concerns, it might be possible to take the job with some mutual understanding that initially it would involve a limited time commitment. To suggest that certain hazards may be avoided by making decisions of this type is not to recommend that issues be straddled. But it is realistic for the counselee to recognize when he is unready to make final commitments and to keep himself as open as the situation permits.

THE ACTION GAP

When there is no follow-through on what has been "decided," it becomes clear that the decision was not genuine. There is no behavioral change. The counselee can give lip-service to a projected course of action, but his ambivalences and anxieties, still unresolved, motivate him to retain the *status quo*. Within himself he is yet at war. Kemp (1967, pp. 46–48) discusses the "inertia of the will" and the hazards and complexities affecting the counselee, especially when the decision is an important one.

> If the will overrides feeling and emotion, anxiety and repression may result. Or if the will is stimulated to act through advice and encouragement, a dependent relationship with the counselor may result.

The counselee needs to raise and gradually extinguish old anxieties in permissive counseling sessions. He needs the time to work through underlying conflicts involved in the way he is accustomed to think about himself. Maybe, as new insights come to him, he needs to "try them out" a little.

The route to a sound decision, when significant behavioral changes for the counselee are involved, is not short or uncomplicated. The hazards are that both counselee and counselor might act as if it were and prematurely terminate counseling.

Manipulative Strategies

Jane was waiting for the counselor to arrive at his office in the high school.

"Mr. X, I've got to talk to you right away! I'm not going to my gym class next period. . . ."

"You're cutting class to see me? What is the problem, Jane?"

"You won't believe how I'm picked on in that class! Just because one day last week I didn't dress out . . . Oh, Mr. X, you've just got to get me out of there!"

This is not an atypical situation. Many counselees, especially high school counselees, feel that the counselor might be the person who would protect or remove them from unpleasant situations. So they proceed quite directly to maneuver the counselor toward that end. They attempt to get the counselor on "their side." They want him to come to feel their outrages or resentments, so that he will act and do something that will fix things. They see him as a person in a position of authority who would be listened to by teachers and administrators and parents and therefore could effect changes. So they attempt to manipulate him in the hope that he will in turn manipulate others.

This strategy of trying to put the counselor in a "fixer" role takes many forms. A counselee may be quite subtle in requesting a small "favor," or in asking the counselor to please sign some approval form about a recommended course change. Often the request is made indirectly and is slipped in during a later counseling session. For example, Bob is a high school senior, who is presently very worried about passing his course in American history. If he fails, it means he will be put off the football team. He has missed being present for the last two tests, and his teacher, Miss Y, has the policy of refusing to give any "make-ups" for announced tests. Bob has been talking about himself and problems that have concerned him in several counseling sessions. He has been gradually leading up to the situation with Miss Y. He explains to the counselor why it was impossible for him to take the tests on the days they were given. So now he says that all that is needed is for the counselor to speak to Miss Y, so that she can understand how things really are. Then Bob would be in the clear!

The counselor could easily fall into the trap. Thinking of himself as a helping person, he could respond to what he might regard as needed action in the immediate situation. He could be blinded entirely to how he was "used" and placed into the role of "fixer." If this hazard should become a reality, Bob will only have learned once again that manipulation works, and he is likely to polish up other strategies for the future. And the counselor, having unfortunately departed from the goals of counseling, will be more vulnerable as a target person for later manipulations.

"PLAYING UP" TO THE COUNSELOR

Because the counselee has become shaky from many past experiences, he may feel an exaggerated need for approval and attention. If he can elicit this response from the counselor he feels less anxious about himself. He wants his present behavior to be endorsed, not changed.

So, especially in the first few sessions of counseling, the counselee "plays up" to the counselor in various ways. He compliments the counselor, or brings a small gift for him to the counseling session. He phrases his remarks and voice inflections to seek the counselor's response of complete agreement. Actually these manipulations to identify with the counselor and to gain present unqualified approval are defensive attempts to avoid any "unmasking" of his deeper self. The counselee is not even likely to be consciously aware of why he is manipulating the counselor in this way.

But to help him to understand the *why* of this excessive desire for approval is precisely the counselor's task. The counselor will help if he can make it increasingly possible for the counselee to explore and understand his anxieties and insecurity needs. He will not help if he is "taken in" and responds at face value to the counselee's manipulative attempts to please, and so closes off the opportunity for counseling to proceed to deeper levels. There is always the subtle hazard for the counselor that he will misunderstand the concept of "acceptance." To accept the counselee as a person, and as he now is, does *not* have to include the dimension of approval. In fact, to do so could dilute or even negate acceptance of the real self and worth of the counselee.

MANIPULATING THE PROBLEM

The counselee's ambivalence about what is troubling him prompts him to use other manipulative strategies as counseling progresses. He wants to uncover his problem fully and realistically to the counselor, but he also shies away from becoming too vulnerable and too *known*. Kell and Mueller (1966, p. 48) refer to these "push-pull" tactics of the counselee in which he attempts to structure the counseling situation to minimize anxiety as "eliciting behaviors":

> The dual intent of the eliciting behaviors reflects the ambivalence of the client about changing. On the one hand, the client may wish to avoid the pain of change and uses eliciting behaviors in an effort to repair the situation without exploring it, since exploration involves pain. Since, however, the success of this kind of behavior also means lack of significant contact, warding-off behaviors arouse anxiety about isolation and this anxiety will activate eliciting behaviors which attempt to reestablish significant interpersonal contact.

The counselor needs to be continuously perceptive and alert in recognizing and coping with these attempted maneuvers. Although the counselee attempts to protect the problem, yet much as in a detective story, he plants clues for the fuller revelation. In spite of the counselee's changing the subject, going off on a tangent, and throwing in "red herrings," the counselor can school himself to be tuned to the central message.

As he initially presents the problem, the counselee might minimize and avoid much of his own responsibility and involvement, while emphasizing, although belittling, the acts and attitudes of others. It should be noted, however, that many such attempts to camouflage or misrepresent the situation may not be consciously practiced by the counselee. They may occur because they are an intrinsic part of his present psychological difficulties. They point to attitudes and conflicts which trouble him as he relates interpersonally. As Sachs

(1966, p. 17) observes, "A student who speaks of nonacademic children as those people 'down there' whom he finds distasteful, has a problem in terms of his own background and sense of values."

TESTING THE COUNSELOR

Many strategic manipulations are directed toward the counselor himself. In spite of trying to partially conceal, deny, or project on others his central problem, the counselee would like satisfying and genuine help from the counselor. He is seeking relief. But, because of his anxieties, he attempts to control the relationship and to test the counselor in various subtle ways. Kell and Mueller (1966, p. 48) note that, "when the counselor is effective, the client will seek to avoid anxiety by trying to render the counselor ineffective; but when the relationship lags, the client will attempt to reactivate it."

There are many tactics by which the counselee attempts to "render the counselor ineffective." Probably strongest in the arsenal are ways in which the counselee tries to put the counselor on the defensive. The counselee may defy, openly challenge, or even insult the counselor, or he may be more subtle. Hiltner (1952, p. 124) cites a counselee as telling her counselor, "You're thinking to yourself how superior you are. You think you are helping me, but inside I'm laughing at you." Other counselee remarks designed to put the counselor "on the spot" could be:

You're supposed to know the answers. Okay. So what would *you* do about it?

You probably have to watch what you say to me, because Mr. W (the school principal) checks up on you, too.

You don't understand me. Why should I expect you to, anyway?

If the counselee can topple the counselor and pull him down into the problem with him, as it were, then he himself would not feel in the "under" position. He, not the counselor, would be in control of the counseling. And of course there always exists the hazard that this could happen! It might, if the counselor allows the hostile or provocative content of the counselee's remarks to "get to him" in a personal way and neglects to keep his attention on the counselee's feelings, which motivate such remarks. But the counselee does not really want this switching of roles. He is testing the relationship; he would really like to be assured that the counselor can withstand manipulation and be strong enough to continue as his counselor. An illustration is provided by Kell and Mueller (1966, p. 49):

> One client . . . whose motivation was that of repairing and reestablishing a relationship, utilized eliciting behaviors which were aimed at revitalizing the relationship. This client went to considerable lengths to convince her wavering counselor that he was adequate and competent to work with her.

Yet the manipulative testings by the counselee continue. The counselee may use hippie jargon and slang terms referring to drugs to see if the counselor understands what he is talking about. Or he may test the counselor's shockability: "You'd be surprised at the thoughts I have sometimes. Last night I thought I might set fire to the dorm."

Counselees who are self-rejecting manipulate the counselor in other ways. Especially for counselees in their teens, self-acceptance and the acceptance of others is likely to be desperately needed. It is too important to take the counselor's apparent regard and concern at face value. So he tests it, even though in other relationships where he has pushed in this way, he has been hurt badly. Jersild (1963, p. 35) explains, "The tragic thing about adolescents who severely reject themselves is that they often do things which cause others to confirm the low opinion they have of themselves."

But now, continuing in this pattern, the counselee may appear at the counseling session dressed slovenly, or unwashed, or with hair uncombed. Can the counselor overlook his external appearance? Does he himself really matter to the counselor? He may try in other ways to see. Will the counselor still see him if he comes late to the appointment? If he calls the counselor at home late at night, will the counselor talk to him? Tyler (1969, p. 169) recognizes these vital needs of the counselee, but also realizes that it is essential for the counselor to maintain certain limits of his own. It is not in the genuine interest of the counselee to permit him to continue trying to gain acceptance through maneuvering acts. "Clients should not get any sort of reinforcement for attitudes of over-dependence on other people or habits of manipulating them."

On occasion, a male counselor may experience manipulation by a female counselee. Maneuvering for a power role, as well as for a certain preferred type of treatment, she may be testing him to see if he is in fact a counselor or is "just like other men." Kell and Mueller (1966, p. 49) describe some of these strategies:

> Often these clients will utilize a tremendous affective barrage involving highly dramatized speech, tears, and marked affective changes, all of which are intended to intensify the power of the communication that they are fragile, and that any show of aggression on the counselor's part will be shattering to the client.

Other behaviors to test the counselor may occur. From interpersonal relationships in the past, the counselee may have learned that presenting himself in certain ways to the other person has resulted in achieving certain ends. Now to present himself to the counselor as helpless, passive, naïve, or as the reverse of these postures may be in the same manipulative pattern. He is again using learned tricks.

In responding to testing maneuvers by the counselee, hazards for the counselor lie primarily in his not dealing with such dynamics therapeutically. Brammer and Shostrom (1968, p. 109) believe that the counselor should cope forthrightly with all manipulations, exposing them to the counselee for his further understanding:

> The counselor . . . may help the client become aware of his defensive pattern of manipulations, or "games" he plays with people, by asking him to indicate the gains he is receiving. They may then discuss the gain values for the client of the various manipulations. . . . The client is helped to see that from a long range point of view they are self defeating, since they tend to alienate him from others, or keep him dependent on them.

Part Three

*

Interaction

6

Barriers to Interaction

When counselor and counselee meet in the counseling relationship, the potential for freedom and discovery and development surrounds them both. The experience can engender involvement and insight and growth, or it can leave both counselor and counselee vaguely (or actively) disappointed and frustrated. As Rogers (1962, p. 416) pointed out, ". . . the quality of the personal encounter is probably, in the long run, the element which determines the extent to which this is an experience which releases or promotes development and growth."

The quality of the personal encounter is a dynamic and fragile thing, influenced not only by what each individual thinks he *should* bring to the relationship, but also by the kind of person he is, what he expects from the relationship, and what he is prepared to contribute to it. The nature of the interaction is determined by factors beyond the control of either individual, for example, age and sex, as well as by the needs and expectations and interpersonal effectiveness of both.

The purpose of this chapter is to

explore some of the barriers to interaction between counselor and counselee. We shall consider circumstantial dimensions such as sex and age and personally inhibiting factors of both counselor and counselee. Also we shall look at the temptation to which either participant might fall prey — exploitation of the relationship for need satisfaction. And finally consideration will be given to that delicate task of communication.

Sex

The focus of this section is upon the sex of the participants in the relationship, not upon matters of sex as the content of counseling interviews. Thus sex as a barrier to effective interaction is here associated chiefly with the persons of the counselor and counselee, and not with their beliefs or value structures. It is assumed, for present purposes, that the counselor is capable of accepting and dealing with the many-faceted subject of sex from both favorable and unfavorable attitudinal stances. The limiting dimension in the discussion that follows is related to the fact of the counselor's maleness or femaleness and to the maleness or femaleness of the counselee — and the influence upon counseling that results from mixing or matching the sexes in the encounter.

Tyler (1969, pp. 55–56) reminds us that counselees — and counselors, too, for that matter — hold "general attitudes toward broad categories of people," and the most obvious and universal classification is that of sex. From early childhood, individuals learn different expectations of Mommy and Daddy. And it is difficult — if not impossible — to think that a counselee entering a counseling room does not notice whether the individual greeting him is a man or a woman. The counselor, too, is aware of the sex of the counselee. Each individual, as part of his social and cultural equipment, has developed an attitude toward male and female. At the time of encounter, whether it be the initial interview or any one of subsequent interviews, these attitudes or concepts or feelings come into play, subtly or obviously, to enhance or to hamper the interaction.

Ordinarily, on first encounter, the counselor does not know the counselee's attitude toward the sex of a person. But he cannot discount the possibility that his sex may be getting in the way if unaccountable signs of hostility develop. Some-times, in counseling, it seems that an interview with the counselee's spouse might be beneficial. Often the counselee himself suggests this. "But," he adds, "I don't think my wife will talk to a woman." Sometimes the husband's assessment of his wife's attitudes is incorrect. He just assumes (his atti-tude comes into play) that his wife relates well to men and therefore cannot relate intimately to another woman, even in a counseling relationship. In such instances, the counselor must keep an open mind and assume that if the wife is willing to engage in an interview, she may be willing to talk on a level that will prove advantageous to continued counseling progress for her husband. Given such a clue, the female coun-selor must guard against conjuring up stereotypes of her own that might preclude effective interaction between herself and the wife.

Often when an individual is engaged in a counseling rela-tionship, the spouse wants to meet the counselor and suggests that the counselee "see what can be arranged." One such instance occurred when a male counselor was approached by his female counselee: "Please let my husband come in here and meet you. I was late getting home after our session last week and my husband was furious. He's just so jealous that sometimes it frightens me." A counseling relationship may be impaired, not by the view the counselee himself or herself has of the sex of the counselor, but by the attitude a wife or a husband or a mother or father holds. The aware counselor must help the counselee talk about the pressure placed upon him by such views of a significant person in his immediate environment.

Split loyalties or guilt feelings are sometimes generated because the husband or wife sees the counselor assuming a role he or she thinks rightfully belongs to him or her by virtue of being the marriage partner. This is what happened in the case of Mr. G, a college senior. A good relationship existed between Mr. G and the counselor and progress was being made. Suddenly two unproductive, frustrating sessions occurred, with no apparent reason. The third week, Mr. G sighed: "My wife resents you because you are a woman and I can talk to you, but I can't seem to talk to her."

It would have been beside the point to remind the couple

at this juncture that the very reason the husband presented himself for counseling was the fact that communication between husband and wife had broken down. To ease the home situation for the counselee, however, the counselor inquired as to whether or not Mr. G would like either to bring his wife in with him sometime or to make an appointment for her to come alone to meet the counselor. He thought about the suggestion and at the next interview asked to make an appointment for his wife. Mrs. G kept her appointment and at the end of the interview commented that she had resented the counselor and had come largely out of curiosity, but found it "much easier to talk than I thought it would be." Several weeks later, Mr. G asked if the counselor would be willing to see him and his wife together "from now on."

Although there is no evidence to support the notion that girls and women relate better to female counselors or that boys and men relate better to males, some schools still mistakenly assign counselors and counselees on the basis of sex. In most schools, however, sex is not the basis of assignment of student to counselor, and an attempt is made to employ both male and female counselors so as to provide students with a choice. Occasionally, a student states a preference with regard to sex of the counselor. Sometimes a girl may prefer to talk with a woman "about this particular matter" or a boy may wish "this time" to see a male counselor. For the most part, however, students do not seem to view the individual only as male or female, but as counselor.

When a preference is stated, it is honored if at all possible. In certain situations, however, a counselor's judgment or availability of counselors may prevail over the stated preference of the counselee — sometimes with unfortunate results. This is what happened to Beth, a college sophomore.

Beth presented herself to the College Counseling Center. During the intake interview she mentioned that she had difficulty relating to men and so she would prefer to see a woman counselor. The intake counselor, who was a woman, argued that since Beth had difficulty relating to men, perhaps this would be a good opportunity to start to learn to feel comfortable with a male. The counseling situation would be non-threatening and in such an atmosphere, Beth could practice talking easily with a man. It was explained, of course, that if the relationship did not work out, Beth could be reassigned. Beth agreed.

Beth did not return for counseling after the first session.

What the intake counselor missed was the fact that Beth was already threatened by the prospect of counseling with anyone. Add a male to the situation, and the outcome could only be what it was — a painful failure for Beth. The experience provided just another reinforcement of her inability to relate to males. As she recounted it, Beth stated that the counselor reminded her of someone she "just couldn't stand" and "all I could think of was the similarity. I just couldn't seem to talk to him. And at the end of the session, he didn't seem to care whether I returned or not — and so I decided I wouldn't go back."

Beth's inability to relate to males was associated with her father's apparent rejection of her. And now, as she saw it, another male, the counselor, had rejected her, too, and the barrier was so great that Beth would not try again.

The case of Beth might have been handled differently. She might have been given an appointment with a female counselor who could have worked with her on exploring and understanding her problem of relating to men. Hopefully, Beth could have reached the point where she would be able to enter a multiple counseling relationship, in which she, her female counselor, and a male counselor could work together. In this protected atmosphere, it would be hoped that Beth would eventually feel sufficiently comfortable to transfer to the male counselor.

The intake counselor made an accurate assessment. Beth did need the experience of relating to a male, but she was not ready to be plunged into that counseling relationship without preparation.

For a reason similar to that which prompted the intake counselor to assign Beth to a male counselor, in an elementary school that can employ only one counselor, a preference is for a male counselor. This decision is especially valid in inner-city or target-area schools where there is a high incidence of fatherless children. The counselor provides a male with whom such children can relate in a warm and friendly atmosphere.

In any elementary school, it is argued, a male counselor is preferred because typically elementary schools have a preponderance of women on the faculty.

For the elementary school child, boy or girl, whose father is a strict, authoritarian figure or is a source of threat to the child, however, the male counselor's task poses a challenge. It becomes important with such children for the counselor to provide a model of an accepting, warm, and friendly male. These children need to learn that not all men are like Dad, and they can learn this only through establishing close relationships with males who are different from their fathers.

Occasionally, the very qualities in counselor and counselee that nurture a close, effective relationship can provide the basis for its complete breakdown, erecting a barrier to the reestablishment of any satisfactory interaction. This type of relationship reversal is most likely to occur when the counselor is male and young and the counselee is a high school senior or college student. It is not unusual, for example, for a young counselor to report, shaking his head in bewilderment:

> I don't know how it happened. We had a good relationship and everything was going along fine. At least I thought so. But when we came back from vacation, she noticed the ring on my finger and wanted to know if I'd gotten married. I told her that I had, and since then she won't even talk to me.

Or similarly:

> Sharon was the best counselee I had — until I told her I was leaving. For a minute or so she was very quiet and then she said, "Oh, so you're running out on me, too. Guess I'll be going now." With that she got up and left and I haven't seen her since.

It is not necessary to explore the dynamics behind these two accounts. It is evident that the young ladies developed strong attachments to the counselors, only to be hurt. Inexperience on the part of the counselors is what allowed the relationships to develop as they did. Young male counselors in a high school or university setting must be aware, as must young teachers, of the possibility of such developments with some of the students they counsel or teach. Counselors are particularly vulnerable because they meet with their counselees alone and do not have the protection of other students and other teachers. Counselors must meet counselees privately. Teachers do not have to place themselves in this position.

Finally, sex of the individuals may create a barrier to interaction when the counselor is female and the counselee is a strong, masculine, authoritarian male. Here is a man who is a "man among men" who cannot allow himself to be helped by females, for it would simply be a sign of weakness. Male superiority is here, masking an underlying insecurity, but no matter, his ego is at stake. Referral to a male counselor would seem to be indicated in a case such as this.

Despite arguments, sound as they are, for a male counselor here or a female counselor there, all the evidence that can be gathered suggests that, in general, the sex of the counselor is secondary. The personal qualities, the warmth and sensitivity of the individual counselor are of greater significance with regard to effectiveness than is sex. The ideal procedure, of course, is to have counselors of both sexes available so that the counselee can make the choice.

Age

Age is another human dimension — like sex — to which people may respond with preconceived notions or stereotypical attitudes. The manner in which counselor and counselee accommodate into their awareness the age factor of the other will at least influence their initial relationship — and at worst, prevent a feeling of interrelatedness so necessary to effective interaction.

Such matters as sex, age, and expectations of counseling are there as facts, even though they may not seem to get in the way. Whether or not they do interfere with the establishment of a working relationship probably depends largely on how the counselor handles feelings that issue from conditions over which neither party has control. The counselor, after all, is the professionally prepared participant in this encounter and has a responsibility here.

Response to the age factor manifests itself in subtle ways: the well-mannered high school junior's solicitous behavior makes the middle-aged female counselor feel like a maiden aunt. Is this the image she projects to him? The attractive high school senior girl approaches the young male counselor as if she were embarking upon a flirtation. Or is it just his imagination? The forty-five-year-old retired army major, now a graduate student, appears for an appointment at the College Counseling Center and finds that his counselor is a brand-new twenty-eight-year-old Ph.D. What does "this kid" know about life?

Are these first reactions obstacles that can be overcome? Or are they inhibiting barriers that cannot be toppled?

Consider for a moment the position of the young counselor in the high school setting. While he is trying to decide whether or not he has accurately assessed the girl's attitude, he is only half listening to her opening words. The counselee stops talking, and he realizes that he is expected to respond — but to what? He hasn't really been attending to her comments. Three possibilities are open to him: (a) he can grasp at any straw and make a general comment; (b) he can ask for clarification; or (c) he can use the "silence" technique and hope that the counselee will continue. Any one of these alternatives may betray him at this point. Effectively he has communicated to the counselee that he is not interested in her. The interview has come to a standstill.

Or, what is the college counselor feeling as he is being scrutinized by the student many years his senior? Is he threatened? Is he, too, wondering what he can do for this man?

It is essential that the counselor be aware of himself, of his own feelings in such encounters. But he must also strive to be aware of the feelings of the counselee. He must be able to catch the nuances of the dynamics operating between counselor and counselee.

Sometimes the counselor will have to retrieve rapport that is flagging by merely being human and, for example, saying to the girl, "I'm sorry, I missed some of what you were saying. Will you pick it up from ———" Or if the counselor in the

College Center is still feeling threatened toward the end of that first interview, he must be secure enough to refer the counselee to someone else who can function more effectively with him.

It is sometimes difficult to sense immediately another person's perception of age, but it is well-known that children and teenagers have their own special view of age. To children in the primary grades, the twelve-year-olds are the "big" boys or girls. As for twelve-year-olds, it is hard for them to believe that they could ever be as old as their parents are. In a theme about his plans for the future, a sixteen-year-old boy wrote, ". . . and when I get to be very old, about thirty or so . . ." Or consider this comment from a nineteen-year-old: "Do you think this pin is appropriate for an older woman?" The "older woman" for whom she bought the gift was twenty-eight. For that matter, a large segment of youth today thinks that if a person is over thirty, he might as well be dead.

The counselor, on the other hand, is the product of a time span different from that of the counselee. His "truths" may not be the "truths" of the counselee — probably are not — and each may have difficulty bridging the age gap. For most counselors are over age thirty, and this alone can present a barrier between counselor and counselee a generation or more apart in age. Or it can cause a temporary block to interaction in an ordinarily effective relationship. It is not so much the *fact* of age in most cases, but rather the stereotype of what each one — counselor and counselee — holds concerning the other's age. It is how one perceives the other in terms of age and expectations of an individual of that age.

If the counselor in the elementary school sees himself as serving as a male model or a father image, he may be able to establish a fairly good relationship with most of the children. And he may be especially effective with fatherless children. During this period of development, adults are significant in children's lives. On the other hand, the high school or college counselor who projects the father or mother image may encounter real difficulty in establishing a satisfactory counseling relationship with young people who are striving increasingly for independence from parental supervision.

Linda, a college freshman, was just not popular with boys — never had been. She had spent most of her first year at college watching her roommate and other girls she knew go off on dates while she studied, or read, or watched TV, or idled away her time on other equally unabsorbing activities. What was wrong with her? Finally she decided to see if she could get some help from the Counseling Center.

When she returned from her first visit, her roommate was waiting for her. "Well, how was it? Was he handsome?"

"Oh, it was all right, I guess. But it wasn't a he. It was a she, and she has mannerisms just like my mother's. I dunno . . . maybe it wasn't such a good idea after all."

Consider another situation.

Dave had been having some trouble with grades, and his father had grounded him. Dave thought this was unfair. The problem was just that the social studies teacher and he couldn't get along. It didn't make much difference what he did or how hard he tried. The guy just had it in for him. He was talking it over one day with his girl, Chris, who suggested that he drop in to see Mr. H, his counselor. To Chris' suggestion, Dave responded:

"You gotta be kidding! You know how that guy is. He'd just side with the old man and tell me the only reason I'm having trouble with Mr. D is that I'm not working hard enough. He reminds me so much of my father!"

In the case of Linda, the resemblance between the counselor and her mother may have been an unfortunate coincidence. How much the similarity of age (plus the disappointment in not being assigned to a male counselor) caused Linda to make associations with her mother will never be known. Perhaps if Linda had returned, that first impression might have been erased, but Linda did not return.

Dave's situation was quite different, however. Mr. H rather prided himself on being a "father" to all the students, especially the boys. After all, he had been working with kids for the past thirty years as teacher and now as counselor, and he

knew what was good for teenage boys. Add to the age gap
between Mr. H and "his kids" encapsulation and a miscon-
ception of what a counselor should or can be, and any chance
for a relationship of a kind the "kids" rarely find at home
and often need is blocked. Mr. H typifies the counselor
who unwittingly dons the paternalistic mantle and consequently creates a barrier between himself and the "kids" he
thinks he understands so well.

Sometimes, although age would seem to be a plus factor in
the relationship, it creates a barrier to effectiveness. When
counselor and counselee are close in age, opportunity for
understanding and empathy would appear to be at its maximum. The probability of effective interaction would seem to
be optimal. But things do not always develop as it seems they
should.

> Mrs. S, a divorcee who returned to college to get a
> teaching certificate, seeks the help of a college counselor.
> As she enters the counseling room, she notices that the
> counselor is about her age and attractive. "Is he mar-
> ried?" she wonders. She decides she had better play it
> cautiously, not expose herself much until she finds out
> something more about him. After all, it might be pos-
> sible . . .

A truly good counseling relationship for this counselor and
counselee is blocked, temporarily at least.

A consideration of the generation gap has purposely been
postponed until last. Complex and well-publicized, it doubtlessly has more relevance as a barrier to the relationship when
the counselee is either a call-in or a reluctant referral. When
the counselee is hesitant about involvement with the counselor
— for whatever reason — interaction is naturally more difficult, though not impossible. A barrier between counselor and
counselee issuing from the generation gap involves much more
than age, however. Hostility is there, as are insecurity, encapsulation, and manipulation. As such, it is beyond the scope
of this section. Any counselor who encounters this problem
will recognize it — and will recognize the need for special
application of skills, or referral. Blocking because of the generation gap — and all its attendant complications — is not

ordinarily present as a problem when the counselee refers himself, despite the age difference.

In general, the skillful counselor transcends age. One elementary school counselor, for example, transcended age so successfully that one of the third-graders he had been counseling — one who considered him her friend — said to him one day: "What are you going to be when you grow up?"

Like sex, age is a fact of life over which the individual has no control. For his part, however, the counselor can keep himself in tune with those younger than he — by being aware, by participating in life, by listening, and by reading. He can keep himself more effective by nurturing that all-important attribute, empathy. Sachs (1966, p. 14) says it well:

> In the loss of his ability to recall his past, the adult loses his capacity to empathize, for empathy carries within it both objective and subjective elements. The empathic person maintains a childlike quality that enables him to remember his past. Indeed, he realizes that all adult behavior is rooted in the past. Thus he is able to perceive more clearly the travails and successes, the sorrow and joy, the aloneness and togetherness of childhood and adolescence with the same identification that he applies to his present condition. In this identification the dignity and autonomy of all children and adolescents are established, for they and he are together a part of the human condition.

Personally Inhibiting Factors

Simply by virtue of their individual and unique humanness, either counselor or counselee or both may feel that satisfactory interaction between them is impossible. The relationship cannot really become a helping relationship because certain personal factors inhibit the process. There may, for example, be a conflict of temperaments, or the relationship may be blocked by prior conditioning for either counselor or counselee, or marked counselor and/or counselee discomfort may render the relationship ineffective.

With reference to counselor-counselee interaction, Stefflre (1965, pp. 262–263) points out that

> . . . what the counselor does is a function of (1) his own
> personality, including knowledge, skills, and needs, (2) the
> client as perceived by the counselor, (3) the instant in the
> history of their relationship in which the counselor is acting,
> and (4) the counselor's notion of what he *should do*, which is
> a value related to his total theoretical position on counseling.

For example, a counselor who is attempting to work out his
own spiritual beliefs has broken away from the religious
tenets with which he was reared. The members of his family
— mother, father, brothers and sisters — are concerned about
him and are questioning his present direction. At this time he
acquires a counselee who espouses the religious beliefs the
counselor is attempting to revise. The counselor views the
counselee's religious background as coloring (indeed, distort-
ing) his perception of his situation. The counselee seems to
him to typify the kind of thinking the counselor has come to
reject — and he wants to "set him straight." But he knows he
must resist this type of behavior in counseling and thus he is
inhibited in his capability of working effectively with this
counselee.

The counselor's deep personal involvement in a matter in
his own life at this instant renders impossible an effective
relationship with this particular counselee at this time. The
aware counselor will recognize his current inability to counsel
this counselee effectively and may refer him to another counselor. The unaware or insecure counselor may attempt to bury
his personal feelings (an impossibility) and see the thing
through, at the risk of damage to both the counselee and
himself.

RECIPROCAL FRUSTRATION

Fullmer and Bernard (1964) stress the reality of "habitual
patterns of behavior" with which an individual approaches
interpersonal encounters, including counseling. An individual's behavior patterns, whether they be those of the counselor or counselee, are not "isolated in time and place," but
are employed habitually in relating to other individuals.
Aware as the counselor may be that he is functioning in the
counseling relationship as a professional counselor, he must
be himself to be effective. The way he functions during the

process of counseling is undoubtedly different from the way he behaves when he is not counseling and is at home with his family or at lunch with his friends. (How insupportable it would be to his family and friends for him to be a "counselor" twenty-four hours a day!) Underlying and intertwined with the professional self is a personal self that must respond in a personal way. The professional self and the personal self cannot — and should not — be separate entities. Sometimes, however, these personal reactions inhibit interaction, just as the counselee's personal responses to content or feeling or circumstances may inhibit the counselor-counselee relationship.

Fullmer and Bernard's postulate that individuals use habitual behavior patterns in responding to all types of interpersonal encounters provides another vantage point from which to view the counseling process. Inhibiting habitual behaviors may be exhibited by either counselor or counselee, causing mutually reciprocal frustrations and further inhibitions. There is the individual, for example, who is habitually defensive. He tends to be cautious, reluctant to expose himself or to commit himself. He plays a hedging game. Consider this type of individual as a counselee, protecting himself against attempts by the counselor to know his essential self by denial or deflection.

Jan is a college freshman to whom counseling was suggested by one of her professors. Capable as she is, Jan probably will be on probation next year. She says she just cannot settle down. At the beginning of each term, she makes resolutions about "getting down to business," but she just does not follow through.

Counselor: Then there are just two of you — you and your older sister.

Jan: Yes, Mona is a senior here. Maybe you know her?

Counselor: I don't believe I do. You've mentioned her occasionally . . . would you like to tell me something about Mona?

Jan: What do you mean, tell you about Mona? She's my sister and she's a senior here.

Counselor: Oh, I guess how you feel about her . . . anything you wish. . . . .

Jan: What do you mean, anything I wish?

Counselor: Well, for example, what do you think when you think of Mona? What are your feelings about her right now?

Jan: Oh, nothing much. She used to make me so mad, but now she goes her way and I go mine and everything's okay. We've got things straight now. So don't worry about Mona. I don't.

This exchange did not accomplish much, except perhaps to make the counselee a bit testy and strengthen her defenses against exposing her feelings about her sister; and it frustrated the counselor. However, if the counselor suspected some strong feelings of antagonism between Jan and Mona, especially on Jan's part, the dialogue served to support the speculation. But for the present, the counselor has been neatly blocked off from further exploration of the relationship existing between the two sisters. And counseling ". . . exclusively oriented toward the *exposure* and *development* of the individual" (Fullmer and Bernard, 1964, p. 140) has presently met an impasse with Jan, for she has employed a withdrawal pattern in her relationship with her sister. Since the problem that brought her to the counselor was her inability to "settle down" with regard to academic assignments, it is possible that Jan uses withdrawal habitually.

CONFLICT OF ATTITUDES AND TEMPERAMENTS

Research suggests that the likelihood of an effective relationship is greater between individuals who are similar than it is for those who differ in major ways from one another. Individuals of like or complementary temperament, similar attitudes and values, accordingly have more potential for interpersonal effectiveness than do those of opposing temperaments and attitudes. In counseling, the burden of understanding and accepting those who are different rests, of course, with the counselor, and most counselors — those who are truly enablers — do value people and attitudes different from their own. Indeed, helping counselor candidates develop the necessary openness and acceptance constitutes a significant portion of the effort in counselor education. But the degree to which achievement of these qualities is possible differs among individuals and in specific situations.

One might question the degree of acceptance a relatively conservative secondary school counselor — and advocate of the status quo — could develop for the student striving for change. He wants change in the curriculum, a change in grading procedures, more voice in student government. (And, furthermore, how *can* he stand that music!) Here is the student who has "everything" and is still not satisfied. The divergence in point of view is sharpened when the youth reaches college and literally assumes the mantle, along with the beard and the long hair, of this group.

How does the counselor, who has learned to put off satisfaction of desires, who takes the long view, work effectively with the current school age population who are far more "now-oriented" than he can ever hope to be? How can he help young people plan for a future that will change markedly from what it is today, in a present that is markedly different from what it was when the counselor attended high school or college?

Many school counselors think work is good and essential and dignified, and it matters not so much what one does but how he does it. How effectively can they convey this idea to students whose world is peopled by individuals who shine shoes, sweep the streets, clean office buildings, or deliver messages day after day? Should they even try? For their part, pupils who come from the ghetto or from a background very different from that currently enjoyed by counselors are suspicious of them and rarely seek them out — so they may not even get a chance. It is much easier for the typical school counselor to work with counselees whose fathers are lawyers, doctors, teachers, engineers, supervisors, or business executives. They speak the same language — at least counselors probably speak the same language the students' parents do.

How much tolerance does the conservative, convergent thinking counselor have for the creative, divergent thinking student? Can he accept this student as a counselee and foster his way-out thinking and behavior, his creativity? Can he understand sufficiently to help the counselee understand himself? Can he support the counselee even at the expense of antagonizing some of the teachers? Can he meet the counselee in a truly effective interpersonal encounter?

Perhaps more than anyone else in the educational setting, the counselor must be open to experience. He must continue to learn — about himself, about his counselees, about change, about value systems, and about differences in value systems. One of the functions of the counselor is to help the counselee resolve his conflicts. The counselor who provides additional conflicts for the counselee does not serve him at all. Helping a youngster develop a value system, for example, does not call for imposing one's own values or prematurely showing him a value system too mature for him to encompass.

Nor is a counselor serving the best interests of the counselee if he exerts pressures counter to those the counselee is experiencing in his own environment. He can, however, help the counselee understand and deal with conflicting pressures by exploring them with him. He can, perhaps, help the counselee sort out the choices available to him.

Sometimes a conflict of personalities prevents the achievement of satisfactory interaction between counselor and counselee. A counselor who moves slowly and deliberately in the process may so exasperate the counselee that he judges the counselor to be uncertain. Having lost the counselee's confidence for this or any other reason, the counselor almost certainly faces failure in this encounter. Or the counselee with a low frustration level may exasperate a counselor who admires maturity, stability, and patience and sees himself as possessing these qualities. If the counselor communicates his feeling to the counselee — and the chances are that he will, for inwardly he undoubtedly wants the counselee to know it — the counselee will back off and the opportunity for effective interaction will be blocked.

Or, again, what chance is there for effective counseling if

the counselor has never really been certain of himself with women and the counselee, a boy less than half his age, is already far more sophisticated than he in heterosexual relationships? Consider the counselor's feeling of inadequacy with this boy, but also consider the boy's attitude toward the counselor.

Some counselors experience difficulty in accepting all counselees, just as counselees sometimes experience incompatibility with certain counselors. When counselor and counselee find themselves in conflict stemming from personal or attitudinal differences, either one may terminate the relationship. But the counselor must be wary of overusing referral. Perhaps it has become his tool to escape all discomfort in counseling. If escape becomes a habitual pattern of behavior, it is time for the counselor to reexamine himself and his motives, and perhaps to seek counseling.

PRIOR CONDITIONING

Counselor and/or counselee may be victims, suspecting or unsuspecting, of prior experiences that condition them unfavorably for this effort toward counseling. Negative feelings a counselee has about counseling or toward a given counselor will cause the counselee to block real counselor-counselee interaction. For example, a friend may have had an unsatisfactory relationship with a counselor. John presents himself for counseling and is assigned the same counselor his friend had. John is predisposed to dislike or mistrust or reject the counselor altogether, rendering interaction difficult, if not impossible.

Or failure in a previous case may have been so devastating to the counselor that he feels the pressure (usually self-imposed) to prove himself with this new counselee. Under such circumstances, he may overreact, become anxious, and fail again.

Prior conditioning of a negative nature may derive from faulty referrals or inadequate preparation for referral. In either case, the counselee feels rejected. Being passed around from one individual to another, from the school counselor, for example, to the psychologist, to a psychiatric case worker, to a mental health clinic, etc., can have seriously adverse effects. Not only does the counselee feel rejected and weary of answering questions but also, and more importantly, he becomes frightened, wonders what is wrong with him, and despairs of ever receiving help. He becomes less hopeful and more suspicious; he anticipates failure and further abandonment.

Although it is on a much more serious level, being passed around from one "helping" person to another is somewhat like being shunted from one office to another in a quest for a simple piece of information. Almost everyone has had the experience of intending to make a "quick" phone call for some information, only to accept defeat an hour or so and five or six calls later. The frustration and feeling of utter helplessness that accompanies such an experience is mild as compared with that felt by a counselee who needs help and support and is disappointed repeatedly.

Akin to being the victim of a faulty referral is the experience of being referred without preparation. Lack of understanding, fear that something is radically wrong, and a sense of rejection may cause the counselee to approach the new counseling experience in a hostile manner. Or he may simply adopt withdrawing behavior. Either way, the establishment of a satisfactory relationship is difficult. Essential to a successful referral is adequate preparation. The counselee should know why the referral is being made, something about the person to whom he is being referred and what he can anticipate. It is helpful to the counselee when an alert counselor, seeing a referral as necessary, begins to prepare the counselee well in advance of the actual referral.

DISCOMFORT IN COUNSELING

A relationship marked by counselor discomfort is almost certain to be a marred relationship. Although either participant in counseling may experience discomfort, the counselor has the responsibility to maintain as well as he can a climate that is conducive to counseling. Because he is the professional member, the counselor is expected to be able to tolerate counselee discomfort and help the counselee overcome the feeling.

Counselor discomfort, handled clumsily or ignored, however, is quickly caught by the counselee, who may himself become uncomfortable, apologetic, or lose respect for the counselor. In any case, unless a counselor deals effectively with his discomfort — and it is reasonable to expect a counselor to be uncomfortable occasionally — a satisfactory relationship is blocked.

Many counselors are not comfortable with certain types of problems. They may experience discomfort when the counselee introduces a particular category of content. Some are unable to relate effectively with counselees who are physically handicapped. In each case, such counselors have failed to be accepting of *all* individuals and/or are so preoccupied with their own problems that they are unable to help the counselees with theirs.

It is not unusual to hear counselors make comments such as, "I just cannot work with homosexuals" or "I don't know what to do with the slow-learning pupil" or "When an unwed pregnant girl comes to me, I simply refer her to Mrs. G" or "I hate to see Jeannie come into my office — I feel so sorry for her" or "After Dick left my office today I felt like opening the windows to get a breath of fresh air." Each comment says, "I have a hang-up and I'm uncomfortable working with these kinds of problems."

There is no doubt that such feelings are communicated to the counselee. At best the counselee senses that something is amiss and although he may not be able to identify the source of irritation, he does not feel at ease in exposing himself to the counselor; thus the counselor's biases inhibit the interaction.

Only through continuous self-examination can the counselor come to know himself better. He must be constantly alert to his own biases that inhibit his relationship with counselees. And, having identified the biases, he must find ways of working with or through them so that he will be capable of serving the greatest number of counselees effectively.

Exploitation of the Relationship

When two people plan to spend time together — for short or long periods — they usually have a particular purpose in mind. The purpose may be that of mutual entertainment or sharing some outside entertainment, exchanging ideas, having a challenging debate, obtaining information, and so forth. Either one or both participants have a need they think can be satisfied as a consequence of meeting with one another. And so it is with counseling. Two individuals meet because one — the counselee — thinks he can profit in some way from an encounter with a person professionally trained to assist individuals. Thus counseling is initiated because the counselee has some unmet needs.

The counselor also has needs, however. For example, his choice of counseling may have been made to meet his nurturant needs. He has other needs as well that he attempts to satisfy through his profession: achievement, self-respect, esteem, confirmation of the self-image, Maslow's self-actualization, and so forth. Being human, both counselor and counselee will inevitably — and justifiably — seek satisfaction of their needs through the counseling relationship.

Exploitation of the relationship to satisfy needs is a misuse of the process, however, and constitutes a barrier to effective interaction. Either counselor or counselee may be guilty of "using" the relationship for his own purpose, at the expense of the process. Or both counselor and counselee may become so involved in using the relationship or each other that they find themselves engaged in a game of one-upmanship — as counseling bogs down.

EXPLOITATION BY COUNSELOR

"The qualified counselor understands himself and his own unresolved conflicts and is aware of how these conflicts may impair his effectiveness as a counselor" (Ohlsen, 1964, p. 94). Self-awareness and self-understanding constitute the first line of defense a counselor can develop as safeguards against using the relationship or the counselee to satisfy his own needs. As Kemp (1967, p. 24) suggests, counselors are increasingly concerned with the "meaning of self" and are coming to view man not simply as a rational being but as one in whom thinking and feeling are "integrally part of the self and part of every significant decision." This view, for one who holds it, has implications not only for insight into oneself but also for understanding counselees, and consequently will be reflected in the counselor-counselee interaction.

Wertz (1957) suggests that counselor security is one of the most important personality patterns in facilitating effective counselor-counselee interaction. Wertz defines security in the counseling context as self-acceptance that involves a candid recognition of both strengths and weaknesses. The insecure counselor, Wertz contends, is likely to project his own feelings of inadequacy onto the counselee, thus deriving for himself a feeling of release (a kind of "second-hand catharsis") as the counselee relates his problem and exposes his emotional reaction. In a situation such as this, one can only speculate as to the genuineness and accuracy of the counselee's feelings. That is, has the counselor communicated his need to the counselee to the extent that it would cause the latter to respond as he did? The dynamics here are undoubtedly subtle. Both counselor and counselee may be unaware of what has happened, but it is entirely possible that the counselee is behaving in a way he thinks the counselor wants him to behave. Here the insecure counselor has used his own weakness to manipulate the counselee, with profit for himself, not for the counselee.

Another, but somewhat similar, exploitative maneuver was undertaken by a counselor who found himself working with a counselee having a problem almost exactly like his own. The counselor was more than empathic. There developed between counselor and counselee a kind of identity that shifted the relationship from that of counseling closer to that of friendship in which counselor and counselee entered into a state of mutual dependency to satisfy mutual needs.

More professional was the young counselor who discovered within himself some hostility towards students on probation who presented themselves for counseling. When he recognized his feelings, he requested that such students not be assigned to him until he could work out his problem. An alternative request might have been that he be permitted to work with more such students. However, the counselor made the choice he did because he did not want to use his counselees to satisfy his need to solve his problem, or indeed to release hostility. Instead, he took advantage of every opportunity to associate with this kind of student outside the counseling relationship. Finally, when he felt he had developed some insight into his own reactions as well as additional understanding of these students, he began to see them again in counseling.

In discussing need satisfactions, Fullmer and Bernard (1964, pp. 180–181) refer to Maslow's hierarchy of human needs and suggest that most counselors have not reached the ideal level of self-actualization but are working at a lower level.

> . . . they are working for esteem and status in the form of certification, improved job status, a master's degree, and the ability to perform counseling work in such a way that they will merit praise from their colleagues and the community.

The implicit danger for a counselor who has strong achievement or status needs is that he must succeed. So strong is this need that he may actually avoid counseling the slow-learner or the potential dropout or the chronic "trouble maker." These individuals are frequently difficult counselees and success in terms of markedly improved learning, a decision to stay in school, or complete adjustment does not come quickly — if at all — or with ease. If counselor "success" is the principal objective, the individual with high achievement/ status needs would do well to avoid these types of counselees. Unfortunately, some counselors simply do not see these students or refer them to others, rationalizing, possibly, that Mrs. G or Mr. H works with them better. Thus some counselors satisfy their own need for achievement or esteem by avoiding counselees who are "difficult," either by refusing to see them in the first place or by referring them when the going gets rough, thereby keeping intact their image of themselves as effective counselors.

There is also the counselor who "turns off" a counselee when he thinks he is about to be confronted with something with which he may not be able to cope. This type of counselor may be found more typically in an educational setting. Consider the exchange between the counselor and Jimmy, a seventh-grader:

Jimmy: I just heard something I think you ought to know, Mr. L.

Counselor: Yes?

Jimmy: I overheard two guys talking in the hall, and they're going to see that the window in the boys' room is unlocked so they can get back in the building tonight.

Counselor: You know, Jimmy, you can't believe everything you overhear. They were probably just talking.

Whether or not Mr. L followed through on this information, his behavior with Jimmy undoubtedly damaged their relationship. It is unlikely that Jimmy will freely confer with Mr. L in the future. The counselor let his need to avoid confrontation or disruption take precedence over his relationship with Jimmy, thus establishing a barrier to future counseling opportunities with him — and possibly several of Jimmy's friends.

The counselor who must always be right or omnipotent soon creates a clear obstacle to effective counselor-counselee interaction. So, too, does the counselor who perceives himself as the expert and feels compelled to alert the counselee to how much he knows.

If we can accept as valid the premise that many counselors choose their work because they expect to derive a sense of fulfillment from it, we can consider the nurturant needs these counselors harbor. It is acceptable and anticipated that the counselor's need to help others will be satisfied in the counseling relationship. For some counselors, however, the need is extremely powerful and creates an obstacle to truly effective interaction with certain counselees. The counselor who cannot tolerate seeing a conflicted counselee in anguish and is prematurely reassuring blocks a truly therapeutic experience for the counselee. In response to a counselee's question, "Do you think I'm crazy?" the quick-to-reassure counselor might simply say, "No, I don't think you're crazy." If he leaves the question as "answered," the counselor cheats the counselee of really knowing how he himself feels; his conflict is unresolved. The counselor's strong compulsion to reassure the counselee caused him to ignore the boy's needs. He responded to words not to feelings, to himself not to the counselee, and in so doing failed to come to grips with the actual problem.

Alternatively, the counselor might have explored with the counselee the latter's reason for the question, his previous and present feelings relating to that area, and so forth. It would be possible during such verbal interaction to communicate reassurance nonverbally or by tone of voice.

Having a powerful desire to help others, a few counselors see in most individuals they meet prospective candidates for their assistance. Projecting perhaps, they assume that everyone has a hang-up and they view themselves as a potential savior. This type of counselor is likely to view the individual who rejects the need for counseling as a rejection of himself personally and may redouble his efforts to convince the individual that he really does have a problem. Such counselor behavior is rare, but occasionally there is one of whom it is remarked, "If you don't have a problem, Mr. S will create one for you."

EXPLOITATION BY THE COUNSELEE

Like counselors, counselees have such needs as security, self-esteem, and fulfillment. Additionally, they need relief from pressures and/or resolution of conflicts. Counselees have every right to expect that the focus of the counseling process will be upon meeting their needs. Research has suggested that although the counselor may be perceived as the "leader" in the process, it is the personality of the counselee that largely determines whether or not the interaction will be successful (Perez, 1965). Thus the counselee, too, has some responsibility for the effectiveness of the counseling process. Chief among his responsibilities are candor or honesty, willingness to communicate with the counselor, and openness to counseling as a therapeutic process. Should the counselee misuse or exploit the relationship for the satisfaction of needs extrinsic to present counseling goals, he will create hurdles that will render attainment of the objective impossible.

The individual who seeks in counseling a means of gaining support for his way of thinking or behaving is exploiting the relationship. Security is a powerful need, and some counselees are simply searching for reinforcement of their present mode of life. One way or another, they are tacitly putting the question to the counselor: "Don't you think I'm right?"

A case in point is the homosexual who wants simply to share his feelings with someone "safe" and perhaps even gain approbation. Or the young woman who presents herself for marriage counseling — because she made a promise to do so — after having firmly resolved to seek a divorce. Their decisions already made, such persons are not really interested in counseling or change. They would like reinforcement, however, and may even attempt to manipulate the counselor (see Chapter 3) to achieve that objective. A counselee who approaches the process with a closed mind is simply using the relationship to further his own purposes.

Popular among teachers is the notion that many students request to see the counselor simply to "get out of class." And some of the teachers have correctly assessed the motive for seeking out the counselor. Students also refer themselves for counseling out of curiosity, to find out what happens in that office or to "psych out" the new counselor. A certain amount of this type of activity is almost unavoidable and is obviously a misuse of counseling services. An aware counselor can rather rapidly curb this use of the counseling office. When the counselor is not sufficiently astute to know when he is "being had" or when the attention is so flattering that he is reluctant to stop it, however, both counselee and counselor become parties to the exploitation. No real purpose is served here. It is unlikely that development in any direction will occur. Counseling as such will be lacking.

RECIPROCAL EXPLOITATION

The situation mentioned immediately above is an example of reciprocal exploitation of the counseling relationship by counselor and counselee alike. Sometimes knowingly, often unknowingly and subtly, the counselor-counselee relationship becomes somewhat like a silent pact to play the game because each thinks the other expects a certain type of behavior, or because both think outsiders expect them to behave this way.

Questing for hidden meanings and probing for deep concerns to satisfy his need to feel that he is "really counseling," a counselor is using the encounter to bolster his own ego. In response, the counselee either exaggerates a concern or creates one simply to satisfy the counselor. In this instance, neither participant is being honest; both are exploiting the process. Real movement is impossible because the problem is not real; counseling for beneficial outcomes is neatly blocked. The relationship degenerates into a kind of profitless role playing.

Both counselor and counselee have responsibilities for the effectiveness of interaction. Should either or both forsake their responsibilities, counseling can become a travesty, as indeed it has in too many instances. The burden of serving as watchdog rests with the counselor, however. He is the professional, the involved one who should know his own role, have realistic expectations regarding counselee role, know intimately counseling's potential, and be capable of communicating all of this to interested individuals. Above all, the counselor must know himself and the extent of his commitment.

Communication

SOME BASIC CONSIDERATIONS

Actually, most of the content of this volume one way or another touches upon communication skills, for they are the "stuff" of which interpersonal relationships are made. Typically, the human organism spends a major portion of his working hours daily in some kind of personal or group interaction for which the skills of communication are required. And yet, making ourselves understood — really understood — as individuals on a person-to-person basis or as statesmen on an international level often is a complex, difficult, and defeating experience.

The paradox in which we find ourselves in this "age of communications" is aptly described by Wrenn (1969, p. vii):

> Man has developed vast technological resources for mass communication — from countless paperbacks and newspapers to computerized translators and TV space satellites. Sometimes we feel overwhelmed by the sheer amount of information available. But, however advanced our techno-

logical ability to communicate, psychologically we are still floundering, in terms of quality and depth of personal communications, modern man is backward and poverty-stricken.

We seem also to be in the "age of groups" — T-groups, basic encounter groups, sensory-awareness groups, sensitivity groups, and group marathons. This mass rush to groups bespeaks man's desperate need to know himself and be understood by others in a world in which proximity with separateness, interdependence with impersonality, human herding with human loneliness and alienation appear to be the warp and woof of the pattern of living. Man wants to reach out, bridge the gap that exists between himself and his fellowman, but frequently he finds himself ill prepared, without the skills or the courage, without the knowledge of where or how to begin.

In treating the matter of making contact with others, Shostrom (1968, p. 48) writes:

> Our greatest problem with our feelings comes in communication. There are two elements to communication: sending and receiving. Like radio transmitters, we are sending out messages constantly. The problem is whether the people about us are getting the messages we send. We all have the problem of trying to make someone understand exactly what we say or feel.

Shostrom follows up this statement by describing sending and receiving errors, centering on the sender's expectations and the receiver's defensive responsive behavior. Cousins (1969), on the other hand, attributes much of the impasse in communications to the inadequate attention education gives to "developing the individual's communications skills," his "need to make himself clear." Of making oneself clear, Cousins (1969), p. 30) states:

> This is less a matter of vocabulary range than of vocabulary control. It has to do with the entire process by which an individual organizes his thoughts for purposes of transmission.

> The prime element in this process is sequence. Ideas have to be fitted together. The movement of a concept or an image from the mind of the speaker to the mind of the

listener is retarded when words become random chunks rather than sequential parts of an ordered whole.

Effective communication is a function of both externals and internals, of intellectual and emotional factors. Misunderstandings are not always caused by words alone or simply a low level of language skills. Schofield (1967, p. 140) notes:

> Man has long been aware that his oral communications are neither given nor received purely in terms of the words spoken (and their explicit or implicit meanings) but that additional and particular meanings are communicated by the general context of their utterance.

Beyond words and their meanings — connotations as well as denotations, the subtleties and nuances of language — the variables that comprise the "general context" of communication are myriad and complex. Particular meanings are derived from the time and place of the encounter. The persons involved, their past experiences and their future expectations, their frame of reference, and their present purposes, all shape meaning. The tone of utterance, the nonverbal facial and bodily behavior, and the "silent language" employed by the conversants communicate meaning, quite apart from words. Any one or a combination of these variables might cause communication to falter or break down entirely.

Our concern here is with communication within the context of counseling. This relationship contains the conditions and elements inherent in any interpersonal encounter, plus one more — the helping nature of the process.

THE PARTICIPANTS

Barriers to counselor-counselee dialogue may stem from what either counselor or counselee does or fails to do. The counselor, for example, must listen to what the counselee says. He must *hear* words, understand underlying meanings, and actually *attend to* the counselee's utterances. Ruesch (1961, p. 33) describes the counselor as one who

> . . . is willing to observe the processes of communication and go through the tedious work of responding in such a way that eventually the other person — the patient — will become aware of both the form and the content of his communication.

Should the counselor fail in this responsibility, should he *not attend to* what the counselee is saying, because he is absorbed in what he is going to say or do next — or for any other reason — his responses will reveal his inattentiveness. The counselor may be "preoccupied with that small voice inside that insists on knowing how to act next" (Benjamin, 1969, p. 103). If he permits himself to become thus preoccupied, he will destroy not only the ongoing dialogue but also the counselee's view of him as a person who wants to understand and help.

The counselee must feel that the counselor is listening to be motivated for further attempts at communication. He gauges the degree of attentiveness not only by the counselor's hearing but also by his responses. As in a computer circuit, one expects a certain quality of output commensurate with the input. Counselor-counselee interaction cannot exist if the counselee is unwilling to communicate. As the more knowing partner to the relationship, the counselor must assume the responsibility for establishing and maintaining a climate that fosters counselee talk.

Another inhibiting element associated with counselee communication is his feeling of shame and anxiety about how the counselor may view him should he reveal his "true self." With the counselor as an object of admiration, whose opinion he values, the counselee may feel that to expose his inner self, his "inner organization" (McKinney, 1958, p. 227), would bring upon his head the counselor's rejection. And so his dialogue with the counselor is guarded, superficial, and random, not allowing for the "quality and depth of personal communication" Wrenn mentions. An experienced counselor should be able to recognize this type of defensive behavior, however, and deal with it by a genuine, receptive, and accepting attitude.

Finally, there are reciprocally inhibiting reactions that either counselor or counselee may "catch" from the other. A cool and distant counselee may cause the counselor to become aloof, and vice versa. Or the overly familiar counselee who has a compulsion to be close both physically and emotionally to the counselor may cause him to feel overwhelmed with a desire to run, to escape. On the other hand, a counselor may come on a bit strong, causing the counselee to exercise more than the usual amount of caution. It is unlikely that if any of these behaviors are present, communication will be free and easy and open. Obstacles block the way to successful counselor-counselee dialogue.

COMMUNICATION AND CULTURE

These days most people are attuned to the concern about the potential for success of a "middle-class teacher" assigned to a school in a poverty area. And there is no doubt as to the meaning of the question, "Can a white (WASP) counselor work effectively with a Mexican-American or black counselee?" We are focusing here upon cultural or subcultural differences which cut across mores and traditions.

Hall (1959, p. 165), who has had vast experience living and working with peoples of other cultures, reminds us that cultural differences are little understood not because of the differences *per se*, but because they are "relevant to the deepest personal concerns." Beliefs, values, attitudes, essence of meanings — these are points upon which cultural differences revolve. Imagine the frustration of a white middle-class counselor who values time (time is money) and punctuality adjusting to a Cherokee Indian school situation in which the student appears forty-five minutes late for an appointment because it simply took longer today to dress after gym. For an individual who has always operated on schedule, it is difficult to understand the person who has never internalized the concept. The two are simply out of step and out of tune. What are the chances for successful communication here?

The judgment of right and wrong, of "good" and "bad" is often a product of acculturation. For some individuals, stealing is simply unlawful and is to be punished. What is the evaluation of the act if the offender is a mother with hungry children at home and the stolen object is food? Or how should one react to this exchange between a man and a social worker after the riots in Detroit a few years ago? The social worker noticed a new color TV in the home of one of his clients and asked, "How did you get this? Did you steal it?" "No," answered the man, "I saved it. It was going to be burned up." The obvious insensitivity of the social worker and the ethical distance between him and the man will preclude their experiencing a profitable relationship.

Potential for misunderstandings that create obstacles to communication are present when a counselor moves into a situation where cultural differences are prevalent. If he is not tuned in to the behavioral patterns and the mode of living of his counselees, he can expect, at best, little more than tolerance, at worst, overt hostility. If he wants ever to be able to communicate in a meaningful way with these counselees, the counselor will have to call up all his sensitivity and patience, be alert to the similarities — there are more similarities than differences — and grasp all opportunities to create touchstones that will enlarge his understanding of his counselees and their cultural world.

Finally, Wrenn's recommendation is worth considering here. In reference to the counselor's personal values, Wrenn (1962a, p. 184) writes:

> There is evidence that these cannot be concealed from the client even though there is no verbal communication of them. What the counselor considers important is communicated in all sorts of subtle ways. It is important that the counselor be explicitly aware of his convictions for these may color his appraisal of a student and also color the counselor's perception of the student that is communicated to him.

VERBAL RESPONSES

Words, which are presumed to constitute the basic vehicle for communication and understanding, can be employed in such a way as to confound, confuse, and compromise a relationship. Counselor use of psychological jargon, too many words, or emotion-laden phrases will block counselor-counselee communication. Professional terminology will either bore the counselee or make him feel inadequate; in either case, the counselor will lose his "audience." If, as Benjamin (1969, p. 98) suggests, the counselor talks as much as or more than the counselee, he will check the flow of messages from the counselee. Or if he repeatedly interrupts the counselee or finishes his messages for him, he may force the counselee into a subservient position. The counselee may actually give up and "let him have it his way." If the counselee becomes a "yes-man" in counseling, this does not necessarily mean that the counselor is right on target. It may mean that the counselee has withdrawn and that the dialogue has become a monologue.

Certain words or phrases tend to arouse hostility or defensiveness in individual counselees. The counselor would do well to be on the alert for any signs indicating counselee discomfort when specific words are inserted into the dialogue. Nichols and Stevens (1957, p. 101) are concerned with "word barriers":

> Emotion-laden words which stand in the way of effective listening [substitute *communication*] are tricky things. Many of them work at subconscious levels where they can be coped with only through deep psychological searching that may require a psychiatrist's help. Others, some of the most troublesome ones, are close to the surface. We can deal with many of them and eliminate their effects as blocks to listening [again, substitute *communication*].

To eliminate the blocking effects of certain verbal expressions, Nichols and Stevens suggest that emotion-laden words be identified and analyzed by the individual for whom they create difficulty. As part of the treatment, a counselor might help the counselee identify, analyze, and thus eliminate some of these troublesome word barriers. Nor is the counselor himself immune. He might do well to start his own analysis. Certain words are fairly generally emotion-laden: nigger, Commie, Bureau of Internal Revenue, LSD, cancer. And in some circles "head-shrinker" would make the list.

The goal of communication in counseling, according to Ruesch (1961, p. 44), is for counselor and counselee to reach agreement with regard to the full content of the message. The counselor must first achieve a "state of understanding." Then he must "acknowledge" the counselee's "intent to communicate," and let the counselee know that the "content of the message has been properly appreciated." Having received and acknowledged the message, the counselor checks back with the counselee to ascertain that they are in agreement with regard to meaning.

Perez (1965, p. 102) states the task simply when he says that the counselor must

> . . . dedicate himself to creating, facilitating, and maintaining the kind of interactive climate which will get across to the counselee that the latter's feelings, communicated via words and behaviors, have gotten through to the counselor.

Should the counselor eliminate or clumsily execute the "check" step, both counselor and counselee may mutually and erroneously assume that the meaning of the message is clear. Not until much later may it occur to either or both that they have been building on faulty assumptions. Untangling misunderstandings belatedly creates a serious disruption of the interactive process, during which period the participants must cope with embarrassment as well as repair communication.

Tyler (1969) admonishes counselors to "listen, think, respond." Impatience to respond may cause the counselor to miss the significance of the counselee's words, and the burden of the message.

Shaffer and Shoben (1967, p. 68) emphasize honesty of communication in the relationship, which can be painful for both participants:

> The therapist has to think and feel with the client. At times the efforts to communicate honestly involve calling painful issues to the client's attention, such as the tendency to feel sorry for himself, his resentment, bordering on hatred for his mother, or his competitive tendencies that are destructive of good relations with others. But much of a therapist's skill lies in his ability to combine this kind of honesty and directness with a sensitive understanding of the client's feelings.

In communicating honestly, it is important to avoid using words that arouse defensiveness (Tyler, 1969). For example, the following statements by the counselor would most certainly cause the counselee to become defensive:

You are feeling pretty sorry for yourself today.

You seem to be the kind of person who always has to win, no matter what the cost.

Too much affect, content that is too heavily laden with emotion or threat causes an interruption of the flow of communication. A case in point is that of a young woman, intelligent and well-educated, with a high degree of verbal facility. She spoke easily and well — until she approached content that was painful for her. At first she faltered just faintly, but as she moved closer to the core of her conflict, she stammered more and more markedly. Occasionally she reached the point where it took her a full ten minutes to complete a sentence.

Some counselees respond to emotional content in quite the opposite manner. Instead of becoming tight, as was the young woman's reaction above, these individuals indulge in an orgy of rambling verbiage. As the words flow out, meaning and sequence become increasingly blurred. Like a child in a wonderland of toys, such persons bounce from one idea to another, leaving a trail of unfinished, illogical thoughts in their wake. Words are being spoken, but meanings are not being transmitted.

Communication fails, too, if counselor and counselee are not functioning within the same frame of reference. To a person who has known St. Bernards, a Dalmatian is not a very large dog. But if an individual's canine experience has been limited to Dachshunds, a Dalmatian can seem like a sizable dog indeed. And so when a counselee says that a large dog chased her, the counselor will want to check out her frame of reference. Similarly, when a student reports in great agitation that his grades have slipped "way down," the counselor will need to know the counselee's concept of low grades. Only after the counselee's base of reference has been established can counselor-counselee dialogue have meaning.

Occasionally one comes across counselees with whom it is almost impossible to establish verbal rapport. Inarticulate and impoverished verbally, they seem able to produce little more than "yes" or "no," with possibly a halting phrase here and there. These persons are not accustomed to engaging in "talk." Individuals who are by habit taciturn, or who are wanting in intellectual capacity, or who have lacked opportunity to learn to express themselves verbally constitute this group. Sometimes, as with children who do not or cannot verbalize in a typical counselor-counselee setting, the counselor might use play materials — things that can be manipulated or explored together — appropriate to the counselee's age to help bridge the communication barrier.

The counselor and counselee who wish sincerely to communicate with one another must, in Seeley's (1969, p. 124) words, "speak and be heard by each other." And each must "speak and be heard by himself."

NONVERBAL RESPONSES

Nonverbal responses may more eloquently convey real feeling than do the words they accompany. People use facial expressions, body movements, and gestures to emphasize and reinforce verbal responses. Sometimes nonverbal actions substitute for words. A raised eyebrow, a slow smile, tapping fingers on a table, leaning forward in the chair, toying with a pencil or a rubber band — all have meaning. These silent actions may serve as "punctuation marks" for verbal exchanges or they may stand alone as signs of communication which are, for the most part, rapidly received and translated.

A man looks at his watch. His partner in conversation says, "Do you have to leave now?" Two people are in earnest discussion when suddenly one flicks his wrist and leans back in his chair. With these quick gestures, one of the conversants has dismissed the entire matter and, we would guess, without having reached a solution. When a mother asks her teenage daughter where the scissors are and the girl shrugs her shoulders (that irritating gesture), her mother knows she must continue her search elsewhere.

Endless examples of familiar nonverbal gestures could be recited. Some of the expressions and motions each of us employs are, of course, within our area of awareness, but others are not. In or out of awareness, however, these gestures are revealing. As Shertzer and Stone (1968, p. 393) point out, individuals develop a repertoire of nonverbal behavior even as they develop a repertoire of behaviors in speech.

Nonverbal responses can be particularly significant in the counseling relationship. Often the messages they convey are ones which neither participant would dare to utter. Perhaps the information transmitted through nonverbal behavior is not available to the awareness of a counselor or counselee and thus cannot be verbalized. For example, a therapist used video tape to record sessions he had with a young child and his mother. Counseling had been under way for several months. One day, as the therapist was reviewing a tape, he noticed that each time the mother spoke of her feelings for her son, her face took on a certain expression, an expression that was not present at any other time. Her facial expression belied her words. The therapist had missed this vital message during the interview. With the tape as evidence, he was able to help his client recognize, accept, and deal with rejection of her son.

Nonverbal communication can aid counselor-counselee interaction, or it can serve as an obstacle. Annoying behaviors that distract one or the other of the participants can interfere with communication. Or nonverbal responses that contradict the spoken word can create barriers between counselor and counselee. Shertzer and Stone (1968, p. 393) remind us that ". . . the occurrence of nonverbal behavior is not random; it derives from elements within the relationship."

Just as a counselee employs nonverbal communications to which the counselor responds, the counselor also has a repertoire of gestures to which counselees are sensitive. On this point Shertzer and Stone (1968, p. 353) state:

> The counselor's nonverbal behavior is of extreme importance in establishing and maintaining a relationship. Many clients are quite able to describe counselor discomfort and, perhaps more importantly, perceive it as a cue to avoid certain content or perhaps even the counseling situation itself.

Spontaneity, warmth, genuineness — these are the facilitative qualities that will help counselors establish and maintain a relationship conducive to effective interaction. Through body movements, facial expressions, and gestures, as well as through his words and his tone of voice, the counselor communicates these qualities to his counselees.

"SILENT LANGUAGE"

In addition to nonverbal responses, body movements, gestures, and facial expressions, there is another set of behaviors we use to communicate ourselves to others. Hall (1959, p. 10) identifies "our silent language" as "the language of behavior." As with verbal responses, silent language can induce or inhibit counselor-counselee interaction.

Some of the behaviors that communicate well the counselor's feelings in an inhibiting manner are counseling with a desk between himself and the counselee, being routinely late for interviews, forgetting the counselee's name or failing to recognize him outside the counseling suite, or making promises he does not keep. In a manner much more eloquent than words, the counselor's "silent language" conveys his disrespect for the counselee and his lack of commitment to counseling. A counselee need not even be especially sensitive to pick up such cues as these.

The counselee, too, has a silent language. Routine tardiness for appointments, frequent cancellation or failing to appear without bothering to notify the counselor, placing his feet on the desk or table, or being exaggeratedly or unnaturally solicitous — all effectively communicate the counselee's real feelings. A counselor will extract meaning from "silent language" such as this that will make interaction between himself and the counselee extremely difficult.

In conclusion, Benjamin (1969, p. 97) speaks well to the counselor on the theme of dealing with obstacles in communication:

> It [the goal] is to become aware of behavior in interviews, to see where we may be creating obstacles, and to try to reduce these as much as possible, all the while recognizing that we remain humanly fallible.

7

Hazards of Inter- action

Finally, some hazards arise in counseling simply because the counselor and counselee are in direct encounter. Risks are shared and are reciprocal. Misinterpretations can cause a good relationship to deteriorate, for example.

Here we have chosen to focus upon five relationship hazards likely to prove problematic: the pacing of the interview; continuing the relationship beyond helpful time limits; misunderstandings occurring in the relationship concerning test information; ethical confusions; and counselor-counselee hazards during periods of crisis.

Pacing

As counselor and counselee interact, the tempo of their communication is important. If either the counselor or counselee is too far ahead or is lagging behind in what he is attempting to communicate, the hazard of failing to understand one another clearly is increased.

Primarily it is the counselor's responsibility to maintain this synchronized interaction. At the start of their relationship, he makes it clear that the counselee can be the pace-setter and open up his problem in any manner he wishes. The counselor is there to listen and to help. However, even here there are hazards to which the counselor must be alert and responsible. With an overly facilitative counselor, the counselee could set too fast a pace. Tyler (1969, p. 61) recognizes that "There are some dangers if we facilitate the release of more emotion than the client is prepared to handle or than we are able to help him handle." Sechrest (1958, pp. 53–54) also sees the counselor's responsibility in this regard and warns that guilt can follow when a counselee is pressured into revealing too much too soon, especially if he is young and immature.

> If the counselor is able to keep this in mind, he will see the importance of upholding the student's ego and defenses, particularly in his early contacts with him . . . so that they may move into deeper confidences gradually and at a rate that is acceptable to the student and not harmful to him.

THE NEED FOR PATIENCE

In this matter of pacing responses, then, impatience is a major hazard for both counselor and counselee. Not only must the counselor on occasion temper the counselee's impatience by "upholding his defenses," but he himself must be sufficiently patient throughout their relationship to allow for the unfolding process to occur. Impatience on the part of either person could cause disruption in the dialogue, by interrupting the communication flow. If it is the counselor who interrupts, it could be because he thinks that he knows what the counselee is going to say next. When this happens, Benjamin (1969, pp. 98–99) comments:

> An interruption creates a major communication obstacle. It cuts short communication that is actually taking place. Our motives may be the best: to show that we understand so well that we can finish the interviewee's sentence for him, to demonstrate our interest by asking questions. Our motives notwithstanding, we are actually choking off what is coming our way, although we may sincerely believe ourselves to be encouraging further flow.

The hazard to communication is less if it is the counselee who interrupts, provided the counselor accepts the interruption.

After all, the counselor's primary task is to be responsive and to listen. And it may be quite important to perceive *why* the counselee is interrupting at this particular point as well as to hear what he says when he does. Counselor patience is needed to understand counselee impatience.

It takes time for the counselee to express deeper meanings, and it takes time coupled with perceptive listening for the counselor to assimilate and understand them. As each counselee has his unique web of complex interrelated experiences, a genuine communication of them is not an all-at-once matter. Hopefully, if the dialogue is reciprocally paced, understandings emerge with increased clarity. Tyler (1969, p. 87), realizing that especially in counseling there is a need for sharpening meaning, describes the process of "successive approximations":

> Something is said by one participant and partially understood by the other. If conditions for the interchange are favorable, Person Number Two will say, 'You mean . . .' and will proceed to paraphrase Number One's remark. Number One in turn will respond, 'Well, not exactly . . .' and proceed to clarify some part of his former message. After five or six of such clarifications, the point Number One was originally trying to make may be completely understood by Number Two.

To achieve this realistic comprehension of Number One's point, Number Two has had to stay patiently and closely attuned. If the counselor, as Number Two, had become impatient after one or two clarifications, it is doubtful whether the opportunity to understand thoroughly the counselee's point would recur.

"Feedbacks" occur in other forms and are of great assistance in regulating and correcting what is said. If, again because of some impatience, the counselor probes or pushes the counselee to "get to the real problem," he is usurping the lead. The feedback response from the counselee could well reveal resentment, resistance, or defensiveness. The hazard illustrated is that the counselor is inwardly tuned to his own readiness and not perceptually sensitive to the counselee's readiness. The counselee may be anxious, confused, embarrassed, or wary. He is not sure that it is wise or good to unveil his "inner sanctum" to the counselor, at least not too quickly. He may show this reluctance by giving very brief noncommittal responses, such as a "yes" or "no," or by replying to a counselor question very guardedly. Nonverbally, too, he shows he is not relaxed. These are warning signs for the counselor: Please be patient. Don't rush me. I don't feel I can tell you yet. Counseling is endangered to the extent that the counselor misunderstands or disregards these clues and fails to subordinate his own readiness and impatience to the counselee's needed and desired pacing. On the other hand, as McKinney (1958, p. 205) understands, counseling progresses when "the counselor encourages him to talk it out, to experience at his own rate the feelings that he has over the years associated with these early feelings of guilt, wrongdoing, or inadequacy."

ELIMINATION OF CURIOSITY

Another hazard to the communication pattern of interaction can occur if the counselor becomes unduly curious. Something the counselee says catches the counselor's personal interest and he identifies with it. Then, to satisfy his curiosity, he is eager to know what happened next. He is more attuned to objective content than he is to the counselee's feelings. As Hiltner (1952, p. 32) observes, the counselor "wants to know what happened, not how or why. He is like the fiction readers who want fast-paced action narratives with a minimum of character and setting." An example:

Counselee: So I called her and told her to meet me in front of the Library. I felt I couldn't take any more, and I sure was going to tell her so.

Counselor: What did she say when you told her that?

Counselee: Uh . . . Well, it wasn't like that. What I mean is, I wanted to tell her . . .

The counselee's response shows he is aware that the counselor has jumped ahead and has bypassed his feelings. Benjamin (1969, p. 41) comments:

When we feel that we require more information or more details, we should not press immediately to obtain them, if this involves cutting off or diverting the interviewee's train of expression. For if we do so, he will then think that we are more interested in what appears important to us than what is significant to him and that he must adapt his interest to ours.

When both the substance and the pacing of the communication interaction between the counselor and counselee become dominated by the curiosity of the counselor, it is no longer a counseling relationship.

SILENCES

Barbara is a college freshman presently having relationship problems with her roommate. As she now tries to tell the counselor about it, she is unsure as to whether he will understand her mixed emotions of hurt, anger, frustration, and self-doubt.

Barbara: I try to be nice to her, but she's so awfully inconsiderate. I think a lot of what she does is on purpose, too — just to see what I'll do about it. I'm getting so upset.

Counselor: It seems that even though you try to cooperate, she still completely disregards your feelings?

Barbara: She *does!* All the time. I . . . I don't know what to do. (*Silence*)

(*Counselor also is silent.*)

What is occurring during this pause? Would it be better if the counselor did not allow for a short mutual silence at this point?

Evidently, Barbara sees that the counselor is "with" her. Her response shows that she feels understood, and so the joint silence which follows is natural and comfortable. It also appears that it will be productive, for during it Barbara can continue with her same thoughts and feelings.

But not all silences are productive. They occur for different reasons and can mean very different things. However, as part of the communication pattern between counselor and counselee, it is inevitable that they will happen and the pacing of the interview must accommodate them. Hazards, for both counselor and counselee, can follow when the need, or purpose, or communicative intent is misinterpreted.

Under what circumstances is silence likely to produce or to indicate hostility? In many respects, counseling is very similar to other relationships. All of us know that when we feel that another person apparently doubts what we say, probes into areas in which our feelings are sensitive, seems to be judgmental, or implies that he is superior to us, our defensive reactions mount. We tend to "close up." We turn away from any further relating and become silent. It is a kind of dead-end, negative silence. Certainly no counselor would intentionally provide the stimuli for such silences, but at any time he could blunder into causing them. Similarly, since counseling is an interaction, the counselee could be the instigator. In response to various "transference" type outbursts from the counselee, for example, some counselors may themselves experience inner hostility and be briefly silent. If for such, or any other, reasons, the counselor feels hostile, what happens is contingent upon his own degree of emotional integration and maturity. Hazards can be avoided if the counselor can resume the interaction, after recognizing and accepting his feelings, as well as those of the counselee.

For some counselees, the tempo of the interview may be too fast. Sensitive, shy, or introverted counselees feel pressured and uncomfortable. Brammer and Shostrom (1968, p. 215) realize the help given to such counselees when the pace is tempered:

> Often the counselor senses that the client is rushing, or that he himself feels compelled to push too hard. He can reduce the intensity and pace to a more tolerable level for both participants in making the pauses longer. The counselor says in effect, 'We are not in a hurry; take it easy.'

For the counselor to sense when and why the longer pauses are needed is very important. As Hiltner (1952, p. 93) says, "There is timing, but there is also awareness of timing." It should be noted, however, that insecure or inexperienced counselors may face a hazard in following through with their "awareness." While pushing may be uncomfortable, silence may be viewed as being even more so. The message of not being in a hurry and of taking it easy needs to be assimilated, in some instances, by both the counselor and counselee.

INTERPRETATIONS

Pacing of the counseling interaction both affects and is affected by interpretive responses made by the counselor. To be sensitively aware of timing is especially important, for many hazards can result when interpretations are prematurely offered. Once given, interpretations may have the impact of considerably modifying the content and rate of subsequent responses by counselor and counselee.

By "interpreting," the counselor hopes to enlighten and enrich understandings for the counselee. But much caution and wisdom are essential. Enough information and understanding may not yet be available for the counselor. Or the counselor may be interpreting heavily from his own biases and point of reference, in addition to responding with his interpretive views to the counselee at the wrong time. The counselee may show that he has neither the readiness nor the willingness to assimilate such analysis. Shertzer and Stone (1968, p. 371) comment:

> Timing is most important. Interpretations should not be blindly made; rather, caution should be exercised until the counselor is sure that the client is ready to accept them. A client can profit from counselor insight only if it also becomes his insight. He arrives at his conclusions at his own pace. To be told that he feels anxiety or is expressing rejection or fear will not help him until he himself can recognize the existence of these feelings and voluntarily acknowledge their presence.

TERMINATION

Hazards are present if the interview is closed too abruptly. The counselee may feel the counselor has wearied of him, and so feels a sense of rebuff and rejection. But as termination is usually the counselor's responsibility, he can, through anticipation and consideration of the closing minutes guide the interaction tactfully. Benjamin (1969, p. 30) suggests that two factors are basic:

1. Both partners in the interview should be aware of the fact that closing is taking place and accept this fact, the interviewer in particular.
2. During the closing phase, no new material should be introduced or at any rate discussed, for closing concerns that which has already taken place.

While it is a mistake to be too abrupt, it is also unwise to prolong and draw out the final moments. Again, what matters is the counselor's perceptual awareness and sensitivity to the temporal dimension as it is maximally helpful to the counselee.

Unnecessary Prolongation

Reference here is not to a single counseling interview, but rather to a series of counseling interviews with one counselee. When should counseling be over? How does either the counselor or counselee know that the relationship probably should no longer be continued? What are the hazards, if any, if counseling continues overlong?

There is, of course, no neat finish line, and each counseling "case" is unique. However, the general goals and objectives which the counselor hopes to achieve with any counselee are similar, and do provide functional guidelines. As counselors, we hope to provide the conditions in which the counselee can realistically perceive his own psychological conflicts and problems and progressively acquire the insights and strength to cope with them more ably. Because of counseling, we hope that he will become a more integrated person and achieve a sufficient realization of self-worth to be able to discard self-defeating manipulations and defenses. In sum, the overall goal is for the counselee to be in more realistic and balanced control of his own life.

SIGNS AND CUES

If counseling has been proceeding normally, after a number of sessions, either the counselor or counselee may note indications of some of these developmental changes. The counselee himself may realize that he finds it easier to discuss "touchy" personal problems and be more honest about accepting his responsibility for them. He may view some personal relationships in a new light, and he may see new alternatives of action for himself. He could then be the one who suggests that he might not need to come in any more. Usually, however, it is the counselor who is alert to these signs and cues, and it most frequently becomes his responsibility to terminate the relationship. There is, of course, the danger that the counselor may fail to understand or perceive these termination signals. But for the most part, hazards are generated, because the closure situation is seldom this optimal or simple. There may be indications that, for a number of reasons, the interaction has become unhealthy or nonproductive. For example, if the counselor perceives that the counselee's problems have become ones beyond his competencies, ethically he should terminate the present relationship and make a referral. Or clues may be present in the interaction revealing hostilities or manipulation so intense that counseling at least in its present form should be discontinued or changed.

RELUCTANCE TO TERMINATE

Readiness to terminate the counseling experience may not be reciprocal. Either the counselor or counselee may feel a reluctance to end the relationship, a reluctance that is not therapeutic to the other. The hazard for the counselee is largely one of "holding on" because of fearing the loss of a certain security; for the counselor, the hazard is letting him become this dependent. Johnson (1967, p. 179) points out the situation:

> The counselor is responsible for the limits of the counseling relationship. He cannot let the anxious person control . . . to the extent of the young woman who felt she must go around the world with her counselor to continue the relationship.

For an insecure counselee, the counseling relationship may be his only personally satisfying one. He has learned that here he is welcomed, not judged, and is attentively listened to. Not going to talk to the counselor anymore would leave kind of a void — he would miss it. Nevertheless, the counselor may know that, partly for these very reasons of growing dependency, the relationship has served its major purposes. To continue the interaction could be hazardous; the counselee needs to venture more widely on his own. He needs to form other and new interpersonal relationships.

To avoid the hazards of a continuation beyond the point of diminishing returns and yet to facilitate as much as possible the new "solo flight," the counselor needs to be alert to these counselee anxieties. And he needs to convey his full empathic understanding to the counselee. The termination of counseling is another time of transition, not too different from the initial phase, and as Fitts (1965, p. 146) realizes, the counselee may be experiencing in part some of the same insecure emotions:

> Many clients experience some of the same kinds of feelings (doubts, fears, conflicts and uncertainty) about terminating that they did about beginning. Fortunately these feelings are not ordinarily so overwhelming nor do they take as long to resolve.

A reluctance to terminate counseling, however, is not always a counselee problem. Inadvertently, the counselor could be the one who would like the relationship to be prolonged. An objective independence and a certain level of acquired emotional maturity are necessary for the counselor to be freed sufficiently from his own anxieties, needs for affection, approval, and so on, to terminate the relationship when it really should be done. Less experienced counselors are probably most vulnerable to the subtle hazards involved. For example, to some extent a counselor could be gratified by the counselee's need to depend on him. (It makes him feel like a "helping person.") Or he may be "taken in" by some of the transition symptoms, sympathizing in lieu of empathizing with the counselee. In other words, as Kell and Mueller (1966, p. 144) realize, the counselor may not understand the dynamics of either his own or the counselee's behaviors:

> At termination time, the counselor may not recognize the meaning of his client's behavior. Perhaps counselor non-

recognition of the possible meanings of such client feelings and behavior relates most often to the fact that the relationship has had and still has deep meaning and satisfaction for him. The counselor may actually be reluctant to recognize the client's feelings, since to do so means that he will lose closeness and contact with someone who is meaningful and rewarding to him. Yet termination must come. . . .

ALLOCATION OF TRUST

It is obvious that counselors view the person of the counselee very differently. Some counselors, in agreement with Rogers *et al.*, see him as potentially able to draw on his own latent resources to resolve his own problems and conflicts. Others do not share this level of confidence and trust, contending that as the counselee is always essentially immature, considerable directive help and guidance is necessary. Behavioral modification is the counselor's responsibility.

These philosophical differences become especially operative in the interaction when the counseling sessions are about to end. Counselors who believe strongly in the strength of the counselee are inclined to feel that when the counselee feels he can "go it alone," he will make the fact known and his choice should be respected. More directive counselors, on the other hand, usually feel that the counselee is not competent to judge when termination would be appropriate. Of course the broad dichotomy here presents an oversimplification. Frequently, external factors can pressure or control the time of ending. Also, many counselees simply fail to return; independently and informally, they terminate the sessions irrespective of the counselor.

Nevertheless, there may be value in considering these two broad counselor orientations and noting some possible termination hazards which could occur from either direction. We are primarily concerned here with the time factor of cumulative sessions. Basically it becomes a matter of the willingness with which the counselor transfers confidence and trust to the counselee and the extent to which he does so, with respect to the counselee's present and future behaviors.

When there is little or no structure, as in the client-centered position, is there a real danger that counseling could continue for longer than is necessary? Can and will the counselee understand and be sufficiently responsive to his own achieved level of readiness to initiate actively a separation from the counselor? In observing the client-centered approach, Carkhuff and Berenson (1967, p. 72) observe that it functions "most effectively when the client's response is enough, and the therapist's response is appropriate." Will the counselor's response be adequately "appropriate" when counselee responses toward termination occur? Should the counselor contribute any broad structure to the situation?

Fitts (1965, p. 144) may be somewhat helpful here. Although he concurs with the general view that the voiced readiness of the counselee should largely be the determinant for termination, he suggests that there also be some goals:

> I have found, however, that sometimes it is helpful to have some goal for termination, just as other goals are helpful. Sometimes I raise the question with clients, after they have made considerable progress in therapy, of whether they would like to set some kind of time goal for themselves for termination.

Fitts adds that all such "goals" should be tentative and flexible. A proposed date would serve only as one to work toward for the final visit, and certainly could be extended if the counselee thought it necessary.

For counselors who are more directive, who believe that behavioral modification in the counselee occurs as a result of specific externally prescribed procedures, are the hazards any simpler? It would appear that because the counselor sets the boundaries and because the planned techniques are usually relatively short in duration, any hazards from needless continuation would virtually be eliminated. But while they may be different, hazards are present and can be complex. The pitfalls may simply be the reverse of those encountered in more extended counseling experiences. Maybe the counseling sessions in many cases should not be as short as they are. Carkhuff and Berenson (1967, pp. 97, 98) observe that a hazard of this orientation for the counselee is that "the approach is not geared to go beyond the fundamental relief of symptomatology," while a hazard for the counselor is that he "might develop inappropriate goals and schedules for behavior modification."

EXPECTANCIES

The duration of any counseling relationship is tremendously influenced by what both counselor and counselee expect. Shertzer and Stone (1968, p. 110) point out that the realistic and practical differences between expectancies and goal statements need to be recognized:

> Perhaps the real difference lies in whether counseling is to be viewed as remedial or generative. Expectancies are likely to stress remediation and repair; goal statements imply that counseling should be preventive or generative in nature.

Counselor and counselee expectations can be, and probably usually are, widely different from one another. The counselee may expect the counselor to "cure" him or to manage him and have little or no understanding of realistic counseling goals. But it is the counselor, in his responsible role as a counselor, who needs the balanced perspectives. If he is to avoid hazards of nonproductive sessions, it is up to him to see that his own expectancies for the relationship are in line as much as possible with his viewed goals. Only when he is integrated realistically in his own perceptions can he be in the position to clarify, respond, and contribute understanding to the counselee as to how long the counseling experience should be continued.

TERMINATION AND REJECTION

A hazard for some counselees is that the termination of counseling (or a referral to another counselor) will be viewed as partial rejection. Even though the counselee himself might recognize that any further continuation would not be too helpful or needed, his feelings are mixed. Some of the old anxieties about himself recur. Maybe he can make it on his own, maybe he will even be glad that he won't have to worry about keeping these counseling appointments anymore. On the other hand, he wonders if the counselor would be glad to see him, should he ever want to come back again. Maybe the counselor is just relieved to see him go now and to be rid of him. As these ambivalences are not uncommon at termination, it would indeed be a hazard for the counselor to minimize or not to be fully aware of them. The continued acceptance of all of the counselee's feelings and the respect for him as a person must be communicated, especially now.

There are other hazards. An insecure counselor could overreact at this time. If some of the counselee's "normal" trepidations are magnified and arouse corresponding doubts in him, he may decide, against his better judgment, to go on with the relationship. Termination would have been natural and was indicated, but the counselor may encourage the counselee to make further appointments. One wonders what positive consequences he expects can be derived from subsequent counseling sessions. Forward movement can hardly happen when both counselor and counselee fear the simple loss of the relationship itself, as Kell and Mueller (1966, p. 81) recognize:

> Clients who are growing and changing and who may be near termination may also precipitate counselors into sometimes undoing their own work. Since counseling relationships are and should be rewarding to both participants, either member, when termination approaches, may attempt to prolong the relationship by returning it to an earlier more regressed stage. The counselor's behavior, in such an instance, sometimes suggests that he believes he may never have another rewarding relationship.

INDIRECT HAZARDS

An unnecessary prolonging of the counseling interviews with one or two counselees limits the number of counselees with whom the counselor can work. In any counseling setting, there are usually many prospective counselees seeking and requiring assistance. In the school situation, particularly, there is likely to be a waiting list. If, for some of the reasons discussed above, a counselor continues overlong with a very few counselees, he is curtailing the potential help he might be extending to others.

For those counselees involved in overprolonged counseling,

a similar curtailment exists. Presumably, at least, they could now be exposing themselves to new constructive activities and experiences.

For both counselors and counselees, the appropriate exit signs should be perceived at the right time.

Misunderstandings Concerning Test Information

Much has been written about tests and their appropriate role in the counseling interview. The counselor's orientation and background will, of course, determine what degree of emphasis and importance he assigns to them. Common to all counselors and counselees, however, are a number of hazards which can occur from the use and interpretation of test information.

GENERAL ATTITUDES

Both counselor and counselee have had many, many prior conditionings with tests. The counselee undoubtedly has been the recipient of approval and acclaim from his parents and teachers whenever he earned high scores on academic tests, and, conversely, he probably experienced certain negative reinforcements when he scored low. In our culture, academic achievement in particular is rewarded highly. Because of various tests and the reactions of others to him in accord with how he scored, important developmental components have indirectly been added to his self-concept. He is not now likely to be neutral in his feelings toward tests. He is likely to be more sensitized and vulnerable.

The counselor, in addition to having had these same experiences, has acquired levels of competency and understanding about tests. Because of his professional role as a counselor, he has been required to specialize to some degree in this area. Of course, counselors vary tremendously with respect to the amount of realistic and functional test knowledge which they have assimilated. They also vary greatly, as we have said, in their perspectives and attitudes concerning the purposes of tests and in the interpretations they give concerning them.

Relying too heavily on test results and overusing tests themselves in counseling are common hazards for many counselors.

INITIAL DIAGNOSIS OF THE COUNSELEE

Even before the counselee and counselor meet in interaction, many diagnostic and evaluative measures of the counselee almost always have been made by others and are available to the counselor. He can use them to whatever extent and in whatever way he chooses. Past test scores, teacher comments, health and family information, and other personal background data are included in a student's cumulative record. In addition, a counselee may have been "screened" for the counseling appointment, and the results from "intake" procedures are also made available to the counselor.

Potentially, there is much of value here for the counselor. General background information can be helpful in receiving the counselee with understanding, and much of the other data can certainly be quite important in vocational and educational planning. But there are also serious hazards involved in how diagnostic information may be used, particularly in personal-social counseling and in psychotherapy. Usually much of the data has been obtained from the person's past, rather than the present. And even when the counselor attempts to secure current measurement information, the whole of it represents an externally evaluative picture which the counselor could be too quick to take over *in toto* into his thinking. It constitutes a "diagnosis" and predictions and expectancies are generated in the counselor's mind because of it. Much of what could more flexibly develop in counselor-counselee interaction becomes preformulated counselor action alone. Also, the form and degree of acceptance and understanding which he, as counselor, extends to the counselee could be subtly changed. Client-centered counselors have been alert to point out these hazards. Tyler (1969, pp. 66–67) notes that the danger can be somewhat lessened if, instead of being rigid and specific in utilizing evaluative information, the counselor forms a comprehensive, flexible "working image" of the counselee. The "image" then can grow, change, and become more complex and accurate as counseling proceeds.

But many voices have been and still are raised against the hazards of forming any type of crystallized diagnosis of the counselee and of believing that diagnosis is an essential foundational part of the counseling process. Brammer and Shostrom (1968, p. 156) make a summary comment:

> There is a principal objection to be stressed in this discussion if the diagnosis is made a separate and formal step. It is our conviction that this diagnostic thinking, though generally coming early in the process, tends to blend into the whole counseling process. Furthermore, this diagnostic process is not the precise definitive act which it is in medicine; in counseling it consists of forming and reforming hypotheses for the most appropriate choices. This formulation is then discussed with the client for assimilation and/or amendment. At this point, it generally becomes the client's hypothesis, and all decisions and consequences are his.

In the counseling interaction, either the counselor or the counselee may feel that taking some tests is indicated. While right and appropriate tests could augment and assist the counselee in realistic self-understanding, there are responsible safeguards to be observed if such benefits are to occur. Fundamentally, for the counselor there is the inescapable and ethical responsibility that he know fully what he is doing. The counselee has the right to expect that the counselor is professionally competent and knowledgeable in this area. If the counselor does not have basic technical and clear understanding of any particular test, he should not venture to use it with the counselee.

Secondly, it can be a mistake if the counselor concurs too readily with a counselee's initial request to "take tests" when he first comes to counseling. Elsewhere, we have spoken of the counselee's facade of defensiveness in this regard; this respectable request can serve to mask many deeper anxieties and conflicts. Proceeding at once to comply, the counselor would face the hazard that he might never be in the position to have a genuine counseling relationship with this counselee. It could turn out to be a "hello-goodbye" interview. Shertzer and Stone (1968, p. 412) realize the danger:

Since the individual thinks tests will help him, all too often
the counselor thinks the same thing and proceeds to test
selection. Clearly, careful exploration of the client's request
is in order to determine whether tests are really needed or
will be useful.

When tests of some type do seem to be validly helpful, how
and by whom should the ones to be taken be selected? Does
it put the counselee in a dependent role if the counselor takes
over and prescribes which ones might be advisable for him?
Is not the counselor again the diagnostician? There has been
much discussion and research concerning the pros and cons of
the counselee's participation in the selection process. Probably
many hazards can be avoided for both the counselor and counselee if it is always remembered that counseling is an interaction, with the growth of the counselee a primary goal. The
counselee has his questions and reveals progressively his
needs. The counselor can respond perceptively to them. He
can supply objective, clear, and nontechnical understanding
about tests with which he is soundly familiar, when he feels
this information would be of assistance in contributing new
and relevant facts for the counselee to consider. The counselor cannot abdicate his technical responsibilities. When
appropriate, the counselee should not be denied knowledge of
the strengths and limitations of the available tests. But it then
becomes the responsibility of the counselee to decide whether
to take the tests at all, and the counselor's responsibility to
accept the decision he makes.

INTERPRETATION HAZARDS

It is in the interpretation and the assimilation of test results
that probably the greatest hazards for both counselor and
counselee are created. As we have noted, the counselee is not
a neutral recipient; the evaluative information he hears from
the counselor affects, now and later, the way in which he sees
himself. And if, in the process, the counselor also should seem
partially to lose sight of him as a unique and important
person, or to minimize his feelings, the counselee's self-esteem
is shaken and hurt the more. Depersonalization of the counselee, while obviously wholly unintentional, can be a more
likely hazard for the counselor than he may usually realize.

Benjamin (1969, p. 95) believes that the pitfall can occur because the counselor tends to use test results defensively, in bolstering his own role:

> Interviewers tend to use another defensive shield. Hiding behind diagnoses and test results, we lose sight of the person and in his stead see the category into which he has been placed.

The counselee may react defensively too, but it is because what he hears makes him feel threatened, or angry, or anxious. The counselor will err seriously in his responsibility as a counselor if he cannot tolerate these emotional reactions with understanding, as Shertzer and Stone (1968, p. 417) know:

> Essentially this means that the counselee is given an opportunity to verbalize his feelings and attitudes and that the counselor recognizes and responds to them. The counselee's feelings cannot be ignored or responded to by defending the validity of the instrument used.

Because the counselor is usually viewed by the counselee as a person who "knows" these matters, his influence on the counselee tends to have considerable impact. Accordingly, the counselee's emotional reactions can be stronger, simply because an authoritative figure is communicating to him information which may not jibe at all with his own present self-expectations.

The manner, sequence, language, and tempo in which the counselor communicates test results to the counselee are very important. Unless the counselor is motivated to make thoughtful interpretations from feelings of genuine respect and empathic understanding toward the counselee, the hazards in the interaction mount rapidly. Tyler (1969, pp. 105–106) makes several constructive suggestions for the counselor. She holds that many pitfalls can be avoided if the counselor plans for the test interpretation interview by organizing the results into a general flexible and coherent pattern and then communicates them to the counselee tactfully in clear, nontechnical, and qualitative rather than quantitative words. Also too much must not be given too rapidly; the counselee requires time to ask questions, to react, to understand, and to assimilate the information.

Special cautions apply when interpretations of projective personality tests are given. After scanning the results from a counselee's projective test, for example, the counselor may feel he is now aware of deeper underlying problems. (Of course the realizations of severe pathologies do need to be recognized and known, and the counselee may be in need of psychiatric referral.) Often there is the hazard, however, that now the counselor will attempt to push and tailor the counselee's responses to "get at" the problems under the surface which the counselor feels are there. Sechrest (1958, pp. 62–63) suggests that this type of counselor behavior in which "some counselors use test results or other confidential information they possess about a student as a device for attacking his defenses" is inimical to the goals of counseling. She adds:

> The counselor's role in working with students who back off from their central problems must be focused on helping the student to explore the problems he is able to discuss, thereby building a relationship that may make it possible for him to look at his deeper problems, too.

It has been found to be helpful and less threatening to the counselee if the counselor makes him an active participant in the interpretation of test results. The counselor should not be the only one to act, while the counselee reacts. If the counselor simply asks the counselee such questions as, "What did you think of that test after taking it?" "Did it bother you to take it?" "Would you like to say how you think you did on this test?" it is better than telling him, "You scored at the forty-second percentile on this test." Counselor and counselee are more likely to retain rapport, when the counselor encourages the counselee to start the interpretive session by ventilating his feelings. His anxieties tend to be decreased. In addition, when the counselee is encouraged to participate and to express himself freely, there are fewer chances that he may be misunderstood. Something he may say to the counselor after his interest inventory has been explained, for example, may reveal that he has not made the distinction between interests and abilities.

Counselees are more comfortable — as we all are — if they feel they are not too different from their peers. It is upsetting if they feel, when personality and interest inventories are interpreted to them, that they may be too "abnormal." Shertzer and Stone (1968, pp. 416–417) suggest that it is probably better for the counselor to avoid using the word "normal." When a counselee's scores on such tests are below the sixteenth percentile or above the eighty-fourth percentile, he can be helped to understand in just what specific ways his scores reflect certain differences.

THE PLACE OF EVALUATION

It is important for the counselor to perceive and be sensitive to exactly what needs of the counselee will be served by taking tests. The counselee may want to continue in a cyclic compensatory pattern, taking further tests in an area where he already knows he scores well. (There may be many other things about himself he may not want to realize or face.) Or, as Tyler (1961, pp. 102–103) points out, a counselee could want to take vocational aptitude tests "as a substitute for his own thinking about life decisions, rather than as an aid to such thinking."

Tests are often given and interpreted for the purpose of predicting which counselees will derive the most benefit from counseling and psychotherapy. Views differ with respect to how efficiently this can be done, but it should be mentioned that it is hazardous to turn away persons seeking counseling on this basis. As Patterson (1959, p. 243) warns, "on the basis of present information, it would appear to be unjustifiable to reject any applicant for therapy on the basis of pretherapy information." He feels that only by experiencing therapy itself can these benefits be known.

For both counselor and counselee, it is hazardous to place an overreliance upon test scores. Test provide one good source of information. But frequently counselors, who should know better, are prone to give more weight to what the test scores appear to reveal than to understandings progressively gained about the counselee. Perspectives need to be retained.

Ethical Confusions

Counseling has become a profession. Like members of other professions, the counselor has been assigned by an agency or institution of society to a role of public social service. And in consequence, he is expected and obligated to discharge all of his counseling responsibilities in accord with high and sound ethical practices.

These ethical procedures have been formally established, and revised as needed, by the American Psychological Association and the American Personnel and Guidance Association. The counselor has a fundamental ethical responsibility to familiarize himself thoroughly with these explicit codes for professional behavior. Many possible problems and aspects of interaction and relationship have been thoughtfully and operationally delineated, and the counselor needs to understand the content of these anchor guidelines, before he himself faces these complexities.

Yet the functional and actual interpretations and implementations are still left up to the individual counselor. And here are the hazards. When involved and confronted with complicated and unpredictable situations in which loyalties may conflict and boundaries are difficult to determine, the counselor may experience ethical confusions. In spite of and in addition to the basic help provided by the stated principles, difficult and discriminating personal judgments are necessary.

SOME PROBLEMATIC SITUATIONS

What should be the counselor's response, when he is faced with ethical dilemmas such as the following?

A counselee tells of his participation in a narcotics group and discloses exactly where and how the drugs are obtained and distributed.

The counselor learns of the unethical conduct of a friend and colleague.

A counselee tells the counselor that two days before the exam in Professor X's class, a copy of the exam was obtained and copies of it were run off for every class member. The counselee and another student procured the exam.

The parents of a counselee invite the counselor to dinner so that they can "learn more" about the serious problems of the counselee.

The counselor feels he has no competent place of referral for a counselee who has been demonstrating acute paranoid reactions and threatening some of his associates.

Both in the APA ethical code and in that established by APGA, we read that the counselor's primary responsibility is to the client. In the APA code it is stated clearly as a first principle that:

> The counselor is primarily responsible to his client and ultimately to society; these basic loyalties guide all his professional endeavors. The counselor is at all times to respect the integrity and guard the welfare of the person with whom he is working as a client.

But in the APA code it is also stated (Sec. 1, p. 2) that "the psychologist's ultimate allegiance is to society, and his professional behavior should demonstrate an awareness of his social responsibilities." And another principle (Sec. 2, p. 5) states "When information received in confidence reveals clear and imminent danger that the client may do serious harm to himself or others, intervention by the psychologist may be required." What do these principles together indicate for the counselor who is as "aware of his social responsibilities" as he is concerned about his counselee who is illegally obtaining and distributing narcotics?

In a similar fashion, the other dilemmas might be discussed and analyzed, referring to the stated ethical principles which appear most applicable. But the counselor may still experience very real confusions and conflicts of allegiance. Ethical codes certainly do provide invaluable ground rules. In the last analysis, however, it is the counselor himself who must decide when there are conflicts and difficult situations with which to cope. Hazards can be very real indeed. What and how the counselor decides depends largely upon his moral character.

Schwebel (1962, pp. 598–599), in an attempt to find the

causes of unethical practice, found that unethical forms of behavior stem from the counselor's desire for personal profit, self-enhancement, and the maintenance of security and status. It can be very much a matter of values and of moral position. When the counselor's values are such that what benefits *him* is more important than what happens to the counselee, sooner or later unprofessional conduct is bound to result.

Wrenn (1952, p. 177) clearly realized the situation:

> The profession has established a code of ethics but its application calls for decisions that will require great personal courage and depth of conviction. It is at this point that the counselor may have to have recourse to the great values and principles of the human race in order to resolve the ethical conflict. The counselor may truly have to think more of others than of himself. Counselors need to strengthen their moral courage as well as their understandings and skills, for it is the constellation of all these qualities that provides true professional competence.

DIFFERING EXPECTATIONS

Because the counselor's role is perceived very differently by the different persons and groups with whom the counselor is associated, many ethical pressures arise. The school counselor is commonly viewed as the one who will resolve certain moral problems, and many students are referred to him for just this purpose. The following example may illustrate how this can happen.

> The school counselor receives a telephone call from a father who asks that his daughter, Marie, be counseled as soon as possible, as she needs to be "straightened out." In talking with Marie, the counselor learns that she and her boyfriend Jim — both of whom are now high school juniors — have been going together for over two years. Marie tells the counselor bluntly, "We're going to be married in June, whether my folks like it or not!"
>
> When she comes in for the third counseling session, Marie is tearful and defiant. She relates how her father has laid down the law, telling her it was necessary since "counseling hasn't done you any good." Jim is now forbidden to come to the house, or even to telephone. Marie

ends up by confiding, "So now we're not going to wait. We're going to run away and get married next week."

The following day, Marie's mother calls in person at the counselor's office. She is distraught, saying she feels "something awful" is going to happen. She begs the counselor to tell her if he knows anything about what Marie might be planning or thinking of doing.

Just where does all this place the counselor? What are his ethical responsibilities? It is obvious that Marie's parents have perceived the counselor as an adult "on their side." Of course both her father and mother are greatly concerned about Marie's future. But the counselor has been counseling Marie and has been the recipient of her confidences. She has "opened up" to him and is trusting him. It would be very easy for the counselor to make several ethical blunders at this point. If he is to avoid these hazards, what should he *not* do?

He does not have the right to reveal what Marie has told him in confidence without first consulting her. Nor does he ethically have clearance to have professional counseling contacts with either of Marie's parents, unbeknownst to her. Patterson (1959, p. 36) is quite explicit:

> The problem arises of what is to be told to the parents or relatives. It usually is not necessary to violate the confidences of the client, or if it seems desirable to do so, it should be done only with the express permission of the client, except, again, where the client is clearly mentally irresponsible.

This is not to say that the counselor closes off all communication with Marie's parents. It does mean that he must understand his ethical obligations to Marie.

ADMINISTRATIVE PRESSURES

Because administrators frequently misperceive the role of the counselor and see him primarily as an adjunct to their own function, both counselors and counselees can experience certain pressures. For example, a student may be referred by an administrator who stipulates that the student must come to see the counselor once every week. Counseling is included as part of the conditional decision for the student to remain in school. A vague threat is now likely to overshadow the relationship between counselor and counselee. Both of them feel that some type of verdict will be made at the termination of counseling and that what comes out of their interaction sessions can make a difference one way or the other. The counselee may understandably be anxious about confidentiality, and the counselor could be confused about his ethical priorities.

We have noted that the counselor's primary ethical allegiance and responsibiilty is to safeguard the confidences of the counselee. Practically implementing this priority can often prove to be difficult, however, as is true in this instance. It takes considerable moral stamina for the counselor to subordinate and place in perspective the administrator's expectations. Wrenn (1952, p. 176) clearly realized the tensions:

> It takes more courage and strength of conviction to take a stand to protect the client than it does to make a decision to protect the employer.

Arbuckle (1961, p. 241) offers some relevant ethical guidelines and suggestions for the counselor:

> It might be that the counselor could, without revealing any particular confidential information, and with the consent of the client, give to the administrator a picture of the [psychological] health of the client, but leave any decision as to whether this is "well enough" or "not well enough" up to someone else.

The counselor needs to understand fully the complications which are involved.

COUNSELOR PROBLEMS AND INADEQUACIES

Ignorance, or a partial lack of current technical understandings on the part of the counselor can generate ethical problems. When, for example, a counselee seeks to learn about certain occupations preparatory to making his vocational choice, he has every right to expect that any information he receives from the counselor will be accurate and current. If the counselor does not really know about that which is requested or needed, to pretend that he knows and to "gloss over" the facts to the counselee constitutes unethical practice. Misunderstandings can easily become compounded. Then, as Schwebel (1962, p. 601) observes, "To the client it is little comfort to learn that the professional blunders may have been due primarily to ignorance." Some of these confusions stemming from ignorance may have seemed initially quite inconsequential to the counselor. Nevertheless, they were closely related to and in violation of principles defined in both the APA code (1953, p. 44) and the APGA code (1961, Sec. B., #6) which state that it is not ethical for the counselor to function either "beyond the boundaries of his competence" or "when he cannot be of professional assistance because of personal limitation."

Other "personal limitations" may make it hazardous for the counselor to continue the counseling interaction. Maybe at some point during counseling, let us say, a counselor senses an unaccustomed tenseness and a general feeling of anxiety. As he tries to understand the cause, he may become partially and uncomfortably aware that some of the counselee's problems are also his own. Is he then able to continue serving the counselee? Ethically, what is his responsibility? If he does continue the relationship, he should be aware of the risks and hazards likely to result. Although the following example is a clinical one contributed by a psychiatrist (Ruesch, 1961, p. 224), it undoubtedly has a general relevance to other counseling settings as well:

A phobic patient who works with a doctor who is basically a somewhat phobic character may at first make rapid progress, only to bog down completely later on.

So, should the counselor feel confused or upset in the relationship, it should be a signal to him that his own needs require attention. Schwebel (1955, p. 258) comments:

The difficulty is compounded when the counselor cannot identify the cause of his uneasiness. The client is in a hopeless position when the counselor defends himself against anxiety by becoming hostile. These dangers and difficulties can be averted in large part when the counselor has become aware of his motives and biases through studied appraisal of himself, personal counseling, or psychoanalysis, and when he works for some time under the supervision of a competent person.

The APA code (1953, p. 3) also objectively defines the counselor's obligations in this regard:

> A psychologist engaged in clinical or consulting work where sound interpersonal relationships are essential to effective endeavor, should be aware of the inadequacies in his own personality which may bias his appraisal of others, or distort his relationships with them, and should refrain from undertaking any activity where his personal limitations are likely to result in inferior professional services.

In summary, the counselor's role is a difficult one. Inevitably, and from time to time, various ethical confusions will arise. Each recurrent dilemma presents its own unique and complex hazards.

Basically, the counselor needs to avoid the hazard of being uninformed, of not thoroughly and functionally understanding the professional codes. He needs also to avoid acting too hastily. When an ethical situation is unclear and complex, the counselor may have to wrestle cognitively with the issues involved. He will need to sort them through in his mind and realize their interrelationships as clearly as possible.

But in the real test of follow-through action, there are no specifics. The route to responsible moral behavior probably always will remain somewhat lonely and uncharted. The counselor has to be guided by his own highest allegiances. Constant to the ideal of doing what he truly believes to be the right course of action to the extent that he can understand it, he gives an "obedience to the unenforceable" and steers himself past any ethical confusions he may encounter.

Periods of Crisis

A psychological crisis must be defined in terms of the person who experiences it. To someone else, the situation may not objectively appear traumatic. But what really matters is the meaning of what has happened, as it is perceived by the person involved. It is a crisis period for him when he feels at a complete loss as to what to do or how to cope. When events in his world, as he sees them, are completely out of hand, it is a crisis.

NATURE AND TYPES OF CRISES

Tyler (1969, p. 31) considers these periods of personal disruption as resulting from a breakdown of the individual's "psychological structures." Normally, from developed learnings, a person "steers his course through his own possibility world" fairly well. His habits, defenses, motives, and perceptions serve as useful and practical guides. But sudden and unexpected changes, especially in the areas of work, interpersonal relationships, or the ability to stand alone may throw him into confusion. He feels unable to go on as usual. He is experiencing a state of crisis.

These feelings of confusion, anxiety, and psychic disorganization are generally common to all crisis periods. The person feels stopped and stymied until he again can get himself "pulled together." Allport (1969, p. 298) gives this description:

> The life of the past and the life of the future seem suddenly to be at cross purposes. There is often an intolerable feeling of suspended animation. Recrystalization is not yet possible.

But there are differences in the degree of the disruptions experienced, as well as differences in their felt urgencies. When Louise, a college sophomore who has been confidently expecting a bid from a certain sorority, suddenly realizes it isn't coming through, or when John, who has been working earnestly and enthusiastically on his first research paper gets it back from his high school history teacher with a large "D" on it, only Louise and John understand their respective degrees of personal crisis. However, it is obvious that some crises are of such magnitude and urgency that they can hardly be misinterpreted. If Louise's parent were suddenly killed in a car accident, the help needed for her shock and psychological disorganization would be fully and immediately realized.

Some periods of crisis are far slower in their development, and because of their cumulative nature, they may be considerably harder to recognize. The person may have been carrying a number of unresolved conflicts and inner tensions for a considerable length of time. Finally there comes that last added straw which is just too much. Underneath, the pressures have been building up; now something happens which triggers the situation. A crisis point is reached.

CULTURALLY PRECIPITATED CRISES

As he talked with the counselor, the young man's face was tight and drawn. He looked and sounded defeated: "My draft papers came yesterday. Ruby and I were going to get married this summer, and then I was going on to school in the fall. . . ."

Young men of draft age are not the only ones who experience personal crises because of the times. No age group really is exempt, nor is war the only current crisis. The stepped-up use of drugs, racial confrontations and conflicts, relentless competitions, fuzzy "situational" ethics, ideational confusions — the list could go on much further. We may think of these serious problems as being "collective" or "social," which helps to blunt our awareness that within them all are agonizing individual crises and confusions. These "social problems" acutely heighten the frenzied search of many individual persons, as they grope for lost meanings or as they struggle to find identity or relationships or security. For some, even children, the pressures of the "rat race" are felt keenly. Others may be bewildered or in despair due to the behavior of loved ones. Consider these examples:

Mrs. W was crying. "Not Ann! Not our Ann! When the letter came that she was going to be suspended from high school because of being in this group involved with drugs, John and I couldn't believe it! We still can't!"

Tommy, age nine, was silent. He kept sullenly staring out of the window. Finally he turned to face the counselor and spoke angrily: "Well, sure. I copied his test paper! All the kids do it. And . . . and besides, if I don't pass, my dad would . . ." Tommy broke off his last words, and tried hard not to cry.

Joan's eyes looked tired, and far older than those of a nineteen-year-old girl. She spoke slowly to the counselor. "I guess I feel kind of loose, and like . . . well, as if there aren't any meanings left any more. I used to go to church, but I don't now. Probably it's like they say — God is dead. But now, when I can't pray and things bad like this are happening . . ."

In short, in today's maximally permissive yet turbulent societal context, there is much to render both the meaning of the person and his purpose unclear. Frankl (1967, p. 121) believes "there are people — and this is more manifest today than ever — who consider their life meaningless, who can see no meaning in their existence and therefore think it is valueless." It is under these conditions that personal despair and crises are born and develop.

RECIPROCAL RESPONSES TO THREAT

These, then, are some of the types of personal crises which find a focus in the counseling office. At these times of emergency, are there special hazards for both counselor and counselee in their relationship?

The counselee is sensitized. His anxiety level is very high. He may tend to overrespond to whatever the counselor says to him. And as he exposes his acute situation, he is very tuned in as to whether the counselor will be shocked or show him any less acceptance. More than ever before, his need is to know with confidence that the counselor cares, keeps on caring, and truly understands.

At such times, almost all of the other hazards for the counselor of which we have spoken are especially applicable and important to avoid. The counselor must be alert and sensitive to what it is the counselee is now trying to tell him. He needs to concentrate and "stay with" him; the pacing of their interaction takes on an added significance. And there is no latitude whatsoever for the counselor to intellectualize or to hand out quick external solutions. The relationship now must be one in which the counselee's perturbed communications do "connect" and "get through." If they do not, the crisis situation for both counselor and counselee will mount. The counselee will feel more anxious, and the counselor will be groping to reach him.

If the counselee is experiencing a real crisis period, there is the hazard that the counselor may overidentify with him emotionally. But at such times there is an added need for calm and stability on the part of the counselor. The more anxious and incongruent the counselee becomes, the more necessary it is that the counselor remain stable and congruent. Psychiatrists understand this balance very well. Ruesch (1961, p. 393) explains:

> In acute anxiety and panic, the knowledge that other persons are not disorganized . . . reduces, through negative feedback, the anxiety of the anxious patient.

It is important that the counselor recognize the nature of the particular actual or approaching crisis as it has meaning for the counselee. Is it a "short-term" disorganization? Or is it a culminating development? How acute and urgent is the present situation? What are the dynamics — in other words, what really is happening here? To be attentive to and understand the meaning of the signs as clearly as possible is the responsibility of the counselor. For only in this way can he give genuine support to the counselee.

The possibility that the counselor will not be able to offer this perceptive depth of empathic understanding at a time when it is most needed by the counselee is a hazard which cannot be averted lightly or immediately. The responses which the counselor gives cannot be "techniqued"; they must come from the person of the counselor himself, from what he is and has become. The counseling interaction must be real. How has the counselor grappled with his own personal pressures and crises? If he is not an *involved* person, if he tends when possible to theorize or escape more than to experience directly and live through whatever it is that happens, he will be found wanting probably in just that measure, when help from him may be quite desperately sought. Carkhuff and Berenson (1967, p. 147) speak clearly here:

> There are no rules for responding at the crisis, no techniques, no rituals. The therapist simply has to "be" to experience the moment and stand the tests. The effective therapist responds most honestly from the deepest wells within him.

We have spoken of the pressures and tensions arising from the complex problems and conflicts of our present society.

Of course as a person, the counselor is not himself immune to them, but it is also hazardous for him in his role as a counselor to fail to be a sensitive observer of the broader social scene. He needs to be very aware of what is happening locally, in his state, in the nation, in the world. (And now, in outer space as well!) He needs to think of these events realistically and empathically with respect to their meanings and implications for students and other persons. In a recent paper expressing some of his views, a graduate student made a plea for this type of awareness:

> Stop and think of the pressures and demands students are being faced with. They have to worry about crowded conditions, confusion of values and many other problems in our jet-pace age. The former and latter make it hard for students to find themselves, to know who and what and why they are, and to understand their relationship to the universe. Students appear to feel somewhat fragmented and purposeless (Graham, 1969).

Hiltner (1952, p. 175) understands the counselor's responsibility for this thoughtful consideration of what is socially relevant:

> It is my belief that our counseling will be more realistic, more helpful, more compassionate and more alert to individuality if its function and its methods are thought out in relation to our more general perspective on the diseases of the time.

THE CRISIS AS OPPORTUNITY

In a sense, whenever a counselee comes for assistance with his personal problems, it represents some form of crisis period for him. His "incongruence" is revealed as being strong enough to motivate him to seek help. The problems he brings may not appear crucial *per se*. But what really matters — and it is indeed a hazard if the counselor fails to discover it— is what he feels these problems are now doing to him. He may be quite desperately struggling to establish and confirm himself as the person he feels himself to be. But he feels confused and blocked. Can he find help if he risks relating with a counselor? Nygreen (1969, p. 292) sees the dilemma as it applies to the adolescent counselee as a struggle between "liberty" and "order":

> ... the counselee in coming to the counselor is uttering a cry for help. His coming represents in some way an awareness that he is unable to reconcile the requirements of liberty and order. He wants to exercise his individuality, to realize himself as a person, to develop an identity meaningful, first to him and then to others. He perceives the social order as denying this to him, as forcing him to accept an imposed order, of requiring conformity as the price of existence. What the counselee may expect to find in the counselor and what he wants to find may be in sharp contrast.

For both counselor and counselee, any period of crisis, because of its climatic nature, holds both risk and opportunity. There is no status quo. Depending on what happens in the counselor-counselee interaction the counselee could now go either forward or backward. The risks and opportunities are sharpened in proportion to the extent to which the counselee presently feels he is at a psychological crossroads. As nonessentials are cleared, Carkhuff and Berenson (1967, p. 148) understand that now "the client seeks his more full emergence or re-emergence, or life, at the risk of death."

In a period of stress or transition, new modes of adjustment are demanded. With the help of a steady counselor, the counselee may be able progressively to organize a new synthesis of meanings. A time of crisis may enable a counselee to change more readily than at any other period. The possibility of future positive growth exists, if the painful realities of any present trauma for the counselee are realistically explored and dealt with by both partners of the relationship. Here is the opportunity.

But there are many hazards, any of which could block such a positive outcome. The latent opportunities for growth, present in the crisis, could be entirely missed through a loss of perspective. What a hazard it is for the counselee when his counselor does not see or really believe that he can grow and change from this experience! The opportunity can also be lost because of subtle hazards. A "well-meaning" counselor might easily slip into the role of just being one who comforts and soothes, who advises, or helps to gloss over the painful facts as they now really are.

The crisis periods in counseling must be shared and faced. Out of them *can* come important new learnings for both the counselor and the counselee. The developmental process for each of them can be deepened and enriched.

8

About Termination

*Terminat-
ing*

Termination of the counseling relationship is really a commencement. In effect, the counselee and the counselor have agreed that the counselee is ready to function on his own. He will begin, unaided, to shape his own future again, utilizing his new insights and understandings concerning himself and his environment.

But even as counselor and counselee move through the final stage of their relationship, difficulties may present themselves. Eagerness for closure on the part of either counselor or counselee, for example, may result in premature termination. Too early a termination may leave the counselee uncertain about how to get on with the business of his life. Or it may afford the counselor a momentary feeling of accomplishment only to be replaced by considerable doubt as to what has been achieved. On the other hand, reluctance on the part of either counselor or counselee to terminate the relationship may place them in a position of unnecessarily prolonging the final stage, a hazard discussed in Chapter 7.

Another major potential hazard

associated with termination issues from the counselor's neglect to make sure that the counselee is committed to continued effort. Without such assurance, the benefits to be derived from counseling are largely lost. In the security of the counseling room, the counselee may feel certain of his future course and commit himself to it. But verbal commitment is often much easier than behavioral commitment. Often unanticipated obstacles develop that make living the commitment far more difficult than the counselee imagined. As mentioned in Chapter 4, the counselee may find himself unable or unwilling to make the effort necessary to behave in accordance with his stated desires. The counselor must be aware of this hazard and attempt to provide a means of circumventing it.

It must be clear throughout counseling that when the counselee makes a commitment to change his actions or behavior in the future, he makes it to himself, for himself, and not for the counselor. Doing something "for the counselor" merely engenders dependency and plants the seeds of guilt, should the counselee be unable to carry through.

Whether the counseling relationship is moving toward termination because the counselee feels ready to work out his own destiny without counseling, or because the school year is ending, or because the counselee is leaving the geographical area — or for whatever reason — the counselor has certain obligations. During the final stage, the counselor needs to guard against leaving the counselee feeling rejected or abandoned. He must let the counselee know that the door is open for future counseling — with him or with another counselor. At the same time, the counselor must help the counselee gather the momentum to carry him through the difficult period that sometimes comes when the "glow" begins to wear off and the counselee's self-confidence is shaken.

It is appropriate during the ending stage for counselor and counselee to consider the counseling experience in terms of what has happened. So that the counselee may gain a final perspective about himself and his experiences, it is helpful to review the counselee's purpose for seeking counseling, to look back upon the process through which he has come, and to consider some ways in which he may proceed. Encouraging the counselee to engage in retrospection in the final stage, to summarize and react to the experience, leads to integration of sometimes seemingly unrelated pieces. It permits the counselee to see this experience as a dynamic process with possibilities for ongoing action with continuing benefits. Thus termination of counseling may be seen by the counselee as a beginning with opportunities not previously available to him.

In Retrospect

In summary, our attempt in this book has been to call attention to a number of commonly occurring situations and factors which could impede the purposes of counseling. We are presuming that a majority of counselors are willing — hopefully, even motivated — to consider all of the functional aspects of counseling which affect the relationship, including those which detract from it.

Because it can be tricky and difficult for a counselor to evaluate his actual role objectively, we have discussed problems of role understanding and role limitations. Although nominally the person may be a "counselor," realistically he could be functioning also in roles of administrator, parent substitute, preacher, or pal, to the considerable detriment of his counselees. The basic key to avoiding all such inappropriate role assumptions and role proliferations would appear to be an adherence to central professional commitment, coupled with an honest and open self-understanding. The counselor who dons many hats does so partially because he wants them. If he is functioning under very negative time and space conditions, he could well have passively submitted to them, to some extent at least.

The counselor needs a clearly formulated philosophical base from which to operate, if he is to have some order and direction in his counseling and understand what happens. Many barriers and hazards can be avoided altogether if he adheres to certain theoretical guidelines. However, no counselor can afford to be encysted in outlook, limited by his own past experience and frame of reference. To avoid engaging in stereotypy and making narrow judgmental contrasts concerning observed behaviors, it is essential that he be open to and aware of change.

Counselors can easily fail to assess many of the emotional

components involved in counselee resistance to counseling. Whether he comes by referral, or possibly reluctantly from his own initiative, his inner barriers to involvement need to be accepted and understood by the counselor. Preconceptions and fears that others in addition to the counselor may learn about his painful personal problems can heighten his instability and feed his defenses. Manipulative behaviors are common, and the counselor needs to realize empathically why they occur and deal with them therapeutically. A continued "unconditional regard" for the counselee may frequently not be easy to maintain, but it is a *sine qua non* if the counselee is to learn to make sound and realistic decisions, begin to follow them through, and gain gradually in feelings of self-worth and self-respect.

Virtually without exception, counselors would agree that their primary responsibility is to focus upon the problems of the counselee; however, certain realistic and subtle complexities frequently cause them to function differently. Fatigue can blunt the counselor's sensitivity, for example. Externalizing or intellectualizing painful and unpleasant counselee dilemmas may meet counselor needs, but evades those of the counselee. If the counselor is to overcome such obstacles, he must first recognize them. Then, in Hiltner's words, he must "take the pain of the insight," acting accordingly.

The counseling relationship itself contains other potentially disruptive elements. Counselor-counselee interaction may be strongly affected by the prior conditionings and response generalizations of the counselee, as he reacts to the sex, age, and unique temperament of the counselor. Occasionally, the personality conflicts may be real. The counselor, however, should be able to work perceptively through most of these difficulties; the clashes need understanding and may prove to be temporary. He should be wary of too quickly and too frequently relying upon referral.

Essentially, the counseling process is one of verbal interchange. If the counselor uses words which arouse emotional or defensive reactions from the counselee, or words not geared to the counselee's understanding, communicative blocks quickly appear. The counselor also must understand and take responsibility for the temporal dimensions of their communication. Their dialogue should be *paced*, so that they move together in understanding. In addition, the counselee may need supportive assistance not to move into deeper problem levels prematurely.

Communicative hazards are also present when test results are interpreted. The counselor needs to be sensitive and tolerant of the ego-involvement of the counselee in this regard, recognizing that test scores often involve real threat. The counselee may need an opportunity to fully vent conflicted reactions.

On occasion, the counselor may be confronted with knotty ethical questions and dilemmas within the counseling relationship. No simple generalizations can of course suffice, as a perceptive analysis of what is involved in each unique situation is necessary. However, the counselor must be well grounded in the Professional Code principles, and he also is well advised not to act hastily.

Finally, in periods of crisis for the counselee, the counselor must take care lest he overidentify emotionally. He needs also to recognize that a crisis can be an opportunity for reorganizing meanings into a new and more constructive synthesis for the counselee.

A Last Word

We now bring our relationship to a close. It is hoped that the reader has not developed an overly negative orientation regarding potential sources of jeopardy in counseling. The intention has never been to create anxiety. The goal has been, rather, to provide some signs, to establish some checkpoints, so that the counselor, being alerted, may with more confidence chart his course between the Scylla and Charybdis of counseling.

In the process, an attempt has been made to give the counselor a greater awareness of himself, of his counselees, past, present, and future, and of his potential as an interacting member of the counseling relationship. The purpose also has been to generate a sufficient quantity of dissonance within the counselor. Dissonance serves as a motivational force. Perhaps for the counselor it will be the catalyst that moves him along in that unending quest for deeper insights as, in his openness to experience, he continues to strive, to revise, to change, to become.

It is hoped too that in some small way this volume has helped better equip the counselor to do what he must do. For, in the final analysis, each individual must extract from what he hears, and sees, and reads, and experiences, the bits and pieces that fit him best. He must select for himself, on the basis of his own judgment, that which is most appropriate for him. And, having made his selection, it is his responsibility to integrate the parts into a whole. For his personal and professional growth, the counselor will be dependent upon his own knowledge and wisdom.

Finally, we wish the counselor well on this high adventure of learning and growing empathically with his counselees. For the ever-present challenge of the complex art of counseling is the achievement of an increasingly compassionate understanding of the human condition.

REFERENCES

ALLPORT, GORDON W. "Crises in Normal Personality Development," pp. 295–303 in *The Young Adult*, ed. G. D. Winter and E. N. Nuss. Glenville, Ill.: Scott, Foresman, 1969.

AMERICAN PERSONNEL AND GUIDANCE ASSOCIATION. "Ethical Standards," *Personnel and Guidance Journal*, 40 (October, 1961), 206–209.

AMERICAN SCHOOL COUNSELOR ASSOCIATION. *Statement of Policy for Secondary School Counselors*. Washington, D.C.: American Personnel and Guidance Association, 1964.

ARBUCKLE, DUGALD S. *Counseling: An Introduction*. Boston: Allyn & Bacon, 1961.

BARCLAY, JAMES R. *Counseling and Philosophy: A Theoretical Exposition*. Guidance Monograph Series. Boston: Houghton Mifflin, 1968.

BATES, MARILYN, AND CLARENCE D. JOHNSON. "The Existentialist Counselor at Work," *The School Counselor*, 16 (March, 1969), 245–250.

BECK, CARLTON E. *Philosophical Foundations of Guidance*. Englewood Cliffs, N.J.: Prentice-Hall, 1963.

BENJAMIN, ALFRED. *The Helping Interview*. Boston: Houghton Mifflin, 1969.

BETTELHEIM, BRUNO. "Autonomy and Inner Freedom: Skills of Emotional Management," pp. 73–94 in *Life Skills in School and Society*, ed. Louis J. Rubin. 1969 ASCD Yearbook. Washington, D.C.: Association for Supervision and Curriculum Development, 1969.

BLOCHER, DONALD H. *Developmental Counseling*. New York: Ronald Press, 1966.

BRAMMER, LAWRENCE M., AND EVERETT L. SHOSTROM. *Therapeutic Psychology*, 2d ed. Englewood Cliffs, N.J.: Prentice-Hall, 1968.

BUCHHEIMER, ARNOLD, AND SARA CARTER BALOGH. *The Counseling Relationship: A Casebook*. Chicago: Science Research Associates, 1961.

CARKHUFF, ROBERT R., AND BERNARD G. BERENSON. *Beyond Counseling and Therapy*. New York: Holt, Rinehart and Winston, 1967.

CLOAK, F. T., JR. "Reach Out or Die Out," *Educational Leadership*, 26 (April, 1969), 661–665.

COMMITTEE ON ETHICAL STANDARDS. *Ethical Standards for Psychologists*. Washington, D.C.: American Psychological Association, 1953.

COUSINS, NORMAN. "Are You Making Yourself Clear?" *Saturday Review* (February 22, 1969), 30–32.

D'EVELYN, KATHERINE. *Meeting Children's Emotional Needs*. Englewood Cliffs, N.J.: Prentice-Hall, 1957.

DUGAN, WILLIS E. "Guidance in the 1970's," *The School Counselor*, 10 (March, 1963), 96–100.

FITTS, WILLIAM H. *The Experience of Psychotherapy*. Princeton, N.J.: D. Van Nostrand, 1965.

FRANKL, VIKTOR E. *Psychotherapy and Existentialism: Selected Papers on Logotherapy.* New York: Washington Square Press, 1967.

FULLMER, DANIEL W., AND HAROLD W. BERNARD. *Counseling: Content and Process.* Chicago: Science Research Associates, 1964.

GRAHAM, DOUGLAS. "My Philosophy of Counseling." Unpublished paper, 1969.

GRANBERG, L. I. "What I've Learned in Counseling," *Christianity Today*, 2 (June 9, 1967), 891–894.

HALL, EDWARD T. *The Silent Language.* New York: Fawcett, 1959.

HILTNER, SEWARD. *The Counselor in Counseling.* Nashville, Tenn.: Abingdon Press, 1952.

HOBBS, NICHOLAS. "A New Cosmology," pp. 114–125 in *Sources of Gain in Counseling and Psychotherapy*, ed. Bernard G. Berenson and Robert R. Carkhuff. New York: Holt, Rinehart and Winston, 1967.

JERSILD, ARTHUR T. *The Psychology of Adolescence*, 2d ed. New York: Macmillan, 1963.

JOHNSON, PAUL E. *Person and Counselor.* Nashville, Tenn.: Abingdon Press, 1967.

JOURARD, S. M. *Disclosing Man to Himself.* Princeton, N.J.: D. Van Nostrand, 1968.

KAGAN, NORMAN. "Three Dimensions of Counselor Encapsulation," *Journal of Counseling Psychology*, 11 (Winter, 1964), 361–365.

KELL, BILL L., AND WILLIAM J. MUELLER. *Impact and Change: A Study of Counseling Relationships.* New York: Appleton-Century-Crofts, 1966.

KEMP, C. GRATTON. *Intangibles in Counseling.* Boston: Houghton Mifflin, 1967.

LOWE, C. MARSHALL. "Value Orientations—An Ethical Dilemma," pp. 119–127 in *Counseling: Readings in Theory and Practice*, ed. John F. McGowan and Lyle D. Schmidt. New York: Holt, Rinehart and Winston, 1962.

McKINNEY, FRED. *Counseling for Personal Adjustment.* Boston: Houghton Mifflin, 1958.

NICHOLS, RALPH G., AND LEONARD A. STEVENS. *Are You Listening?* New York: McGraw-Hill, 1957.

NYGREEN, G. T. "Counseling Adolescents," pp. 290–294 in *The Young Adult*, ed. G. D. Winter and E. M. Nuss. Glenville, Ill.: Scott, Foresman, 1969.

OHLSEN, MERLE M. *Guidance: An Introduction.* New York: Harcourt, Brace & World, 1955.

———. *Guidance Services in the Modern School.* New York: Harcourt, Brace & World, 1964.

PATTERSON, C. H. *Counseling and Psychotherapy: Theory and Practice.* New York: Harper & Row, 1959.

———. "The Place of Values in Counseling and Psychotherapy," pp. 145–155 in *Counseling: Reading in Theory and Practice*, ed. John F. McGowan and Lyle D. Schmidt. New York: Holt, Rinehart and Winston, 1962.

―――. *Theories of Counseling and Psychotherapy.* New York: Harper & Row, 1966.

PEREZ, JOSEPH FRANCIS. *Counseling: Theory and Practice.* Reading, Mass.: Addison-Wesley, 1965.

ROGERS, CARL R. "The Interpersonal Relationship: The Core of Guidance," *Harvard Educational Review,* 32 (Fall, 1962), 416–429.

RUBIN, LOUIS J., ed. *Life Skills in School and Society.* 1969 ASCD Yearbook. Washington, D.C.: Association for Supervision and Curriculum Development, NEA, 1969.

RUESCH, JURGEN. *Therapeutic Communication.* New York: W. W. Norton, 1961.

SACHS, BENJAMIN M. *The Student, the Interview, and the Curriculum: Dynamics of Counseling in the School.* Boston: Houghton Mifflin, 1966.

SAMLER, JOSEPH. "Change in Values: A Goal in Counseling," pp. 129–137 in *Counseling Readings in Theory and Practice,* ed. John F. McGowan and Lyle D. Schmidt. New York: Holt, Rinehart and Winston, 1962.

SCHOFIELD, WILLIAM. "Some General Factors in Counseling and Therapy," pp. 137–146 in *Sources of Gain in Counseling and Psychotherapy,* ed. Bernard C. Berenson and Robert R. Carkhuff. New York: Holt, Rinehart and Winston, 1967.

SCHWEBEL, MILTON. "Some Ethical Problems in Counseling," *Personnel and Guidance Journal,* 33 (January, 1955), 254–259.

―――. "Why? Unethical Practice," pp. 597–603 in *Counseling: Readings in Theory and Practice,* ed. John F. McGowan and Lyle D. Schmidt. New York: Holt, Rinehart and Winston, 1962.

SECHREST, CAROLYN A. *New Dimensions in Counseling Students: A Case Approach.* New York: Bureau of Publications, Teachers College, Columbia University, 1958.

SEELEY, JOHN R. "Some Skills of Being for Those in Service of Their Education," pp. 111–129 in *Life Skills in School and Society,* ed. Louis J. Rubin. 1969 ASCD Yearbook. Washington, D.C.: Association for Supervision and Curriculum Development, NEA, 1969.

SHAFFER, LAURANCE F., AND EDWARD J. SHOBEN, JR. "Common Aspects of Psychotherapy," pp. 63–70 in *Sources of Gain in Counseling and Psychotherapy,* ed. Bernard G. Berenson and Robert R. Carkhuff. New York: Holt, Rinehart and Winston, 1967.

SHERTZER, BRUCE, AND SHELLEY C. STONE. *Fundamentals of Counseling.* Boston: Houghton Mifflin, 1968.

―――. "The School Counselor and His Publics: A Problem in Role Definition," *Personnel and Guidance Journal,* 41 (April, 1963), 687–693.

SHOSTROM, EVERETT L. *Man, the Manipulator.* New York: Bantam Books, 1968.

STEFFLRE, BUFORD, ed. *Theories of Counseling.* New York: McGraw-Hill, 1965.

TYLER, LEONA E. "Minimum-Change Therapy," *Personnel and Guidance Journal*, 38 (February, 1960), 475–479.

———. *The Work of the Counselor*, 2d ed. New York: Appleton-Century-Crofts, 1961.

———. *The Work of the Counselor*, 3d ed. New York: Appleton-Century-Crofts, 1969.

WERTZ, HENRY. "Counseling as a Function of the Counselor's Personality," *Personnel and Guidance Journal*, 35 (January, 1957), 276–280.

WRENN, C. GILBERT. *The Counselor in a Changing World*. Washington, D.C.: American Personnel and Guidance Association, 1962a.

———. "The Culturally Encapsulated Counselor," pp. 214–244 in *Guidance: An Examination*, ed. Ralph L. Mosher, Richard F. Carle, and Chris D. Kehas. New York: Harcourt, Brace & World, 1965a.

———. "Editor's Introduction," pp. vii–viii in *Group Counseling in the Schools*, by Clarence A. Mahler. Boston: Houghton Mifflin, 1969.

———. "The Ethics of Counseling," *Education and Psychological Measurement*, 12 (Summer, 1952), 161–177. Also pp. 171–186 in *Counseling and Psychotherapy: Classics on Theories and Issues*, by Ben N. Ard, Jr. Palo Alto, Calif.: Science and Behavior Books, 1966.

———. "The Fault, Dear Brutus ———," pp. 561–572 in *Counseling: Readings in Theory and Practice*, ed. John F. McGowan and Lyle D. Schmidt. New York: Holt, Rinehart and Winston, 1962b.

———. "A Second Look," pp. 53–66 in *Counseling, A Growing Profession*, ed. John W. Loughary. Washington, D.C.: American Personnel and Guidance Association, 1965b.

APPENDIX A
Cases For Discussion and Development*

The cases that follow illustrate various "crises" or problems counselors might experience. For each case, questions are posed for discussion, with the possibility of further development by means of role playing. Several types of problems are represented. Note the potential hazards and barriers inherent in each situation.

1. Problems resulting from
   (a) lack of technical or professional knowledge, or
   (b) one's own values.
2. Problems resulting from poor judgment or unfamiliarity with a particular situation.
3. Problems resulting from excessive self-interest on the part of the counselor, involving such matters as (a) profit motive, (b) self-enhancement, or (c) security and/or status needs.
4. Problems resulting from overwork, i.e., becoming insensitive, perhaps hostile, because of too much sustained exposure to human problems.

Case 1

A counselee expresses feelings and values that are contrary to those of the counselor. The counselor recognizes that some hostility and resentment toward the counselee is developing. The counselor can refer the counselee to someone else, but this is only a temporary reprieve.

Should the counselor refer the counselee or should he work out his feelings as he continues to counsel this individual? What are the implications for the counselor in either case?

What can the counselor do about his own feelings toward those that do not fit his "mold"?

Case 2

A counselee (a female college senior) informs the counselor that a professional colleague is behaving in an unprofessional and unethical manner.

Should the counselor initiate an investigation of the possibility on the basis of this information? How should he proceed?

Should the counselor discount the counselee's report? Why or why not?

* The cases and questions in this section were provided by David Redfering, a doctoral student in Counseling and Guidance at Ball State University. Some of the situations are based on personal experience and some are hypothetical.

Should the counselor confront his colleague? If so, how should he approach his colleague?

Should he report it to the professional organization? What are some of the implications of such an action?

CASE 3

The counselor has a maximum work load but feels obligated to accept additional cases, even though it interferes with his evenings and weekends. He feels growing resentment toward his counselees' infringement on his time. He considers dropping some of his cases (no referral resources are available) but is reluctant to do so.

What should the counselor do?

What professional and/or ethical responsibilities does a counselor have with regard to counselee load?

CASE 4

The counselor is becoming discouraged by the lack of progress with a counselee over a long period of time. The counseling relationship has been marked by ever increasing complexities of human behavior. The counselor begins to resent having to counsel this counselee. The counselor wants to terminate; the counselee feels rejected.

What is happening here?

Are the counselor's needs and expectations becoming more important than the counselee's needs? If so, what can he do about it?

What obligation does the counselor have to the counselee with regard to continuing the counseling relationship?

Is a referral in order? Why or why not?

What professional responsibility does the counselor have to himself in this case?

CASE 5

The female counselor is a close friend of the counselee's (a high school freshman girl) parents. Knowing this, a colleague reveals to the counselor some shocking facts about the girl, saying, "You'd better do something about this before it gets out of hand."

Should the counselor disregard the information or view it as untrue? What if the information involves unlawful activity? Immoral activity?

Should the counselor confront the girl with the facts?

Should the counselor go, instead, to the parents with this information?

What should the counselor do?

CASE 6

A male counselor is experiencing excessive positive transfer toward an attractive female counselee. The possibility of a romantic attachment is present.

Should he refer the case?

Should he express his feelings to the counselee?

What should he do if the counselee's problem is relatively severe and she refuses to see another professional person?

Should he continue the relationship but with increased awareness of his feelings? If so, can he be objective?

Which one is "counseling" the other?

CASE 7

The counselee, a high school senior, faces serious problems in the home situation involving unnatural advances by her father. The male school counselor feels it necessary to intervene and defend the counselee. The parents object to the school's attempt to tell them how to run their family. The counselor has committed himself to "helping" the counselee with an apparently insoluble situational problem.

Did the counselor make a mistake by intervening with the parents? Why or why not?

What might he have done instead?

What are some alternatives open to him?

What impact will the counselor's actions have upon the counselee?

CASE 8

A teacher requests the counselor to speak with a ten-year-old boy in her class. She is concerned about his erratic attendance pattern and has heard that the boy's home environment is deteriorating. The parents were divorced about two years ago. The boy and his twelve-year-old sister are living with their mother, whose behavior is extremely unstable. From counseling interviews with the boy, the counselor learns that among other things the mother disappears from the home for several days at a time, leaving the children without food or money. The father maintains a small apartment in the same city, but is frequently out of town on business. During the mother's absences, the father—if he is in town—provides food and money for the children and often keeps them at his apartment.

What is the counselor's responsibility to the boy?

Should he counsel the older sister? The mother? The father? What implications are there for the counselor's relationship with the boy if the counselor works also with the sister, the mother, and the father?

What responsibility does the counselor have to the teacher who referred the boy?

CASE 9

The mother of an eight-year-old boy asks the counselor, who is a close family friend, to talk with her son. The boy's behavior has changed recently, and the parents are concerned. During the counseling interview, the boy reveals conflict between his parents and reports that he has seen his mother kissing another man. The counselee says that his mother does not know he saw this, and says, "Please don't tell my mom what I told you, not anything. She'd be awful mad at me." The next day, the mother phones the counselor for a report of the interview.

Should the counselor ignore the child's request and tell the mother the problem? (As the person who referred the boy, the mother is entitled to some report.)

What is the counselor's responsibility to the counselee?

How might being a close family friend influence the way the counselor works with this case?

CASE 10

The counselor feels that one of his cases is an extremely challenging one and is not certain of his competency in handling it. He realizes that a referral is warranted but does not want to admit that he may not possess the professional knowledge and skill needed to deal with the case.

Should the counselor continue in order to learn of his limitations? Why or why not?

If the counselor decides to continue, what are some possible outcomes? For the counselor? For the counselee?

CASE 11

A counselor at a trade school is evaluating a man referred by the Vocational Rehabilitation Office. The individual is uneducated and unskilled; his work experience has been limited to manual labor. His family is dependent upon him, and until a year ago he managed to support the family in a meager but adequate manner. At that time he suffered a heart attack and has not worked since. He must restrict himself to jobs requiring only a minimum of physical effort. The months of inactivity and dependence on the family are jeopardizing his emotional well-being. The counselor administers a battery of psychological tests and discovers that the man's test scores are not high enough to qualify him for rehabilitative training.

Should the counselor accept the test scores and recommend "no training"?

Should the counselor "fudge" on the test scores so that the man can qualify for rehabilitative training?

What is the relative importance of the test scores as opposed to the welfare of the man?

How much reliance should be placed on test scores? On motivation?

If the counselor decides to recommend the man for training, how would he justify this decision?

CASE 12

The counselor is caught up in the "halo effect." The counselee has appeared as the ideal type of student and person, but is now expressing strong feelings of inadequacy and incompetence. The counselor sees the counselee in the light of his past perceptions of him and attempts to minimize the intensity of the counselee's feelings. The counselee finally lets the counselor have it with both barrels, insisting that he (the counselee) exists under a tremendous amount of pressure to perpetuate the image of the typically "carefree and happy youth." The counselee is considering some "changes" that will relieve the pressure but will possibly develop some behaviors which he would find "undesirable."

How can the counselor communicate to the counselee that he accepts and understands his predicament without giving the impression that he is encouraging "undesirable" changes?

Should the counselor encourage the counselee to continue as he is? On what basis can the counselor justify this reaction? What approach should the counselor take?

Should the counselor encourage the counselee to "do his own thing"? Why or why not?

APPENDIX B
Suggested Films and Audio Tapes

The following 16 mm. films and audio tapes are currently available for rental or purchase. They were selected for their potential value in stimulating class discussions and might be integrated with various chapters of the book. They are listed here with film information and publishers' annotations.

American Crises: Values in America—The Individual, 1964

60 min. 2 reels. sd/b & w. (#81487, $10.40. NET: Visual Aids Service, University of Illinois)

Focuses on the problem of the individual in finding a meaningful personal identity in our modern mass society with its large-scale, complex organizations. Presents interviews with a Pennsylvania farmer whose pattern of living is threatened by a gigantic river-basin development scheme, a Chicago housewife who finds her new home in a high-rise urban renewal project sterile in comparison to the friendly disarray of her former tenement neighborhood, and a New York assembly line worker who is frustrated in a job of monotonous routine. Edwin Land, president of the Polaroid Corporation, and psychologist John Kenney of Princeton, discuss the problems of the individual in a mass society.

American Crises: Values in America—The Parents, 1964

60 min. 2 reels. sd/b & w. (#81486, $10.40. NET: Visual Aids Service, University of Illinois)

Presents a documentary report on the changing problems of today's American parents. Focuses on the confusion and lack of assurance that mark the attempts of parents to find fulfillment in their own lives and in relationships with their children. Dr. Benjamin Spock and Dr. Paul Popenoe point out that if parents use their children as status symbols and as sources of identity, they are not meeting their children's need for mature and responsible parents who know who they are and can be firm models for their children.

American Crises: Values in America—The Young Americans, 1964

60 min. 2 reels. sd/b & w. (#81485, $10.40. NET: Visual Aids Service, University of Illinois)

Shows a cross-section of American youth, both the uncommitted majority and the minority who have attempted to define themselves and their beliefs. Discusses who the youth of the nation are, what they want, where they fit in, how they affect society, what they believe in, and why.

Behavioral Therapy or Client-Centered Therapy: A Dialogue Between John D. Krumboltz and C. H. Patterson, 1969

40 min. sd/b & w. ($25.00. APGA Film Series, 1607 New Hampshire Avenue, N.W., Washington, D.C.)

Two of the foremost spokesmen for varying approaches to counseling compare similarities and contrast differences in their methods, and discuss the role and function of the counselor.

Changing Attitudes Through Communication

24 min. sd/color. (Audio-Visual Centers, University of Michigan/ Michigan State University)

Developing a strategy for change to avoid resistance, tension and conflict with employees. Creating acceptance of new policies and change by persuasion. Resistance by rejection, distortion and avoidance overcome through effective communication.

Client Centered Therapy

30 min. sd/b & w. (Part I, $5.75. Audio-Visual Centers, University of Michigan/Michigan State University)

Documentary of interview between Dr. Rogers and a female graduate student, superior in scholastic achievement but perturbed about her social isolation.

Client Centered Therapy

30 min. sd/b & w. (Part II, $5.75. Audio-Visual Centers, University of Michigan/Michigan State University)

Documentary between Dr. Rogers and a client. Shows 32nd session in case of middle-aged mother experiencing conflict with husband and daughter. Summarized by Dr. Rogers; brief explanatory notes throughout.

The Contemporary Counselor, C. Gilbert Wrenn, 1969

35 min. sd/color. ($25.00. APGA Film Series, 1607 New Hampshire Avenue, N.W., Washington, D.C.)

The author of *The Counselor in a Changing World* deals with the role and function of the counselor, especially the school counselor, in an age of rapid social, economic, and technical change.

Counseling Interviews, Winter Quarter, 1964 (Egyed)

28 min. sd/b & w. ($5.50. Audio-Visual Centers, University of Michigan/Michigan State University)

High school student discusses aspirations in entering college; her personal family and educational problems; an interview with a University of Minnesota counselor.

Counseling Interviews, Winter Quarter, 1964 (Gilbert)

28 min. sd/b & w. ($5.50. Audio-Visual Centers, University of Michigan/Michigan State University)

A college student discusses some of the problems that worry her as a student and person in an interview with a University of Minnesota counselor.

Eye of the Beholder, 1953

30 min. sd/b & w. ($5.75. Audio-Visual Centers, University of Michigan/Michigan State University)

How an artist who is involved in the supposed killing of a girl appears to different witnesses. How no two people see the same thing in the same way.

Games People Play: The Practice

30 min. sd/b & w. (ES–853, $5.40. NET: Audio-Visual Center, Indiana University)

Interviews psychiatrist and author Eric Berne concerning his use of the terms "game," "script," "ego state," and others. Describes why he uses the term "transactional" rather than "interaction" to distinguish his method of analysis. Relates the problem of one of his patients to a fairy tale which he says can be used to explain the "script" which the patient is unconsciously following.

Games People Play: The Theory

30 min. sd/b & w. (ES–852, $5.40. NET: Audio-Visual Center, Indiana University)

Presents a series of interviews with Eric Berne, psychiatrist and author, during which he explains the assumptions upon which his theory of transactional analysis is based. Describes the relationship of his method of transactional analysis to the more traditional methods of psychoanalysis. Mentions games such as "RAPO" and explains their functions in his theory.

Guidance and the Role of the Counselor, E. J. Shoben, Jr., 1969

25 min. sd/color. ($25.00. APGA Film Series, 1607 New Hampshire Avenue, N.W., Washington, D.C.)

Dr. Shoben considers the nature of man, how competing values affect the counselor, counseling theory, and the role and function of the school counselor.

Interpreting Test Scores Realistically, 1961

18 min. sd/b & w. (#51122, $2.40 ETS: Visual Aids Service, University of Illinois)

Shows that standardized test scores take on meaning only as they are interpreted properly. Discusses the use of scores as only an estimate of ability, the value of percentile bands, and the necessity of comparing scores with various tables of norms.

The Task of the Listener, 1956

30 min. sd/b & w. ($5.75. NET: Audio-Visual Center, University of Michigan)

Discusses the relationship between personality and communication. Explains human behavior in terms of the self-concept. Defines self and shows how it differs from the self-concept. Illustrates the way in which the self-concept controls acceptance or rejection of a message. Stresses the importance of non-evaluative listening.

Three Approaches to Psychotherapy, 1965

2 hrs. 15 min. sd/b & w. (Available for sale or rental from Psychological Films, 205 W. 20th St., Santa Ana, Calif. 92706)

A three-part film series illustrating three distinguished approaches to psychotherapy. Film #1 is of Dr. Carl Rogers (48 min.), Film #2, Dr. Frederick Perls (32 min.), and Film #3, Dr. Albert Ellis (55 min.). Each therapist describes his system of therapy. He then demonstrates his work with a patient, "Gloria," and finally comments briefly on his interview.

AUDIO TAPES*

The Decision-Making Process: Experimental Findings and Implications

Harold Borko. 19 min. Recorded 1963. #75947.

An analysis of the major stages of the decision-making process.

Process: Organization of Psychotherapy I

Charlotte Buhler. 19 min. Recorded 1953. #75744.

An examination of the concept of psychotherapy as an organized growth process with developmental phases corresponding to human growth.

Process: Organization of Psychotherapy II

Charlotte Buhler. 21 min. Recorded 1953. #75745.

The phases and criteria of the successful psychotherapeutic process.

Process: Organization of Psychotherapy III

Charlotte Buhler. 20 min. Recorded 1953. #75746.

The criteria and characteristics of the incomplete and unsuccessful psychotherapeutic process.

The Structure of a Motive

William Fischer. 16 min. Recorded 1967. #75789.

An introductory inquiry into the various aspects of the process of motivation. The relations of motives to choices, causes, time and meaning are discussed. The orientation is eclectic.

* All audio tapes are available from McGraw-Hill Sound Seminars, McGraw-Hill Book Company.

Psychotherapy: A Socio-Cultural Perspective

Thomas S. Szasz. 23 min. Recorded 1968. #75561.

Examines the triangular psychotherapeutic relationship involving therapist, client, and society.

Ten Commandments of Meaningful Communication

William C. Wester. 23 min. Recorded 1968. #75513.

An examination of the receiving, sending, understanding, accepting, and action elements of the communication process.

INDEX

PB-6437-10